Rooted in Movement

In Memoriam

JYTTE LAVRSEN

Acknowledgements

The research leading to the results presented by the editors has received funding from the European Union Seventh Framework Program (FP7/2007-2013) "Forging Identities" under Grant Agreement no. 212402. The publication of these papers, developed during the 2010 winter semester, was only possible thanks to a bequest from the estate of archaeologist Jytte Lavrsen. Therefore, this book is dedicated to Jytte Lavrsen. Special thanks to those whose commitment enabled the high quality of the contributions, the editors and to Helle Vandkilde for her scientific support and motivation. Additional thanks go to Jesper Laursen for introducing us to the craft of editing a printed volume and to Rob Lee for his assistance in making the English corrections.

Rooted in Movement

Aspects of Mobility in Bronze Age Europe

Edited by
Samantha Reiter, Heide W. Nørgaard,
Zsófia Kölcze & Constanze Rassmann

Foreword by Helle Vandkilde

JUTLAND ARCHAEOLOGICAL SOCIETY

Rooted in Movement
Aspects of Mobility in Bronze Age Europe

Layout & prepress: Louise Hilmar
Cover: Louise Hilmar
Type: Palatino Linotype
Printed in Denmark by Narayana Press, Gylling
Cover photo: Theresa Airey, Avebury circle

ISBN 978-87-88415-88-9
ISSN: 0107-2854

Jutland Archaeological Society Publications Vol. 83

Published by:
Jutland Archaeological Society
Moesgaard Museum
DK-8270 Højbjerg

Distributed by:
Aarhus University Press
Langelandsgade 177
DK-8200 Aarhus N
www.unipress.dk

Published thanks to a bequest from the estate of archaeologist Jytte Lavrsen and funding from the European Union Seventh Framework Programme (FP7/2007-2013), grant agreement PITN-GA 212402.

Content

Foreword

The title of this book is highly appropriate; mobility has always been a key issue in human life, both at home and abroad. Almost everything we do is concerned with movement rather than idleness. Movement involves dwelling: one dwells while one travels by ship, horse, or wagon and one both responds to (and of course transmits) culture while underway. Paradoxically, even dwelling involves movement. When we dwell, we often move on a small scale within our homes and residential neighbourhoods. Houses and settlements could be considered places of decelerated movement in which people socialise and engage with material culture. The reception and transmission of culture (itself intrinsically materialised) is built into every movement, be it short- or long-distance. It is important to note that almost anything can move either on its own or when aided by human interaction, agency or travel: ideas, things, technologies, people, plants and animals. We easily recognise this state of affairs from our own globalised present. The actual scale of movement and interaction and the response to transcultural flows has varied over time as well as within the metaphorical and literal expanse of culture and geography.

Historically, some periods and societies in human history were more dependent on corporeal and material movement than others. Today's level of movement, for example, is much higher than that in the prehistoric past. Nonetheless, the portrait of the European Bronze Age which emerges from current research is a period in which the world was in motion, albeit varying with such factors as geography, culture, economy, and class. In temperate Europe, the Bronze Age lasted from circa 2000 BC to 500 BC and saw two clear and important socio-economic turning points during this 1500 year time span: in c. 1600 BC and again in c. 1200 BC. During these times of upheaval, waves of change in cultural and religious trends characterised an interconnected Europe. Current research suggests that the trait common to these breaking points was increased mobility.

Increased macro-regional interconnectedness often occurred in the past. However, with the onset of the Bronze Age, movement on different scales became both a necessity as well as a new way of life for a dominant section of society. This connectivity was based on the demand for bronze, that new, pliable metal with geographically restricted sources. If one wanted to be part of 'project' Bronze, one had to either move in order to obtain the metal, or arrange for said metal to be delivered to one's own doorstep.

This process of increased connectivity across Europe notably triggered parallel innovations in other social sectors. More effective axes enabled the production of new plank-built ships, specially-designed weapons enabled warfare to be enacted on a larger scale to more deadly effect and intricate jewellery effectuated and created social distinctions between different genders, classes and cultures. Bronze also became intertwined with religion, cosmology and ritual, as did those distant voyages that brought the metal back home. Bronze was not just a metal; it was imbued with complex meanings which were rooted in movement as well as in adjacent social mentalities. Bronze changed the world, making it both more complex and open.

However, this dependence on a foreign material also made societies potentially more vulnerable to societal transformations in other parts of Europe. When bronze disappeared in the mid first millennium BC generating the emergence of the Iron Age, a whole way of life among an internationalised upper echelon vanished, leaving behind some key innovations for further development. The articles of this volume (nine in number) all touch upon a number of different themes which each convey the Bronze Age as a crucial period in the history of Europe.

"Rooted in Movement" has roots of its own. It grew out of a MA course about Bronze Age mobility which took place in the autumn of 2011 at Moesgård under the auspices of Aarhus University's Section for Prehistoric Archaeology. That course (as well as this manuscript) can be considered an offshoot product of the EU-project 'Forging Identities – the Mobility of Culture in Bronze Age Europe' which developed within the dynamic framework of a Marie Curie Initial Training Network. The project was coordinated by Aarhus University and included seven network partners and eleven associated partners from leading research institutions across Europe. Starting in 2009 and running until 2012, the project and its partner institutions hosted ten PhD fellows and four post-doctoral fellows.

The four editors of this book were affiliated with the 'Forging Identities Project' in various ways. Samantha Reiter, Heide Wrobel Nørgaard and Constanze Rassmann undertook research with the Marie Curie project as PhD fellows and Zsófia Kölcze has cooperated closely with the project as an AU-Arts PhD fellow. The 'Fabulous Four of Forging' have furthermore formed a close team during the lifetime of the Marie Curie project as they participated in the diverse conferences, research and training activities associated therewith. For four years, mobility was a constant. It comprised not only their principle topic of research, but was also literally built into their lives. This text is not only a reflection of their mobile state, but is also the coalescence of a specific attitude towards movement in a Bronze Age setting. The sum of these experiences impacted a series of parallel activities, such as the editorship of this book. Simultaneously, the editors have positively influenced – and in an international manner – the doctoral and study environment at Aarhus University's Sections for Archaeology and Anthropology here at Moesgaard.

Therefore, this book represents an international spirit of collaborative research training. Its contributors are a blend of PhD fellows and MA students who were much inspired by the passion expressed by their young teachers. The contents demonstrate not only creativity of thought but also persistence, ambition and the command of archaeological and theoretical knowledge. In writing this book, the contributors engage in the bold presentation of new ideas rather than long-established scholarship. While the authors are not experienced researchers, both the publication process and the end product glimpse present and future scholarly excellence. This book opens a window, providing a fresh new look on Bronze Age research.

Helle Vandkilde

Introduction
Should I stay or should I go

Constanze Rassmann

Everything is movement.[1] People move. Fauna migrates. Objects, raw materials and ideas are made mobile. Even the archaeological study of movement is subject to cyclical shifts within the theoretical spotlight. Thus, the very beginning of our field of research is interwoven with the study of movement (cf. Beaudry and Parno 2013, 5). After years in shadow, movement and mobility have once again come to the fore and are particularly visible in the great number of publications (e.g. Barnard and Wendrich 2008; Colburn and Hughes 2010; Vandkilde 2007), research projects (e.g. the EU-funded Marie Curie Actions "Forging Identities – the Mobility of Culture in Bronze Age Europe" project) and conferences (e.g. "People in Movement: Migration, Mobility, and Exchange" at Brown University) which engage with this topic.

As a result of this newly awoken interest, Aarhus University's Section for Prehistoric Archaeology held a course which concentrated on mobility, especially within the context of the European Bronze Age. The papers published in this volume were inspired by this course. These contributions approach mobility and movement from different angles, both in regard to their theoretical approach as well as the materials upon which they focus. Although the majority of these papers are oriented towards Southern Scandinavia, there are a few, notable exceptions which address mobility from a wider, global standpoint or the long-distance movement of objects or design patterns across continental Europe.

Archaeology and Movement – a long-term relationship

The study of movement is "concerned with the relationship(s) among time, object, person, and space" (Beaudry and Parno 2013, 1) and, therefore, resembles

the study of archaeology very closely. Unsurprisingly, both concepts are tightly connected. Their long conjoined history has resulted in various terms which refer to "movement", its conceptualisation and its effects at different points in time. In some cases, movement appears as a hidden paradigm, disguised as "networks" or "transmissions".

In the beginning of the 20th century, "migration" was used to explain the spatial distribution of artefacts (Burmeister 2000, 539). Furthermore, this early worldview was closely connected with the idea of diffusionism, as well as the work of Vere Gordon Childe (1928) and Gustaf Kossinna (1911), who each associated the spread of culture with the migration of peoples. These interpretations were not only problematic with regards to their political use or cultural understanding, but also due to their generally poor methodological and theoretical conceptualisation (Eggers 1959). These definitions were heavily criticised by proponents of 'New Archaeology' and, at least within the world of anglophone archaeology, migration was allowed to fall by the wayside until its return in the 1980s (Burmeister 2000, 539). Since then, the study of archaeology and migration/mobility have each had different foci. However, they also have much in common, including both broader aspects, such as underlying economic and social factors (e.g. Renfrew 1988; Kristiansen 1989) and smaller studies, such as the ways in which roads influence and shape movement (Gibson 2007). In recent years, the study of movement has come back with a vengeance. Although this is possibly at least partly explicable by the use of a more thorough methodological definition, it seems likely that the main explanation for this phenomenon stems from a fresh bloom of awareness within both archaeology and sociology of the globalised and mobile world in which we are living (Urry 2006). This awareness has been complemented by the "strontium isotope revolution" which enabled scholars to determine whether or not people, animals, plants and (other) organic materials were foreign to the places in which they were recovered (Price *et al.* 2002). Moreover, these new possibilities also demonstrated how variegated mobility was in prehistoric times, enabling the archaeologist to separate the study of the mobility of things from the mobility of people, as is exemplified by work at the Early Bronze Age cemetery of Singen (Oelze *et al.* 2011).

Although discussion has thus far focussed on the relationship between archaeology and movement, the partnership between mobility and the European Bronze Age is of equally long standing. As raw materials were available from only a select few regions, investigations involving mobility in the Bronze Age were less a question of *if*, but more of *how* and *why*. Therefore, provenance studies on metal have played a major role and called for an application of the natural sciences earlier than might otherwise have been the case (e.g. Junghans *et al.* 1960). Despite the name of the period, metal has not been the sole focus of Bronze Age studies. The transmission of metallurgy, exchange networks, and local responses to foreign influences have all played important roles in the study of the European Bronze Age. The papers included in this volume join in as part of this long discussion.

Approaching Mobility

In her paper, Reiter focuses on globalisation and its impact on cultural settings as well as individuals. She argues that the Neolithic could be distinguished from the Bronze Age world not by the connection of formerly distant areas, but rather by increased connectivity. Indeed, the increased connectivity of a mobile world created an awareness of people, places and things that were both foreign and different. However, it is not only globalization and movement which are typical Bronze Age phenomena, but also the importance that was placed on the individual in the creation of grave identities. Both a focus on identity and the awareness of difference made it possible to manipulate, creatively use and/or integrate said differences into one's own cultural setting or identity. Reiter focuses on three denominations and possible manipulations of identity: cultural synthesis, adoption, and sublimation. While cultural synthesis describes the creation of something new from different cultural aspects, adoption and sublimation are

two diametrically opposed (but related) phenomena. She argues that identity adoption refers to occasions in which a local person would take on the mantle of a culture which is not their own, whereas the dominance of one culture over the other – as expressed in grave goods – can be described as sublimation. The choreography of identity and the implication of "foreignness," therefore, is a carefully controlled dance between these static concepts.

Tollaksen also applies these ideas within her article on "The Social Identity of the Oak-Coffin People" insofar as her discussion concerns the ways in which visual recognition enfolds itself across geographic areas in terms of identity. Her study material includes the so called oak coffins, a burial form dated to 13th century BC. The oak-coffin burials are characterised by the excellent condition of the organic materials found inside and were – with few exceptions – geographically restricted to the Cimbrian Peninsula. While this burial custom was neither restricted to a special gender nor to a certain age group, the grave goods included suggest that those who were buried were subject to some social restrictions. Following the same reasoning as Reiter, Tollaksen suggests that the (physical) appearance of an individual was affected by their membership within a group as well as their identity. In the case of the oak-coffin burials, it is clear that both grave goods as well as clothing reflect the role of the individuals within a wider geographical scope. Artefact decoration, by contrast, shows smaller geographical distribution patterns. Tollaksen points out a very interesting conundrum: while women's jewellery in the Bronze Age occasionally limited their day-to-day mobility, the selfsame items seem to reflect a greater geographical mobility, as these costumes often point to distant regions.

Rather than examining society as a whole, Nørgaard's text narrows in focus. In "Are Valued Craftsmen as Important as Prestige Goods? Ideas about itinerant craftsmanship in the Nordic Bronze Age", she attempts to trace the individual in the material and to examine whether smiths left individual traces in the crafting processes. By tracing the works crafted by different smiths, it is possible to gain a better understanding of how Bronze Age metallurgy was organised. Ethnographic evidence supports the idea that smiths were differentiated into two groups: "subsistence craftsmen" and specialists (the latter rely on surplus economies). Nørgaard stresses the close connections between the social elite and specialised craftsman. Indeed, she suggests that the mobility of craftsmen might have taken place within the context of elite networks. The analysis of working traces on Krasmose type neck collars revealed both technical similarities and differences between artefacts. This study lead to some exciting results. Her examination of the collars from Jomfrugård and Vorup showed that the minimal changes and addition of local ornamentation make it likely that the same person produced both collars.

Johannesen's work pulls away from the individual, engaging instead with the movement of ideas and objects. She analyses the relationship between bronze and flint daggers as well as the different networks comprised thereof. She combines the idea of a network with the core periphery model. Both dagger groups can be differentiated not only on the basis of their diverse materiality, but also by the different mental templates which were applied to them during the production process. Apart from these obvious distinctions, the connotations connected to the daggers were translated across materials. At least in South Scandinavia, Johannesen argues, it seems as if it was not the material that was responsible for symbolic use, but rather the artefact itself.

Where Johannsen concentrates on the way in which ideas are translated across materials, Simonsen studies the way in which one type of decoration was translated in different geographic regions. She understands translation as the creation of a new version based on a foreign template. The changes which occur during this translation effectively make a new addition understandable within the new cultural setting in which it finds itself. The principle subject matter of the article is the spiral, a widespread decorative motif in 1600 BC. One of Simonsen's central questions is whether the sword (which was popular during the same period and had a similar distribution) might have acted as a carrier for the spiral. In order to understand how the spiral might have been translated, she qualitatively discusses its appearance within three principle areas of study: Denmark, the Carpathian Basin and Mycenae. By means of this comparison, she shows that the spiral occurred on different types of objects in these different regions, making it unlikely that the sword was the means of transporting the idea of the spiral between these regions. In fact, it is likely that the spiral was accepted so whole-heartedly over such an expanse because of the translation phenomenon in which it was detached

from its former carrier and applied to objects which were familiar within the local context.

Kölcze chooses a similar chronological and geographical scope in her analysis of "The Fårdrup-type Shaft-hole Axes: Material Hybridity in Bronze Age Europe c. 1600 BC". Her paper examines the Southern Scandinavian Fårdrup axe occurrences which combined Nordic shape traditions with southeastern European decorative style. Kölcze focusses on movement in terms of transmission and reception. Kölcze utilises hybridity (Stross 1999) as a means of understanding this mixture of socio-cultural traditions. In this way, Kölcze analyses the axes with regards to their so-called growth capacity, progenitors, temporal and spatial context and the mechanisms of hybridisation. These various analyses show that Fårdrup axes were employed both actively and consciously to establish cross-cultural borders and to negotiate power and identity. As some artefacts demonstrate heavy-use wear, a long period of circulation and a resultant change in the perception of that artefact group is assumed.

Spliid's paper on the Skallerup wheeled cauldron approaches mobility from yet another angle, namely in terms of its materialisation and conceptualisation. Furthermore, Spliid also examines who was buried in a cauldron as well as why that very special burial treatment was chosen. Naturally, the focal point of the paper is on the wheeled cauldron found in a barrow at Skallerup which dates from around 1300 BC. Spliid discusses the symbolism and use of both the container and the wheel in particular (as well as material culture in general) as part of the negotiations of meaning involved in the cognitive processes. This article argues that the Skallerup wheeled cauldron refers to a number of different metaphors, such as the womb. Furthermore, the wheels themselves reference other artefacts (such as the sun wagon from Trundholm) and iconographies which conceptualise a mobile world. Spliid additionally links mobility to the concept in which the deceased travelled to the afterlife. The grave goods in the cauldron style the deceased as part of a warrior elite, thereby also connecting this social group to the conceptualisation of a mobile world. A similar connection between mobility and the afterlife is stressed by Damkjer in her paper about the cosmological significance of ships. She investigates different cosmological models in regard to Bronze Age ship wrecks, rock carvings and other depictions of ships.

It was this selfsame understanding of movement that inspired Knudsen's work with hand stones and their meanings. Hand stones began to appear in mortuary contexts around 1100-900 BC. As is suggested by their name, this artefact group comprises the rather abstract depiction of hands on stone slabs and, although geographically widespread, is quite uniform in execution. Knudsen favours a semiotic and cognitive approach for reconstructing the meaning of this fascinating rock art. According to his approach, prehistoric art was intentionally made; the shape and version of the hand depicted were, therefore, the result of conscious choice. He additionally discusses the hand as a metonym: as a part of the body which refers to the body as a whole. Moreover, the hand can also be understood as a very special part of human interaction, namely because it is one of our principle means of contact with the world. As a result, Knudsen reasons that hand stones were a medium through which the transition from one world to the other might have been made tangible and manageable.

The papers presented in this volume each analyse mobility from a different angle. They trace the movement of individuals via material culture and discuss the influence of the 'foreign' on the creation and manipulation of identity. They debate the transmission and reception of foreign influences on material culture, as well as the conceptualisation of mobility within a burial context. Due to the variety of the approaches, this book will hopefully be the rootstock from which further analyses of movement can spring.

Note

1. In this article, movement and mobility are understood in a spatial sense; social mobility is not discussed.

Bibliography

Barnard, H. and Wendrich, W. 2009: *The archaeology of mobility: Old World and New World nomadism*. Los Angeles.

Beaudry, M.C. and Parno, T.G 2013: Introduction: Mobilities in Contemporary and Historical Archaeology. In: Beaudry, M.C. and T.G. Parno (eds): *Archaeologies of Mobility and Movement*. New York, 1-14.

Childe, V.G. 1928: *The most ancient Near East: The oriental prelude to European prehistory*. London.

Colburn, H.P. and Hughes, R.C. 2010: Movement and materiality: Mobile cores and the archaeology of political boundaries. *Archaeological Review from Cambridge* 25 (2), 43-56.

Eggers, H.J. 1959: *Einführung in die Vorgeschichte*. München.

Gibson, E. 2007: The archaeology of movement in a Mediterranean landscape. *Journal of Mediterranean Archaeology* 20 (1), 61-87.

Junghans, S.; Sangmeister, E. and Schröder, M. 1960: *Kupferzeitliche und frühbronzezeitliche Bodenfunde aus Europa*. Studien zu den Anfängen der Metallurgie 1. Berlin.

Kossinna, G. 1911: *Die Herkunft der Germanen: Methode der Siedlungsarchäologie*. Würzburg.

Kristiansen, K. 1989: Prehistoric migrations: The case of the Single Grave and Corded Ware cultures. *Journal of Danish Archaeology* 8, 211-25.

Oelze, V.M., Nehlich, O. and Richards, M.P. 2011: ‚There's no place like Home' – No Isotopic Evidence for Mobility at the Early Bronze Age Cemetery of Singen, Germany. *Archaeometry* 54 (4), 752-778.

Price, T.D., Burton, J.H. and Bentley, R.A. 2002: The Characterization of Biologically-Available Strontium Isotope Ratios for the Study of Prehistoric Migration. *Archaeometry* 44 (1), 117-35.

Renfrew, C. 1988: *Archaeology and language: The puzzle of Indo-European origins*. Cambridge.

Stross, B. 1999: The Hybrid Metaphor: From Biology to Culture. *The Journal of American Folklore* 112 (445) 254-267.

Urry, J. 2007: *Mobilities*. Cambridge.

Vandkilde, H. 2007: *Globalisation, battlefield and economics: Three inaugural lectures in archaeology*. Aarhus.

A Choreography of Place
Globalisation and Identity in the Bronze Age

Samantha S. Reiter

Introduction

Although the extreme connectivity of the modern world might suggest otherwise, globalisation is not the sole intellectual property of recent human history. Despite the fact that it might initially appear counterintuitive to speak of 'globalisation' in a historical context in which the inhabitants of planet Earth were perhaps unaware that the landmass on which they existed was, in fact, a globe, that is precisely the intent of this paper. Globalisation in its current incarnation is vastly different from globalisation in the past, and people have engaged with the phenomenon in varying ways over time. The purpose of this article, therefore, is two-fold. Firstly, it aims to discuss the width and temporal depth of globalisation, particularly in relation to the European Bronze Age; secondly, the text builds upon the theoretical foundation established by the preceding section and provides a framework for the archaeological analysis of small scale cultural and personal engagements with the wider phenomenon of globalisation.

What's in a Name?

The term 'globalisation' is unfortunate enough to have been severely abused in recent times. Despite – or perhaps because of – this poor conceptualisation (Giddens 1996), it has come to be generally understood as a sort of catch-all idiom cataloguing the changes occurring on a worldwide scale within recent history (Rothschild 1999). Linguistically, it is surprising that so comparatively young a term could accrue such muddied usage and multitudinous interpretations. Although the invention of the word 'international' dates from the 1780s (Betham 1948, 326; Suganami 1978), 'globalisation' first entered a dictionary in 1961 (Gove 1961, 965). Almost every language uses the term 'globalisation' (or has a native equivalent).

However, the superseding of concepts contributing to globalisation with the latter term are not uncommon (see Carron 2009). This persistent ambiguity has brought about considerable scepticism in the academic community towards globalisation as a concept, and has resulted in the coinage of such mocking turns of phrase as 'globalony', 'global babble' and 'glob-blah-blah' (Rosenberg 2001).

Despite the negative press, globalisation is not a premise without analytical use. Indeed, the conceptual conflation of globalisation with other phenomena lead Scholte to argue that many (if not all) analyses which make use of globalisation are flawed by this inherent redundancy; the four main approaches to globalisation have mistakenly used the term as a proxy for either internationalisation, liberalisation, universalisation and/or westernisation (Scholte 2002, 8). Globalisation, he writes:

> "…[is] the spread of transplanetary – and in recent times more particularly supraterritorial – connections between people…[it] involves reductions in barriers to transworld contacts" (Scholte 2002, 13-14).

Larsson has referred to the same phenomenon as a process of "world shrinkage" (Larsson 2001, 1), resulting in a wider, more inclusive shift in the nature of social space. As a result, people become more able to engage with each other within a single and – most importantly – more *connected* world.

This notion of an increasingly united social space borders upon the ancient Greek concept of *oikoumene*, in which the space occupied by humanity was thought to be a single realm (Kroebner 1945). The global *oikoumene* would be "a region of persistent culture interaction and exchange" (Kopytoff 1987, 10; Hannerz 1989). Sociology speaks of global social space as one which also cannot be defined in geographical terms. For sociologists, globalisation has no three dimensional aspect. It is defined as a "space of *flows*" rather than a "space of places" (Castells 1989, 348, emphasis added). This idea is echoed by Appadurai in terms of what he calls the "ethnoscape", a term which refers to the autopoietic tendencies of the shifting landscape of humanity, the world and the politics therein (Appadurai 1990, 297; 1996).

History is Past Politics, Politics is Present History

No discussion of globalisation – be it concerned with the past or the present – can ever be apolitical. Today's world is very much embroiled in globalisation inasmuch as it is an increasingly coalesced and intertwined social space. The European Union is under pressure not only by separatist interests like those present in southwest France, Catalonia and Brittany, but also by the imbalance between the economic powerhouses of the Union and the poor fiscal decisions of their brother constituents. Over the past decade, a host of editorials have hawked the great transformative powers of globalisation as a means to bring together all peoples into one socially, culturally, politically and fiscally equal society (i.e. Ali 2001). These opinion pieces represent an inherently inaccurate view of the phenomenon of globalisation; namely, that it is a process that will one day be complete. Perhaps because of this somewhat rose-tinted promise of a future dawn, current government policy makers are very much interested in the *process* of globalisation as well as its functionality. How does it work? When did it begin? Unfortunately for world politics, a study of the history and development of globalisation on a social scale indicates that the prospect of an eventual unified global culture is remote.

In recent years, many academics have drawn parallels between the onset of globalisation and the advent of the European Bronze Age (see Earle and Kristiansen 2010), but this association is far from being without challengers. Chanda posited that globalisation began in the Neolithic (Chanda 2007, 23), while still other researchers push the origins of the phenomenon even further back into the Paleolithic era (Fernández-Armesto 2002). Another scholar proposed a compromise in which the globalisation phenomenon was divided into three temporal phases: archaic, proto-modern

and post-colonial (Hopkins 2002). If history has a pre-history, then can globalisation not also have a prototypical phase? Armitage addresses this very question:

"There is no single universal process of globalisation within which all forms of human interaction move in lockstep towards an inexorably globalized condition. Globalisation's histories are multiple, and its pre-histories just as various. It would be fallacious to seek a single prehistory of globalisation, both because it has had many paths and because none of those paths has been unbroken" (Armitage 2004, 173).

Globalisation is not about the final creation of what some have poetically termed the "borderless world" (Ohmae 1990) or the advent of "distancelessness" (Heidegger 1971, 165-66). A fully integrated world culture would be impossible without the formation of a single world state (Featherstone 1990, 1), an idea which current politics clearly banishes to the realms of science fiction. Globalisation has neither start- nor endpoint, nor can it possess any final 'global culture' goal. The fragmented spatial and temporal nature of globalisation makes it possible to speak of what one might call *multiple* global cultures (Featherstone 1990, 10) rather than one, singular, invariate pathway towards a final and united cultural end.

Politics and Paradigm Shift

If the current of globalisation has no clear temporal point of origin, then why has the Bronze Age been so often mentioned in conjunction with the advent of that global movement? If one views globalisation as a socially-centralising influence, present in fits and bursts throughout the history of humanity, then the globalisation which occurred in the Bronze Age was somewhat different to that which had occurred in previous time periods. As a whole, academics have tended to temporally misplace globalisation as a modern phenomenon because of the degree and rapidity with which peoples are connected today (i.e. telephone, fax machine and the great inclusive and magnetically connective force of the world-wide web). The Bronze Age witnessed a rapid increase in connectivity which, although it represented but a miniscule portion of the connectivity present today, was proportionately enormous for that time. It was, arguably, during this period that the first real pan-European community was created (see Earle and

Kristiansen 2010). Certainly, the rapid expansion of borders and the coalescence of social space occurring during the European Bronze Age was analogous to what Barabási calls the breach of the threshold of one:

"When you add enough links such that each node had an average of one link, a miracle happens: A unique giant cluster emerges. That is, most nodes will be part of a single cluster such that, starting from any node, we can get to any other by navigating along the links between the nodes… Mathematicians call this phenomenon the emergence of a giant component, one that includes a large fraction of all nodes. Physicists call it percolation and will tell you that we just witnessed a phase transition, similar to the moment in which water freezes. Sociologists would tell you that your subjects had just formed a community" (Barabási 2003, 18).

Given that globalisation appeared in many different places at many different times, this paper argues that the permutation of the globalisation process which took place in Europe from c. 2000 to 1500 BC was the first occasion in which European society bypassed this critical threshold. This is not to say that other periods were not socially connected or even that they did not form communities. It is clear that they did; studies of the homewards orientations of LBK long-houses and the intricately detailed work that has been done on polished stone axes proves that people in the Neolithic were far from being isolated (Bradley 2001; Chappell 1966, Cummins 1980; Fisher 1982). However, Bronze Age connectivity was the first spate of globalisation in which it is clear that our ancestors not only aggrandised their social sphere, but also presented some resistance to the changes brought about by their presence on a wider social stage. Indeed, the same resistance to the changes ensuant to rapid social expansion is clearly visible within modern society through the regionalisation and rise of ethno-nationalist politics mentioned above (Scholte 2000). These very human responses of resistance or acceptance are particularly visible in Bronze Age contexts because of the particular ways in which Bronze Age society functioned on a social level.

For the first time in human history, the optique of culture and society demonstrably changed from a backward-looking, ancestral focus to one which projected outwards from the individual (Clarke *et al.* 1985; Renfrew 1974; Shennan 1982). This is clearly demonstrated by the switch from Neolithic communal mortuary monuments and their associated ancestor cults to Bronze Age traditions of individual burial with the associated inclusion of grave goods as well as other structural indicators of definitive social stratification. The very nature of globalisation as an integral movement necessitated an awareness of places, peoples and things that were *different*. People in the Bronze Age expressed concepts of difference on and with their bodies through regionally-specific jewellery sets and/or states of cleanliness and body hair (or the lack thereof) (see Jöckenhovel 1995, 1991, 1980; Wels-Weyrauch 1989; Bergerbrant 2007; Treherne 1995; Stig-Sørensen 1997; Rebay-Salisbury *et al.* 2010). Difference in the Bronze Age was not only determined by virtue of spatial or geographical factors, but also by vertical social criteria, such as social status and gender. Spatial, vertical and horizontal differences are of interest to globalisation because of the fact that Bronze Age people were not only aware of these various social contexts, but also utilised and manipulated them in ways that were radically different from everything that had come before.

The Gender of the Gift is most often associated with Neolithic populations because of the partitive, socially referential structure of the author's concept of the 'dividual' (Strathern 1990). According to Strathern, the dividual is constituted by his or her social relations (Strathern 1990). Because of the birth of vertical social difference in the Bronze Age, researchers tend to think of that period as the origin of *individuals* (i.e. people who are socially unique from each other). However, the emergence of social rank in the Bronze Age does not automatically coincide with social diversification. People in the Bronze Age may have been *individuals*, but the *types* of individuals they could be were still very much predetermined. These 'individuals' would have been analogous to the 'individuals' present in Terry Jones' 1979 cult classic *The Life of Brian*; that is, the social positions held by Bronze Age persons were carefully controlled. One could, for example, assume the mantle of the beautiful warrior, or perhaps even that of chief or foreign woman/other rich female. Men and women were even buried in a strict, socially-mandated left or right *Hocker* fashion (a pattern from which archaeologists have observed very little deviation). It is almost as if Bronze Age society created a typology of roles which people could choose (or were chosen) to fulfill. Shakespeare accurately describes such a situation: "All the world's a stage/And the men and women merely players" (Shakespeare in Knowles

2009, 696). Due to this confined cast list within Bronze Age societies, it is much easier for archaeologists to determine where and when (and how) those peoples engaged with, or rejected, the changes brought about by foreign contacts.

Playing Backwards: Unpicking the Choreography of Difference

There is one principle means of discerning the individual cultural steps taken in the Bronze Age as a response to the pressures of increased social exposure caused by globalisation: through people and identity. Archaeologists know that the types of identity available for Bronze Age social actors were strictly prescribed. However, the investigation of small-scale responses to foreignness as would be brought about by globalisation in prehistory is not impossible. By comparing the socially perceived (local or non-local) in-grave identities of individuals with the evidence for their geological place of origin (see Fig. 1), one can determine how receptive individual culture groups were to foreign peoples and exotic material culture.

The individual steps taken in this choreography of place and social change are determinable by examining individual burials within a known culture group. Were they wholly resistant to change, adopting foreigners into their culture through an absorptive process akin to osmosis? Or, alternatively, were such Bronze Age persons so keen on the social clout brought about by the possession of foreign objects that they flaunted their foreign contacts by dress-

ing (or perhaps acting) like those foreigners with whose non-local material culture they surrounded themselves? Perhaps even a third scenario is possible. Were such persons open enough to the experience of change to create something new out of the broadening of both contacts and social world? The creation and manipulation of the in-grave identity of an individual can take three different forms. The first two of these – namely, cultural synthesis and adoption – occur in instances in which in-grave identity characterises a local person interred with foreign objects. The final instance (that of foreign persons interred with local objects) is indicative of the sublimation of an individual's place of origin. The next portion of this paper engages with each of these denominations of identity and the possible manipulations thereof.

Cultural Synthesis

Due to the fact that it is the most unlike its fellows, cultural synthesis[1] is perhaps the best choice for beginning any discussion of these three denominations of the manipulation and creation of identity. Unfortunately, cultural synthesis is possibly also the most difficult of the triad to identify in an archaeological context, as its causality can be difficult to define. Was a local person interred with foreign objects a symptom of foreign contact, or could they be said to be a harbinger of material culture change? This concept can perhaps be best illustrated via concrete example. Although there have been some recent challenges to the argument that no copper was mined in Scandinavia in the Bronze Age (Ling forthcoming),

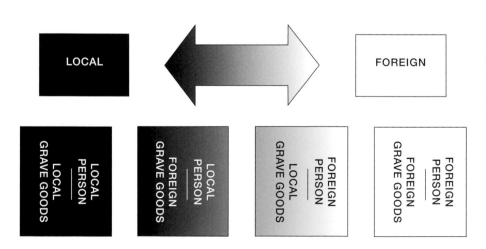

Figure 1. Schema for analysis of archaeological identity-in-grave, cross referencing isotopic status as 'local' or 'foreign' and the stylistic and material origin of the objects with which persons were buried.

bronze alloying – if only by virtue of the inclusion of tin – must have arrived in those Northern European climes from the outside (be it via Cornwall or the European continent) (Kristiansen 1998; Montelius 1872). If the wide scale usage of objects made from this alloy could be grouped together in the loosest sense as a 'culture of bronze,' then the first individual to be interred in Scandinavia (or the northern portion of the European continent, for that matter) would be a prime example of cultural synthesis.

Unfortunately, such an individual has not yet been found, and the fine-grained dating required for recognising him as such an important figure would render it unlikely that archaeologists would be able to recognise such a personage should they be fortunate enough to uncover him. However, the presence of bronze and bronze working in Scandinavia speaks to a wider *cultural* interaction with globalisation. Although it is unlikely that the inhabitants of ancient Scandinavia were able to produce the alloy themselves, their work on this new, foreign material was so highly developed as to be regionally specific and distinguishable even within the confines of modern-day nations (see Nørgaard 2011). If only in terms of the metals needed, bronze alloying could not have been a local Scandinavian phenomenon, and yet through trade, exchange and the wholehearted cultural adoption of an erstwhile foreign material and technology, ancient Scandinavians created a social and material culture different from its predecessors. In this instance, cross-cultural *mélanges* became so intermeshed that they seceded from both host cultures.[2]

Although difficult to pinpoint on an individual level in archaeological contexts (it is impossible to know which specific individual represented that elusive 'first' contact to bring about cultural synthesis and a resultant hybidity), cultural synthesis is perhaps the most clear-cut example of globalisation. Certainly, it is clear that it was strong both biologically and culturally; integration through cultural synthesis was the backbone of Roman foreign policy and the foundation upon which that ancient world empire was constructed (Millett 1990; Woolf 2004). Be it the heights of bronze crafting in a land without the materials to make that alloy or even in the expansionist might of a toga-clad empire, this denomination of globalisation – the synthesis of something new out of a merger between two cultures – became something greater than the sum of its parts.

Adoption

Where cultural synthesis refers to the creation of something new, adoption[3] speaks more to a cultural reference of a distant, but otherwise extant culture. This pattern of interaction, evidenced within a funerary context by individuals interred with objects that are foreign to the land in which they were born, is of particular interest in the Bronze Age. A traditional *Kulturkreis* culture-historical interpretation (see Kossinna 1911) would always view non-local objects as indications of the distant origins of the people with whom they were associated. More recent theoretical developments allow us to consider "foreign" objects in light of trade connections with exotic places, or even autochthonous, concomitant developments. However, when one considers the social importance placed upon exotic goods in the Bronze Age (Vandkilde 2007; Helms 1994), it is conceivable that the processes behind the presence of non-local grave goods in Bronze Age funerary contexts could be more nuanced than was previously thought.

Recent isotopic work on the Early Bronze Age site of Singen conclusively demonstrates a prevailing pattern of stasis rather than mobility, despite clear-cut evidence for the presence of foreign trade goods (Ölze *et al.* 2011). The fact that Price's comprehensive work on Bell Beaker skeletal material showed an overwhelming pattern of (admittedly, primarily female) long-distance movement (Price *et al.* 2004) would suggest a deviation from the established pattern. Perhaps individual difference as expressed in the Bronze Age was thought to have best been represented in terms of long-distance contact akin to the trade patterns uncovered in Melanesia by Malinowski (Malinowski 1922). Certainly, this pattern seems to resonate with recent isotopic work on Batora's Early Bronze Age material from Jelšovce (Reiter and Frei, forthcoming). De Castro argues that the desire to reach beyond the confines of the known is a natural human desire:

> "If humans were immortal, perhaps society would be confounded with the cosmos. Since death exists, it is necessary for society to be linked with something that is outside itself – and that it be linked socially to this exterior…" (de Castro quoted Sahlins 2008, 177).

It is perhaps possible to study Bronze Age social contacts not only in terms of the exoticism element established by Vandkilde and Helms (Vandkilde 2007; Helms 1994), but also in terms of mimicry. Can archaeologists have misconstrued the social importance and status belonging to exotic objects? In 1917 Ezra Pound wrote: "[t]ransportation is civilisation" (quoted Urry 2007, 17). Perhaps power in the Bronze Age came not from lived experiences in exotic locales, or even the assembly of exotic objects, but rather the ability to bring those exotic locales, cultures and material objects to heel in one's own backyard.

Sublimation

Given the importance that exotic objects and materials had within Bronze Age societies as a whole, it is difficult for modern minds to imagine an instance in which past persons would have downplayed their foreign connections or birth. However, the vagaries of the political clashes inherent in any coming-together of peoples is such that this phenomenon is commonplace within our modern world.[4]

Although not strictly archaeological, an excellent illustration of the sublimation of identity[5] in a funerary context would be a comparison of Achilles' treatment of Hector's body after their fateful battle at the gates of Troy to that of Antigone's care with the corpse of Polyneices. In the first instance, Achilles went mad with grief at the loss of Patroclus, and planned to dishonour Hector's memory by feeding his corpse to carrion-eating dogs and vultures. However, he had an additional horror to lay upon his erstwhile nemesis:

> "[A]nd now bent on outrage, on shaming noble Hector.
> Piercing the tendons, ankle to heel behind both feet,
> he knotted straps of rawhide through them both,
> lashed them to his chariot, left the head to drag
> and mounting the car, hoisting the famous arms aboard,
> he whipped his team to a run and breakneck on they flew,
> holding nothing back. And a thick cloud of dust rose up
> from the man they dragged, his dark hair swirling round
> that head so handsome once, all tumbled low in the
> dust…" (Fagles' translation The Iliad 1990, 554-555).

Although he later relented, Achilles' initial refusal to cede an honorable burial to Hector is an excellent illustration of the sublimation of identity. By treating the prince of Troy as if he were a criminal and not a warrior defending his city of birth, to the Greek mind, Achilles would have dishonoured the deceased (Griffin 1980, 161). Antigone, by contrast, was willing to die herself rather than allow dishonour to fall upon her brother:

> "Quickly she scattere[ed] earth over the corpse. Then she lift[ed] up a bronze jug and pour[ed] a sacred offering of milk, honey and water over him [Polyneices]" (McDonald's translation of Antigone 2000, 18).

However, the sublimation of identity need not always have a negative connotation. Within a funerary context in which a foreign individual was interred with local objects, the sublimation of identity must indicate some level of social acceptance and participation. If a foreigner were not welcomed and/or part of society (as would have been the case for Hector had Achilles proceeded with his plan), then it is difficult to imagine how he or she would have been buried in a style and place consistent with local standards. In its most basic form, the sublimation of identity is the expression of the dominance of one culture over another. One individual gives up his or her traditional dress and objects and adopts those of the people with whom he or she is living. This sort of phenomenon could characterise situations in which there were slaves, prisoners or particularly within an exogamic patrilocal or matrilocal society.

Conclusion

Identity, like globalisation, is so large and convoluted a topic that it is impossible to investigate in its entirety. The tripartite synthesis/adoption/sublimation framework presented here does not exhaust all possibilities for the creation and manipulation of identity under the inductive pressures made by globalisation. Nonetheless, it is hoped that the suggestions provided might open up a dialogue about the ways in which human beings respond to the pressures of an increasingly smaller world both today as well as in prehistory. Were individual differences in the Bronze Age crafted by first-hand experience of faraway places, or did people content themselves to being the prehistoric equivalent of armchair travellers? While it is certain that Bronze Age peoples were interested in exotic places and items, the conundrum facing archaeologists is just how those exotic items and ideas arrived: with people travelling to distant lands, themselves privy to the same interest as the foreign items they brought along with them, or through a down-the-line system of trade, bringing only the objects and ideas of the outside world into their nuclear one? Initial results from Jelšovce suggest it was ideas and objects that were moving and not people, and this evidence is echoed by recent studies at Singen (Ölze *et al.* 2011). Perhaps power in this region of the world in the Bronze Age came not from lived experiences in exotic locales, but rather from the ability to bring those exotic locales to heel in one's own backyard.

Notes

1. In this paper, cultural synthesis refers to the creation of a new (local) material culture brought on by contact with the peoples, ideas and objects of another area.
2. It is difficult to know what to call such mixtures. Unfortunately, most terms that come to mind have negative connotations. The word *creole* comes from the Spanish *criollo* or *criolla*, (origin: *crier*, meaning "to breed" or "to raise"). It was a term created in 18th century New Orleans to refer to individuals of 'pure' or 'mostly pure' European ancestry born in the colonies (Stewart 2007, 178). Hybrid, perhaps, would be more appropriate, due to its biological origins (Stross 1999, 254). Feldman supports this biological inclusion in cultural studies by arguing that hybridity in culture mimics that in the biological world. She posits a cultural application of the notion of hybrid vigour (the phenomenon in which hybrid plants and animals grow stronger and faster than their parents) (Feldman 2006, 62).
3. In the terms of this paper, adoption refers to the adoption of non-local traditions or material culture by local persons.
4. During World War I, US restaurateurs re-labelled sauerkraut and frankfurters 'liberty cabbage' and 'hot dogs' in a culinary protest against the Central Powers. Recent events mimic those sixty years their senior; because of Gallic refusal to support US military action in Iraq, republican Bob Ney moved that all eateries at the House of Representatives replace the 'French' in French fries and French toast by the word 'freedom' (Loughlin 2003).
5. The sublimation of identity is understood to refer to situations in which a foreign identity would be subsumed and the mantle of local funerary tradition and grave goods would be assumed in its place.

Bibliography

Ali, A.J. 2001: Globalisation. The Great Transformation. *Advances in Competitiveness Research* 9, 1-9.

Appadurai, A. 1996: *Modernity at Large. Cultural Dimensions of Globalisation.* Minneapolis.

Appadurai, A. 1990: Disjuncture and Difference in the Global Cultural Economy. In: Featherstone, M. (ed.): *Global Culture. Nationalism, Globalisation and Modernity.* London, 295-310.

Armitage, D. 2004: Is there a pre-history of globalisation? In: Cohen, D. & M. O'Connor (eds.): *Comparison and History. Europe in a Cross-National Perspective.* London & New York, 165-176.

Barabási, A.L. 2003: *Linked. How Everything is Connected to Everything Else and What It Means for Business, Science, and Everyday Life.* New York.

Bauman, Z. 1990: Modernity and Ambivalence. In: Featherstone, M. (ed.): *Global Culture. Nationalism, Globalisation and Modernity.* London, 143-170.

Bentham, J. 1948: *An Introduction to the Principles of Morals and Legislation.* London.

Bergerbrant, S. 2007: *Bronze Age Identities. Costume, Conflict and Contact in Northern Europe 1600-1300 BC.* Stockholm Studies in Archaeology 43. Lindome.

Bradley, R. 2001: Orientations and Origins. A Symbolic Dimension to the Long House in Neolithic Europe. *Antiquity* 75, 50-56.

Chanda, N. 2007: *Bound Together. How Traders, Preachers, Adventurers and Warriors Shaped Globalisation.* New Haven & London.

Chappell, J. 1966: Stone Axe Factories in the Highlands of East New Guinea. *Proceedings of the Prehistoric Society* 32, 15, 96-121.

Clarke, D.V., T.G. Cowie & A. Foxon 1985: *Symbols of Power at the Time of Stonehenge.* Edinburgh.

Cummins, W.A. 1980: Stone Axes as a Guide to Neolithic Communication and Boundaries in England and Wales. *Proceedings of the Prehistoric Society* 46, 45-60.

Earle, T. & K. Kristiansen 2010: *Organizing Bronze Age Societies.* Cambridge.

Fagles, R. 1990: *The Iliad.* New York.

Featherstone, M. 1990: Global Culture: An Introduction. In: Featherstone, M. (ed.): *Global Culture. Nationalism, Globalisation and Modernity.* London, 1-14.

Feldman, M.H. 2006: *Diplomacy by Design. Luxury Arts and an "International Style" in the Ancient Near East, 1400-1200 BCE.* Chicago.

Fernández-Armesto, F. 2002: Review of A. G. Hopins (ed.): *Globalisation in World History* (London 2002). *History Today* 52, 5, 76-77.

Fisher, A. 1982: Trade in Danubian Shaft-Hole Axes and the Introduction of Neolithic Economy in Denmark. *Journal of Danish Archaeology* 1, 7-12.

Giddens, A. 1996: *Essential Matter. Globalisation Exerpts from a Keynote Address at the UNRISD Conference on Globalisation and Citizenship* [Homepage of United Nations Institute for Social Development], [Online]. Available: http://www.unrisd.org/80256B3C005BE6B5/(search)/3F2A5BF8EF7300D480256B750053C7EC?Opendocument&highlight=2,anthony,giddens&fromsearch=yes&query=anthony+giddens [2012, 02/22].

Gove, P.B. 1961: *Webster's Third New International Dictionary of the English Language Unabridged.* Cambridge MA.

Hannerz, U. 1989: Notes on the Global Ecumene. *Public Culture* 1, 2, 66-75.

Helms, M.W. 1994: Essay on Objects. Interpretations of Distance Made Tangible. In: Schwartz, S.B. (ed.): *Implicit Understandings. Observing, Reporting and Reflecting on the Encounters between Europeans and Other Peoples in the Early Modern Era.* Cambridge, 355-377.

Hopkins, A.G. 2002: *Globalisation in World History.* London.

Jockenhövel, A. 1995: Zur Ausstattung von Frauen in Nordwestdeutschland und in der Deutschen Mittelgebirgszone während der Spätbronzezeit und Älteren Eisenzeit In: Jockenhövel, A. (ed.): *Festschrift für Hermann Müller-Karpe zum 70. Geburtstag*. Bonn, 195-212.

Jockenhövel, A. 1991: Räumliche Mobilität von Personen in der Mittleren Bronzezeit des westlichen Mitteleuropa. *Germania* 69, 49-62.

Jockenhövel, A. 1980: *Die Rasiermesser in Westeuropa*. Prähistorische Bronzefunde VIII, 3. München.

Knowles, E. 2009: *Oxford Dictionary of Quotations*. 7ᵗʰ edition. Oxford.

Kopytoff, I. 1987: The International African Frontier. The Making of African Political Culture. In: Kopytoff, I. (ed.): *The African Frontier*. Bloomington, 3-83.

Kossinna, G. 1911: *Die Herkunft der Germanen. Methode der Siedlungsarchäologie*. Würzburg

Kristiansen, K. 1998: *Europe Before History*. Cambridge.

Kroebner, A.L. 1945: The Ancient Greek *Oikoumenê* as an Historic Culture Aggregate. *Journal of the Royal Anthropological Institute of Great Britain and Ireland* 75, 9-20.

Larsson, T. 2001: *The Race to the Top. The Real Sotry of Globalisation*. New York.

Loughlin, S. 2003: House cafeterias change names for 'French' fries and 'French' toast. CNN [online] Available from: http://articles.cnn.com/keyword/freedom-fries [Accessed 28 December, 2011].

Malinowski, B. 1922: *Argonauts of the Western Pacific. An Account of Native Enterprise and Adventure in the Archipelagoes of Melanesian New Guinea*. London.

Marcuse, P. 2000: The Language of Globalisation. *The Monthly Review* 52, 3, 23-27.

McDonald, M. 2000: *Antigone*. London.

Millett, M. 1990: Romanization. Historical Issues and Archaeological Interpretation. In: Blagg, T. & M. Millett (eds.): *The Early Roman Empire in the West*. Oxford, 35-40.

Mittelman, J.H. 2002: Globalisation: An Ascendant Paradigm? *International Studies Perspectives* 3, 1, 1-14.

Montelius, O. 1872: *Sveriges forntid. Försök till framställning af den svenska fornforskningens resultat*. Atlas I, Sternåldern och bronsåldern. Stockholm.

Nørgaard, H.W. 2011: *Die Halskragen der Nordischen Bronzezeit*. Bonn.

Ohmae, K. 1990: *The Borderless World. Power and Strategy in the Interlinked Economy*. New York.

Ölze, V.M., O. Nehlich & M.P. Richards 2011: 'There's No Place Like Home'. No Isotopic Evidence for Mobility at the Early Bronze Age Cemetery of Singen, Germany. *Archaeometry* 1475-4754, 1-27.

Price, T.D., J.H. Burton & R.A. Bentley 2002: The Characterization of Biologically-Available Strontium Isotope Ratios for the Study of Prehistoric Migration. *Archaeometry* 44, 1, 117-135.

Rebay-Salisbury, K., M.L.S. Sørensen & J. Hughes 2010: *Body Parts and Bodies Whole. Changing Relations and Meanings*. Oxford.

Renfrew, C. 1974: Beyond a Subsistence Economy. The Evolution of Prehistoric Europe. In: Moore, C.B. (ed.): *Reconstructing Complex Societies*. Bulletin of the American Schools of Oriental Research 20. Cambridge MA, 69-95.

Rosenberg, J. 2001: *The Follies of Globalisation Theory. Polemical Essays*. London.

Sahlins, M. 2008: The Stranger-King or Elementary Forms of the Politics of Life. *Indonesia and the Malay World* 36, 105, 177-199.

Scholte, J.A. 2000: *Globalisation. A Critical Introduction*. New York.

Shennan, S. 1982: Ideology, Change and the European Early Bronze Age. In: Hodder, I. (ed.): *Symbolic and Structural Archaeology*. Cambridge, 155-161.

Simmel, G. 1950: *The Sociology of Georg Simmel*. New York.

Sørensen, M.L.S. 1997: Reading Dress. The Construction of Social Categories and Identities in Bronze Age Europe. *Journal of European Archaeology* 5, 1, 93-114.

Stewart, C. 2007: Introduction. In: Stewart, C. (ed.): *Creolization. History, Ethnography, Theory*. Walnut Creek CA, 1-25.

Strathern, M. 1990: *The Gender of the Gift. Problems with Women and Problems with Society in Melanesia*. Berkeley.

Stross, B. 1999: The Hybrid Metaphor. From Biology to Culture. *The Journal of American Folklore* 112, 445, 254-267.

Suganami, H. 1978: A Note on the Origin of the Word 'International'. *British Journal of International Studies* 4, 3, 226-232.

Treherne, P. 1995: The Warrior's Beauty. The Masculine Body and Self-Identity in Bronze Age Europe. *Journal of European Archaeology* 3, 1, 105-144.

Urry, J. 2007: *Mobilities*. Cambridge.

Vandkilde, H. 2007: *Culture and Change in Central European Prehistory 6ᵗʰ to 1ˢᵗ Millennium BC*. Aarhus.

Wels-Weyrauch, U. 1989: Mittelbronzezeitliche Frauentrachten in Süddeutschland. In: Mordant, C. (ed.): *Dynamique du Bronze Moyen en Europe Occidentale Actes du 113e Congrès National des Sociétés Savantes*. Strasbourg, 117-134.

Woolf, G. 2004: Becoming Roman. The Origins of Provincial Civilization in Gaul. In: Champion, C.B. (ed.): *Roman Imperialism. Readings and Sources*. Oxford, 231-23.

The Social Identity of the Oak-Coffin People

Majken Tessa Tollaksen

Introduction

"She feared that she would be married off to a gentleman from a distant foreign tribe, so she would never see her family again. Wirsla, wife of Assur came from a country far to the south. Joril's grandmother had told them that Wirsla was very beautiful when she came to the chief's camp. Her hair was darker than that of most women, her jewellery was different, and you could not understand what she said. She cried for many days before she calmed down" (Poulsen 1990, 10; author's translation).

Poulsen (1990) brought the Egtved woman to life, his dramatization describing a hard life filled with stark gender differentiation in terms of power, hierarchy and life course. This introductory quote was chosen specifically because it mentions mobility, a concept which dovetails admirably with the social differentiation in the funerary patterns of the oak-coffin burials from Northern Europe; Wirsla was perceived of as a stranger principally because of visual differences in her physical appearance and dress.

This article addresses the ways in which mobility is affected by visual recognition and acceptance across geographic areas, specifically in terms of the oak-coffin people's social identity, self-identity and social cohesion.[1] Appearance plays a large role within inter-group relations and individual perception. For example, Boye (1896) emphasizes the presence of blond hair on the oak-coffin people in burials. As was aptly demonstrated by Poulson, even so simple a thing as hair can create a feeling of familiarity. Perception and signal value extend beyond the immediate social group.

The empirical material on which this study is based is comprised of the well-preserved published oak-coffin finds from Denmark which date from the 13th century BC.[2] This text assumes that there was a correlation between the oak-coffin burials and social perception. It is the presentation of the deceased in the grave which illuminated the social group as context. Unfortunately, due to space constraints, a selection of the best-preserved examples rather than the entirety of oak-coffin burials were included in this investigation. This article also acts as a test of whether the graves can be examined within a larger social context by examining geographical and physical mobility from a feminine perspective. While the focus will be on women, both sexes will be investigated in terms of the material aspects of costume and dress. This concentration in turn necessitates a theoretical engagement with social identity and mobility.

The Oak coffins' Stories about People

The first step in the investigative process is to categorise object types within a larger context, namely to characterize the funeral object repertoire of the oak-coffin people and the trends implied by any patterning therein. For example, while a dagger remains a dagger, the oak-coffin material shows the presence of important differences between different daggers in terms of their decoration and design. For the sake of coherency, it is the presence of the dagger and not the finer details of its uniqueness that are brought in focus within the confines of this article, as a more involved investigation would be beyond the scope of this paper. This article examines the overall recording of object trends, the ways in which they were absorbed and maintained within society, and their

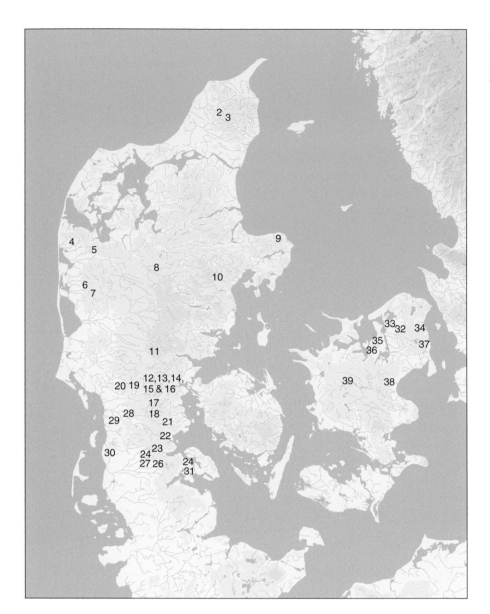

Figure 1. Distribution map of the recovered oak-coffin burials. The numbers refer to the list in Appendix 1.

social meaning as part of burial practice. The research of Boye (1896) and later Jensen (1998a) made it possible for researchers to have an extraordinarily good overview of the oak-coffin burials in Denmark and their find contexts.

The Oak coffins

Excepting the coffin from Melhøj (which is made from a culvert), as their name implies, the coffins are generally made out of a hollowed-out oak trunk (Jørgensen *et al.* 1982). Again, with one exception (the cremation at Store Ørnhøj), individuals within the oak coffins were inhumed (Boye 1896, 46-48). While the coffins mostly contain adults, examples from Guldhøj, Store Kongehøj and Trindhøj (Fig. 1, 15 and 16) have been interpreted as children's graves due to the

shorter lengths of the coffins (1,3 m and 1,4 m) or (in the last instance) the small size of a bracelet found inside (Boye 1896, 76-85 and 93-95).

The coffins tend to be lined with animal skins; cattle hide was the most popular material used for this purpose, although a child in Guldhøj was buried with sheepskin (Jensen 1998, 132) and the Skrydstrup woman's coffin was additionally lined with a layer of grass and forest chervil (Jensen 1998, 154). In nine cases, the bodies of the deceased were protected by the inclusion of a woolen blanket. The personal items included in the burials are worthy of particular note. In 18 separate cases, daggers were included, each with different decoration and the occasional wooden scabbard, some of which were lined with fur. Knives were included in four cases. Daggers and horn combs (nine cases) are counted as personal equipment, as they were interred with both men and women. Leather cases, wooden sticks, a flint spearhead, the handle of an awl as well as complete items, tweezers, flint tools, iron pyrite, pieces of burned bone, a ball of wool, small stones, one chisel, a saw blade, ox horn and razors also count as personal equipment. In two out of ten cases, these personal items were placed in a box.

Other larger finds include the fabric-wrapped bones of a cremated child (5-6 years of age), wooden vessels (eight cases), ceramic pots (two cases), a bucket of mead and a horn spoon. Items that would have been notably prestigious and/or exotic are exemplified by wooden vessels with pewter pins in a star motif (six cases) and folding chairs (two cases, see example Fig. 2). The weapons which were included were either swords (14 cases) or bronze axes (five cases). Swords were most commonly found with a lined wooden scabbard. Interestingly, a wooden scabbard was found without a sword at Storehøj (Boye 1896, 41). It is unknown whether the scabbard was missing either sword or even a dagger, as was the case in Borum Eshøj where an individual was interred with a dagger placed in a sword scabbard (Boye 1896, 56-57).

The Question of Sex

Although many items from the oak coffins in Southern Scandinavia can be divided according to sex,[3] unisex objects are also present. The latter include daggers,[4] costume needles, fibulas and/or horn combs (Bergerbrant 2007, 8; Jensen 1998).

Male Objects and Costume

Male objects consisted of weapons (swords and bronze axes) and personal items (razors, tweezers and belt buckles). Only men were buried with belt buckles and wooden pins (Boye 1896; Jensen 1998).

Costume remains have been found in 32 instances; in 15 of these, it is possible to determine the type of dress (Boye 1896; Jensen 1998). These costumes had various similarities. Men were commonly buried wearing knee-length kilts (i.e. Borum Eshøj) or a woolen coat with a belt (such as at Muldbjerg and Trindhøj). Men additionally had kidney-shaped cloaks, leather-wrapped textiles on the feet and a hat of some variety, with the exception of the younger male at Borum Eshøj (Boye 1896; Bergerbrant 2007, 52f.; Jensen 1998).

Figure 2. The Guldhøj objects – after Aner and Kersten 1986, 29-33, Tafel 18-19.

Female Objects and Costume

Female objects were generally related to jewellery (e.g. belt plates and bronze pipes). Women's jewellery from different regions seems to have been used in the same way despite cosmetic and typological differences in form and shape (Bergerbrant 2007, 8f). In general, the jewellery from within the Danish oak-coffin burials included bronze needles, *tutuli*, fibulas and different kinds of buttons.

The most common women's costume was a blouse with three-quarter length sleeves, a long skirt held up with a belt and (as was also the case with men) leather-wrapped textiles on the feet (see Fig. 3). Long hair was common; some individuals (i.e. the Skrydstrup woman) wore their hair in a hairnet. Other female dress was similar to that of the Egtved woman: a three-quarter length blouse above a short cord skirt and short hair (Bergerbrant 2007, 63f.; Nielsen 1979, 6f.). Women's physical movement would have been

Figure 4. A figure from Grevens Vænge, approximately 5 x 5 cm – after Rud 1966, 209.

more limited than that of men due to the limitations of their clothes and heavy jewellery. A cord skirt would have given more overall freedom of movement, if the bronze figure from Grevens Vænge (Fig. 4) is reliable. However, these skirts tightened at the knee and thus limited leg movement (Bergerbrant 2007, 64; Jensen 2001, 176).

This apparent limitation of leg movement within some female costume did not prohibit the overall migration of women. Jockenhövel's (1991) study of women in Central Europe concluded that, when they migrated, women generally covered distances between 50 and 200 km. Other studies concluded that, when they migrated, most women moved within local social groups (Bergerbrant 2007, 118).

Kinship and Individuality

Do graves show the individual or are they representative of the group? Bergerbrant believes graves to be indicative of the individual (Bergerbrant 2007, 14). Each part of the costume can be combined with a part of the social understanding of a person's identity. In this way, it is possible to have multiple, overlapping identities (Sørensen 1997, 93).

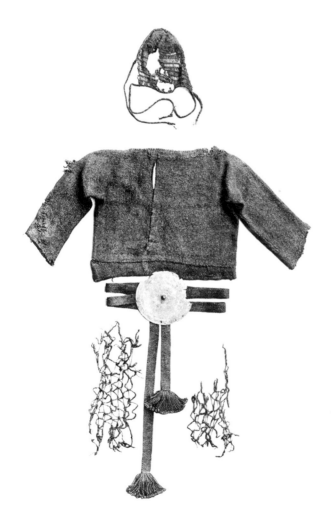

Figure 3. Part of the Borum Eshøj woman's clothing – after Broholm 1952, fig. 229.

> *"Identity, as used here, refers to the characteristics of an individual or group that are assigned and assumed by the group and others as a result of perceived differences from and similarities to others. These identities are created and assigned qualities, which result in both cohesion and separation, and material culture is employed in a variety of ways to express them. It is thus different from, for example, subjective personal self-identity."*
> (Sørensen 1997, 94).

The perception of identity must exist in relation to other people and groups. Variations in dress and material accessories played upon this idea of recognition and served to mark the difference between groups as well as individuals within a group. While the objects a person possessed (as well as the specific style of those objects) would have been important within a specific local group, if we widen the scope, the importance placed on objects expands not only from their ownership and style, but also to their symbolic value. In terms of identity, differences between groups can be divided into two categories: inter-group and intra-group (Sørensen 1997, 93-96).

Naturally, these differences play a role in social rules. For example, women might not have been allowed to maintain their original identities after marriage. If a woman did maintain her original identity after matrimony, this could be due to an acceptance of and respect for the woman's heritage or perhaps as a means of emphasizing a man's contacts and alliances. However, when any individual has lived in another group for a longer period of time and been witness (and perhaps subject) to other traditions, languages, costume styles and objects, it is likely that some physical adornments would have changed according to a new group status while others would remain the same. The object types of the different areas can affect the production of items in more than one area (Fig. 5).

The similitude of social groups can be shown through similarities (or, indeed, differences) in religion, burial methods and social understanding of personal

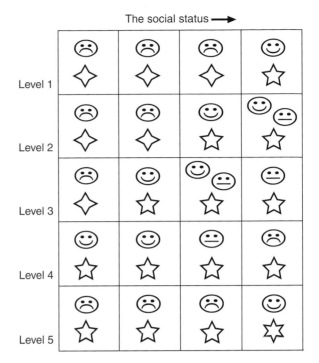

Figure 6. An expansion of Miller's emulation model. Level 1: the upper class has acquired status through objects. Level 2: the second highest social tier adopts a similar material object to those used in Level 1 (either the same or an imitation); the upper echelons of society remain satisfied, imitation being the sincerest form of flattery. Level 3: the middle group acquires a similar item. As a result, Level 1 is unhappy as it no longer has a means of material distinction. Level 4: The more common the status symbol, the lesser the power it possesses. Level 5: the highest social level regains/maintains its status by obtaining new material tendencies and continuing the pattern of material social differentiation – based on Miller 1985, 186.

appearance (e.g. the signal value placed on dress and jewellery). A group within a specific geographical area could potentially have partially recognised elements of the material from other groups, but, as is shown in Fig. 5, the extent to which the materials were known varied (Miller 1985, 165-170). For example, studies on Kalahari San rock art show the same sort of shamanic art over a large geographical area with variations in the use of weaponry. Arrows are common in some areas, and are rarer in others (Eastwood 1999). The possibility remains that some groups lacked an awareness of those which existed nearby. Identity is somewhat dependent upon what a person has achieved in his or her life, and this can be visualized through grave material. The identity displayed in a grave can be joined with an individual's social status and identity as well as the identity of the overarching group (Sørensen 1997, 95). When an individual or group tries to raise their status, they will attempt to imitate or copy the habits, belongings or trends

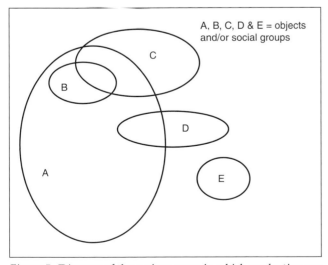

Figure 5. Diagram of the various ways in which production can be affected – after Miller 1985, 167.

present in the upper echelons of society (Fig. 6). The possession of a new object can be either the means by which to achieve higher status, or the means by which to maintain personal or familial status.

Human consciousness is tied to a common understanding of objects and their meanings (Berger and Luckmann 2003, 58). A conceptualization of the ways in which new objects are acquired and accepted is shown in Fig. 7. An item will be accepted by the new group if it contains something recognizable which appeals to the common knowledge base of that group. According to Berger (1974) and Miller (1985, 167), a person can only have an individual identity if that identity is recognised by the persons by which he or she is surrounded. A specific costume, therefore, signals differences (rather than individuality) through the combination of different hairstyles and/or ornaments (Sørensen 1997, 98). It is this combination that shows social belonging. However, it does not eliminate or supercede individuality, as Bergerbrant (2007, 14) concluded.

Burials are connected to social understanding.[5] Changes in burial reflect changes in social relations. Burials are a means of maintaining the status of a social group after they lose one of their own (Sørensen 2004a, 283f.). At the beginning of the period of the oak-coffin burials, a change in burial praxis occurred (Sørensen 2004a, 290). Even if a person was buried individually, their interment was unlikely to have been an expression of purely individual burial

because of the fact that burial mounds contained multiple persons. Nonetheless, different types of and variations within style allowed for individual expression.

Individuality and Mobility

As described in the previous section, it is difficult to separate the individual from the group. This is a problem which will be examined further below. However, to facilitate the best understanding of the individual within the group in terms of the material culture in question here, it is necessary to first investigate the connection between Jutland and Germany in the Bronze Age.

German Connections

In southern Germany, women's costumes were known to look like the ones seen in the north, albeit with the addition of other types of jewellery (Laux 1971, 131-148; Wels-Weyrauch 1994, 59-64). The costume traditions and equipment most similar to those of the Jutish oak coffins are those from what is now northern Germany. One must then question the manner in which variations in style (such as is visible in the daggers) were employed. As with the example from the Kalahari San, the oak-coffin men possessed the same types of equipment differentiated by slight differences in style or ornamentation. While this line of enquiry deserves a study of its own, some conclusions can be drawn from general observation. That all of these individuals had the same type of equipment implies that the Danish group must have been in contact with groups within Bronze Age Germany (Kubach-Richter 1994, 54-58). In Germany, there are not as many preserved textiles and costumes as there are in Denmark (Kubach-Richter 1994, 54). Therefore, when Danish male dress is used in the depiction of a German male, he could almost be mistaken for the man from Guldhøj (Fig. 8, see also Fig. 2).

One reconstruction of a male grave northwest of Vaale near Itzehoe, Schleswig-Holstein is worthy of particular note. In addition to containing costume items typical of Denmark, the grave contains items similar to those found at Trindhøj (Boye 1896, 88-92; Jensen 1998, 61-63): a fibula, two swords, a hanger for a sword scabbard, a dagger, a bronze axe, a folding chair similar to the one found at Guldhøj (Boye 1896,

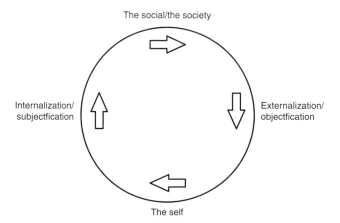

The social/the society

Internalization/
subjectfication

Externalization/
objectfication

The self

Figure 7. This illustration demonstrates a Bronze Age example of how a group that has created an object can be capable of transferring and maintaining its signal value. In this fashion, an object goes through a process in which its meaning is potentially changed when it is discovered by a new person (or group) – after Berger 1974, 1-88; Berger and Luckmann 2003, 205-216.

Figure 8. Reconstruction of a male grave from northern Germany based on the grave goods from Vaale, Schleswig-Holstein – after Kubach-Richter 1994, 55.

70-79; Jensen 1998, 129-134)) and a clay pot (Kubach-Richter 1994, 55). This resonates well with Miller's theory concerning socially-connected groups insomuch as they absorb some of the same objects (Miller 1985, 167). Berger and Luckmann extrapolated further (1974), arguing that objects could be accepted as long as the ability to recognise new material was maintained (see also Berger and Luckmann 2003).

Metal objects and dress were not the only similarities between these two regions. Fourteen separate instances of fragments of wooden vessels with pewter pins have been found in Denmark and northern Germany (Boye 1896; Jensen 1998). These vessels are interpreted as being part of a drinking ritual (Jensen 2002, 296-301) used in social kinship and exchange connections.

Further Geographic Connections

The distant connections associated with the oak-coffin material go even further afield. Folding chairs such as the one from Guldhøj (and its compatriots in Germany and Sweden) have also been found in Egypt and Greece (Fig. 9). One of the best examples comes from Thebes and has been dated to 1450-1400 BC (Jensen 1998, 129-139; Jensen 2002, 269). But Egypt was not alone in influencing Bronze Age Scandinavia. The tradition of mound burial began with culture groups north of the Alps and spread northwards through southern Germany to Scandinavia (Jensen, 1998, 140).

To explore these differences, it is necessary to look at burial in greater detail. Women can be seen as status markers because of the signal value expressed by their burial material. In the Lüneburg area they used

Figure 9. The folding chair from Guldhøj (left) and the one from Thebes, Egypt (right) are very similar in formal appearance and date approximately from the same time period – after Broholm 1952, fig. 213 (right); Jensen 2002, 269 (left).

hair jewellery (*Haarknotenfibeln*). It has been suggested that these may have worked as ethnic markers (Laux 1971, 32-34; Sørensen 1997, 104). These hair pieces were not worn by all women. Indeed, those who carried them were often buried with non-local jewellery pieces typical of Southern Scandinavia (Sørensen 1997, 104). Perhaps the cord skirt best known from the Egtved woman could be considered an ethnic marker similar to the *Haarknotenfibeln*. Remains of similar garments have been found at Borum Eshøj (Jensen 1998, 15-18) as well in parts of southern France in the Late Bronze Age (Jørgensen *et al.* 1982, 53).

Individuality or Group Identity

According to Treherne (1995, 107f), development in the Bronze Age was an ideological change which emphasized personal status without individualisation. The interesting part of personal display was that while the individual seemed more prominent, as far as burials were concerned, the body was less visible than was the case with earlier megaliths (Treherne 1995, 112). Although mounds varied in size and shape, they differ from megalithic graves in a very important way: they are closed. In this way, the individual could be said to be anonymously visible. Even in new graves, the corpse would have been visible for a short period of time, since the body did not undergo extensive pre-burial treatment (Treherne 1995, 113).

In the beginning, trade in or the possession of bronze helped to sustain a group's status because of the mystique and wealth that were associated with the possession and production of bronze. When trade increased, it could have been a key factor in the development of religion and ideology because of the mystery associated with working bronze. These changes were adopted by the upper echelons of local society (Miller 1985). With ideology came fashion, either in terms of clothing or in the possession (and perhaps display) of certain object types (Boye 1896; Jensen 1998). An examination of Scandinavian material shows that there were variations in the styles from different regions. Jewellery followed a recognizable pattern over a larger geographical area across groups. However, it had a local touch that differentiated between groups without separating them from the accepted ideology (Treherne 1995, 114; Wrobel 2009, 1-7). The challenge was to create connections out of individual identity. Identity required the existence of mutual trust between the groups involved. In other words, if subtle differences were to be noticed and interpreted correctly, the various groups connected by those selfsame patterns of difference could not move beyond a common perception of the body. The body became an object through the signal values of a person's appearance (Treherne 1995, 120; Miller 1985, 167; Berger and Luckmann 2003, 58). Treherne (1995, 126) suggests that the oak-coffin people had a self-identity more than a personal identity based on the answers to the perennial questions of 'Who am I?', 'Where am I from?' and 'To what do I belong?'

Self-identity depends on a person's age as well as their gender (Gowland 2006, 143-152; Sofaer 2000, 390). Besides objects being an expression of a person's perceived needs in the afterlife, it is interesting to see how objects depended upon the person's status at their time of death. This concept is illustrated by the child's grave from Guldhøj. The length of the coffin is 1,3 m (the one beside it measures 2,7 m) and, as well as crab apples, contains an object that has been interpreted as a toy (Boye 1896, 76f.; Jensen 1998, 132f.). The coffin length would indicate the burial of a 6-8 year old child. The combination of these items and the burial parameters evoke the image of a child rather than that of a young man growing toward adulthood. For instance, spiral arm or leg rings could be adjusted to fit an individual regardless of their chronological age. In this way, a piece of jewellery could be attached to (and potentially associated with) someone over an extended period. The removal of such a piece could perhaps then have been greatly significant for the individual concerned (Sofaer 2000, 398). These items reflect the status of the social group and affect a person's self-identity in connection to the aforementioned three questions. While such questions are potentially answered by such a piece of physical ornamentation, at the same time, these types of pieces create the ability to recognise and be recognised by others wearing similar adornments. These patterns of recognition are generally thought to display the type of persons that were displayed through burial material (Johansen *et al.* 2003, 35f.).

Jewellery partially demonstrates the contrast between male and female (Sofaer 2000, 392). Although male and female jewellery was produced from the same material, its shape suggested different meanings (Boye 1896; Jensen 1998).Women can often be recognised by the presence of bronze jewellery around the neck, ankles, arms, fingers and/or ears (Johansen *et al.* 2003, 46). Examples at Taarnholm include a jewellery set consisting of rippled diadem-shaped neck jewelry,[6] two arm rings and a thin spiral ring. A jewellery set consisting of a bronze earring, belt plate and two arm rings was found at Egtved (Boye 1896, 149-152; Jensen 1998, 15-18). Such jewellery made the status and identity of women very visible. However, it also affected their mobility, as is addressed in the following section.

Female Mobility

While women are less well-represented than men within the oak-coffin dataset (Randsborg 1975, 203-205), their presence is strong enough to make a study of their long-distance mobility and physical movement worthwhile.

Women's Geographical Mobility

As was mentioned earlier, although some women in Central Europe moved between distances as great as 50-200 km, the majority moved within their local social groups (Jockenhövel 1991, 60; Bergerbrant 2007, 118). There are examples of women buried in Lüneburg costume in Southern Scandinavia as well as examples of women buried in a combination of Lüneburg costume pins and Nordic bronze objects (Bergerbrant 2007, 119). These might represent marriage alliances both between northern Germany and Southern Scandinavia and Southern Scandinavia and more northern areas in Period II. As far as costume and physical adornment is concerned, after Period IB, alliances were forged across local regions. Bergerbrant (2007, 131) concludes that an overwhelming importance was placed upon appearance and action in the Bronze Age and that this in turn affected social understanding. At the same time, room for regional differences and differentiation remained. These regional differences could be described as a combination of fashion and sets of rules. In certain instances, however, items were also an expression of or reference to exotic places (e.g. the glass pearl from Ølby), and this latter case should also be taken into consideration. While there are many similarities between the Danish oak coffins, these similarities were based around lifestyle, contact areas and overarching group identities. Therefore, it is easy to pick out grave trends. However, there was always room for a local touch – however small – which could be indicative of migration (Bergerbrant 2007, 131).

Women's Physical Mobility

Costume ornaments of the same type as those found in burials are also found on settlements. The objects are therefore likely to have been used *in vivo* by virtue of a symbolic value associated with costume and identity. This relation became further established when a certain arm ring could not have been removed after its initial attachment. This was determined by the presence of rings whose diameter made it possible to be easily put on and taken off (Sørensen 1997, 102). The grave of a woman was found near Upflamör south of Reutlingen in Baden-Württemberg in which the deceased wore two leg rings which were attached by a chain below the knees (Bergerbrant 2007, 64; Jensen 2001, 176). This would have certainly limited her physical movements. Similar pieces (i.e. either exceedingly large or placed in such a way so as to hinder general movement) have also been recovered elsewhere (Sørensen 1997, 108; Wels-Weyrauch 1994).

Scientific studies have shown that clothing was normally produced from wool with natural brown mottling. The Skrydstrup woman's belt was constructed out of specifically selected lighter wool (Nielsen 1979, 6f.). This costume was standardized (as described earlier) and would also have somewhat limited physical movement. What is not yet known is the way in which the skirts found at Borum Eshøj, Skrydstrup and Melhøj (Jørgensen *et al.* 1982, 49f.) were worn (Jensen 1998, 155f.). Interestingly, the Melhøj woman is the only female within the dataset to have been buried with a cloak (Jørgensen *et al.* 1982, 52). Upon examination of the Danish oak coffins' jewelry, it seems that it was mainly belt plates which limited the movement of women, as such plates required upright posture and made it difficult

to bend at the waist. Belt plates have been found in five graves, of which Egtved is the best known (Boye 1896; Jensen 1998, 15-18). Even if women were less well-represented in graves, the oak-coffin period was a time in which women became more visible via their material identity because of the jewellery. The more a woman's physical mobility was limited by jewellery, the richer her relatives and connections were assumed to be. The limitation of physical mobility and its associated high status was not limited to cultures of Bronze Age Europe. Han China's practice of foot binding had similar status connotations and was also a natural part of female gender identity within a specific social caste (Ko 1997, 12 and 21). One must recall that the limitation of women's mobility in the Bronze Age should not be viewed from a modern, feminist approach; it was likely to have been a natural part of the identity in the period. In connection to the oak-coffin burials, the identity that a person

Muldbjerg/Trindhøj (male) Guldhøj (male) Borum Eshøj (young male)

Lille Dragshøj (male) Egtved (woman) Skrydstrup (woman)

Borum Eshøj (woman)

Figure 10. A schema of the various hairstyles of Bronze Age persons: Muldbjerg (hair combed back); Trindhøj (male with thick mid-length hair); Young man from Borum Eshøj (curly hair); Guldhøj (male with short hair); Lille Dragshøj (short hair on the sides and a long part from the forehead down the back); Woman from Borum Eshøj (long hair); Egtved woman (short hair); Skrydstrup woman (hair up). Their hair colour was probably light to medium blond. However, we are missing some details as to the exact lengths of the various hairstyles. The Borum Eshøj woman has been depicted with her hair down, however it is also possible that it might have been pinned or tied up in some way. The males from Muldbjerg and Trindhøj are shown together, due to lack of information on their hairstyles – based on Boye 1896; Jensen 1998.

possessed in life and at their time of death continued into the afterlife.

Conclusion

The impression Poulsen (1991) gave of Wirsla in the fictional rendition of the Egtved woman's life cannot be a reflection of past reality because of its emphasis on her specifically foreign nature. The exotic and the rare were not fungible. However, given that there were many similarities between people over large geographical areas, it has to be the aforementioned capacity for recognition which created the connections between social groups. Object types were often repeated in oak-coffin burials, while styles varied. These differences were due partly to gender divisions (Bergerbrant 2007), but also to the age divisions which were also highly dependent upon a person's gender (Gowland 2006).

Bronze Age persons were certainly concerned about their appearance. The bodies of men were shaved, the nails rounded (recognisable in two separate instances). Both men and women varied in terms of hairstyle (Fig. 10). Hairstyle and the length of the hair held meaning, as hair could often reflect what an individual's style was in life. Upon study of the bronze figures from the period (Fig. 11), it appears that there was no specific connection between hairstyle and costume; bronze figures are found with cord skirts accompanied by both short (like the Egtved woman) and long locks (Jensen 2001, 176; Rud 1966, 209f.).

Even if there were room for a personal touch, the individual must still adapt to the norm. There were no signs of deviance within the oak coffins, perhaps due to the fact that friends and relatives arranged burials rather than the deceased. Due, however, to the hierarchical structure of society, there was not enough social room for people to deviate from the norm. People were held in place and held a place by means of their costume, jewellery and perhaps their hair and the type of knife in their belt, as suggested by Miller (1985) and Berger and Luckmann (2003). The Egtved woman is often depicted as being both mysterious and unique. However, when other cord skirts were found in Denmark and elsewhere in Europe and the material evidence from bronze figurines was examined, it seems more likely that this type of dress was common in its time, perhaps representing a social group that has yet to be properly understood.

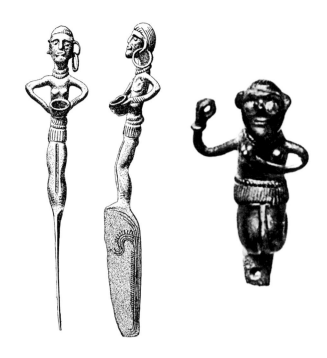

Figure 11. Two examples of bronze figures with cord skirts and different hairstyles. The figurine on the razor (left) has short hair which has been combed back and the kneeling goddess from Faardal, Denmark (right) has long hair – after Rud 1966, 209-210 (right); Kristiansen and Larsson 2005, 261 (left).

The most surprising thing revealed by this study is that women cannot be categorized as easily as the men. For example, because of his folding chair, the man from Guldhøj was categorised as a man of importance, possessed of external contacts. The young man from Borum Eshøj was thought to be a person from a wealthy family, but the absence of a cloak and the inclusion of a dagger instead of a sword in the scabbard are thought to be indicative of him having died before being able to take up the mantle of a more important man within society.

Women showed status in terms of their grave goods, but they are harder to place according to the function they must have had when alive. Grave goods alone could be indicative of age, status and place of origin. The discipline has yet to come to grips with the appropriate way by which to consider the signal value of the deceased. It is possible that hairstyle might have been indicative of group status or some form of prestige. This idea is supported by the Danish National Museum's find of plaited hair (sacrificed around 350 BC) Fårup and Thorup.

Identity can change through change of jewelry or hairstyle. But some identities become a part of the body. As mentioned earlier, some types of jewellery are impossible to remove. However, there is another consideration of bodily decoration which has yet to be addressed: Wels-Weyrauch (1994, 59) writes that tattoos are known from both male and female Scythians burials. Certainly the awls found in the grave good repertoire of the North European Bronze Age could have been used for the production of such bodily adornment. Unfortunately, for the time being, the lack of a volume of very well-preserved awls hinders such a study.

In conclusion, identity and mobility are very complex, and exist on many levels. In many ways, the body is connected to identity, but identity is also connected to place of origin. It seems people could maintain the old and yet at the same time augment their identities with the addition of new parts. In this way, perhaps it is best to speak of a single person's identities rather than identity.

Appendix 1

1. **Melhøj**, Mjallerup at Aalborg, dated 1220 BC (Jørgensen *et al.* 1982, 19, 22-23).
2. **Mound at Jerslev I and II**, Jerslev, Hjørring amt (Boye 1896, 15-18).
3. **Langhøj at Svennum**, Jerslev, Hjørring amt (Boye 1896, 19-21).
4. **Fladhøj**, Flynder, Ringkøbing amt, northwest Jutland (Jensen 1998, 74; Boye 1896, 21-23).
5. **Bredhøj**, Måbjerg, Ringkøbing amt; two oak coffins (Jensen 1998, 126; Boye 1896, 24-29).
6. **Muldbjerg**, Hover, Ringkøbing amt; three oak coffins dated to 1365 BC (Jensen 1998, 110; Boye 1896, 30-37).
7. **Store Mound**, Barde, Vorgod, Ringkøbing amt, dated around 1373 BC (Jensen 1998, 105; Boye 1896, 38-44).
8. **Mound at Ungstrup**, Torning, Viborg amt (Jensen 1998, 126; Boye 1896, 45).
9. **Store Ørnhøj**, Hemmed, Randers amt; two oak coffins, one cremation (Boye 1896, 46-48).
10. **Borum Eshøj**, Borum, Aarhus amt; three oak coffins dated to 1351 BC and 1345 BC (Jensen 1998, 83; Boye 1896, 49-64).
11. **Egtved**, Located west of Vejle, Vejle amt, dated ca. 1370 BC (Jensen 1998, 9-10).
12. **Storehøj**, Located at Kongeådal (Jensen 1998, 127-128).
13. **Guldhøj**, Vamdrup, Ribe amt; three oak coffins, one of them was a child burial located at Kongeådal (Jensen 1998, 128; Boye 1896, 70-80).

14. **Mound at Vester Vamdrup**, Vamdrup, Ribe amt (Boye 1896, 81).
15. **Store Kongehøj**, Vamdrup, Ribe amt; four oak coffins, one of them was a child burial (Jensen 1998, 129; Boye 1896, 82-87).
16. **Trindhøj**, Vamdrup, Ribe amt; three oak coffins, one of them was a child burial dated ca. 1347 BC (Jensen 1998, 61; Boye 1896, 88-95).
17. **Jels**, Near Gram in southern Jutland, dated ca. 1348 BC (Jensen 1998, 148-149).
18. **Skrydstrup**, Near Jels in southern Jutland, date from the beginning of the 12th century BC (Jensen 1998, 9, 150-165).
19. **Mound at Foldingbro Krogaard**, Folding, Ribe amt (Boye 1896, 96-97).
20. **Fladshøj**, Føvling, Ribe amt (Jensen 1998, 128; Boye 1896, 98-100).
21. **Stevnhøj**, Marstrup, Haderslev amt (Jensen 1998, 49; Boye 1896, 101).
22. **Mound at Dybvadgård**, Rise, Aabenraa amt (Jensen 1998, 78; Boye 1896, 102-104).
23. **Mound at Stamplund**, Hjortkjær, Abenraa amt (Jensen 1998, 42-43; Boye 1896, 105-106).
24. **Mound at Nybøl**, Hjortkjær, Aabenraa amt, dated 1275 BC (Jensen 1998, 127; Boye 1896, 107-108).
25. **Toppehøj**, Bjolderup, Aabenraa amt (Jensen 1998, 35; Boye 1896, 109-111).
26. **Mølhøj**, Uge, Aabenraa amt (Jensen 1998, 44; Boye 1896, 112).
27. **Mound at Terkelsbøl**, Tinglev, Tønder amt (Jensen 1998, 79; Boye 1896, 113).
28. **Lille Dragshøj**, Højrup, Haderslev amt, dated ca. 1373 BC (Jensen 1998, 54; Boye 1896, 114-116).
29. **Tvillinghøj**, Skjærbæk, Haderslev amt (Jensen 1998, 49; Boye 1896, 117-118).
30. **Nøragerhøj**, Emmerlev, Tønder amt (Jensen 1998, 45-46; Boye 1896, 119-120).
31. **Rønhøj**, at Nydam in southern Jutland (Jensen 1998, 158).
32. **Store Firehøj**, Slangerup, Frederiksborg amt (Jensen 1998, 122; Boye 1896, 121-122).
33. **Lundehøj**, Græse, Frederiksborg amt (Boye 1896, 123-125).
34. **Vallerødhøj**, Hørsholm, Frederiksborg amt (Jensen 1998, 122; Boye 1896, 126-128).
35. **Mound at Vejlby**, Ferslev, Frederiksborg amt (Boye 1896, 129-131).

36. **Mound at Vellerup**, Vellerup, Frederiksborg amt (Jensen 1998, 124; Boye 1896, 132-133).
37. **Løfthøj or Garderhøj**, Gjentofte, Copenhagen amt (Jensen 1998, 124; Boye 1896, 134-136).
38. **Mound at Ølby**, Højelse, Copenhagen amt (Jensen 1998, 122; Boye 1896, 137-139).
39. **Mound at Tårnholm**, Tårnborg, Sorø amt; three oak coffins (Boye 1896, 149-152).

Notes

1. This paper has deliberately used the term 'social group' rather than 'society,' as the latter is a human product. Mankind, by contrast, is a social product. Likewise, the term 'community' would be too modern an idea to use in the Bronze Age. Berger and Luckmann's (2003) concept (in which it is the individual who chooses to act in concert with others who creates social unity) is used it its stead.
2. See Appendix 1. (Distribution map with additional information about the 39 burial mounds referenced in this article).
3. This is not unusual, other mound graves are also divided according to sex, e.g. seen in Single Grave Culture burials (2800-2400 BC).
4. Daggers are unisex objects, the difference is that men are more often found with daggers than with swords (Jensen 1998; Boye 1896).
5. Social understanding refers to non-verbal communication through different kinds of signals and signal values.
6. A neck collar type that is spread over the whole Nordic Bronze Age region (Wrobel 2009, 1-7).

Bibliography

Aner, E. & K. Kersten 1986: *Die Funde der älteren Bronzezeit des nordischen Kreises in Dänemark, Schleswig-Holstein und Niedersachsen*. VIII. Ribe Amt. Neumünster.

Berger, P.L. 1974: *Religion, samfund og virkelighed elementer til en sociologisk religionsteori*. København.

Berger, P.L. & T. Luckmann 2003: *Den sociale konstruktion af virkeligheden*. København.

Bergerbrant, S. 2007: *Bronze Age Identities. Costume, Conflict and Contact in Northern Europe 1600–1300 BC*. Stockholm Studies in Archaeology 43. Lindome.

Boye, V. 1896: *Fund af egekister fra bronzealderen i Danmark et monografisk bidrag til belysning af bronzealderens kultur*. 1986 (reprinted). København.

Broholm, H.C. 1952: *Danske Oldsager. Ældre Bronzealder*. København.

Eastwood, E.B. 1999: Red Lines and Arrows. Attributes of Supernatural Potency in San Rock Art of the Northern Province, South and South-Western Zimbabwe. *The South African Archaeological Bulletin* 54, 169, 16-27.

Gowland, R. 2006: Ageing the Past. Examining Age Identity from Funeral Evidence. In: Growland, R. & C. Knusel (eds.): *Social Archaeology of Funerary Remains*. Oxford, 143-152.

Hornstrup, K.M. 1997: Chronological Problems the transition from the Early to the Late Bronze Age in Denmark. In: Jensen, C.K. & K.H. Nielsen (eds.): *Burial and Society. The Chronological and Social Analysis of Archaeological Burial Data*. Aarhus, 65-69.

Jensen, J. 1998: *Manden i kisten. Hvad bronzealderens gravhøje gemte*. København.

Jensen, J. 2001: *Oldtiden i Danmark. Bronzealder*. København.

Jensen, J. 2002: *Danmarks Oldtid. Bronzealder, 2.000-500 f.Kr.* Viborg.

Jockenhövel, A. 1991: Räumliche Mobilität von Personen in der mittleren Bronzezeit des westlichen Mitteleuropa. *Germania* 69, 1, 49-62.

Johansen, K.L., S.T. Lauersen & M.K. Holst 2003: Spatial patterns of social organization in the Early Bronze Age of South Scandinavia. *Journal of Anthropological Archaeology* 23, 33-55.

Jørgensen, L.B., E. Munksgaard & K. Nielsen 1982: Melhøjfundet. En hidtil upåagtet parallel til Skrydstrupfundet. *Aarbøger for Nordisk Oldkyndighed og Historie* 1984, 19-55.

Ko, D. 1997: The Body as Attire. The Shifting meanings of the Foot Binding in Seventeenth-Century China. *Journal of Women's History* 8, 4, 8-27.

Kubach-Richter, I. 1994: Nadel, Schwert und Lanze-Tracht und Bewaffnung des Mannes. In: Jockenhövel, A. & W. Kubach (eds.): *Bronzezeit in Deutschland*. Stuttgart, 54-58.

Laux, F. 1971: *Die Bronzezeit in der Lüneburger Heide*. Veröffentlichungen der urgeschichtlichen Sammlungen des Landesmuseum zu Hannover 18. Hildesheim.

Miller, D. 1985: *Artefacts as categories a study of ceramic variability in Central India*. Cambridge.

Nielsen, K.H. 1979: *Kvindedragten fra Skrydstrup – beretning om en ny rekonstruktion af en 3000 år gammel dragt*. Haderslev.

Poulsen, J.A., 1990: *Pigen fra Egtved. En skæbne fra bronzealderen. Vojens.*

Price, T.D., C. Knipper, G. Grupe & V. Smrcka 2004: Strontium Isotopes and Prehistoric Human Migration. The Bell Beaker Period in Central Europe. *European Journal of Archaeology* 7, 1, 9-40.

Randsborg, K. 1975: Befolkning og social variation i ældre bronzealders Danmark. *Kuml* 1973-74, 197-206.

Rud, M. 1966: *Jeg ser på oldsager*. København.

Sofaer, J.D. 2000: The Role of Early Metalwork in Mediating the Gendered Life Course. *World Archaeology* 3, 3, 389-406.

Sørensen, M.L.S. 1997: Reading Dress. The Construction of Social Categories and Identities in Bronze Age Europe. *Journal of European Archaeology* 5, 1, 93-114.

Sørensen, M.L.S. 2004a: The Grammar of Drama. An Analysis of the Rich Early Bronze Age Grave at Leubingen, Germany. In: Kienlin, T. (ed.): *Die Dinge als Zeichen: Kulturelles Wissen und materielle Kultur*. Universitätsforschungen zur prähistorischen Archäologie 127. Bonn, 283-291.

Sørensen, M.L.S. 2004b: Stating identities. The use of objects in rich Bronze Age graves. In: Cherry, J., C. Scarre & S. Shennan (eds.): *Explaining Social Change: Studies in honor of Colin Renfrew*. Cambridge, 167-176.

Treherne, P. 1995: The Warrior's Beauty. The Masculine Body and Selfidentity in Bronze-Age Europe. *Journal of European Archaeology* 3, 1, 105-145.

Wels-Weyrauch, U. 1994: Im Grab erhalten, im Leben getragen. Tracht und Schmuck der Frau. In: Jockenhövel, A. & W. Kubach (eds.): *Bronzezeit in Deutschland*. Stuttgart, 59-64.

Wrobel, H. 2009: Die Halskragen der Nordischen Bronzezeit. *Mitteilungen der Berliner Gesellschaft für Anthropologie, Ethnologie und Urgeschichte* 30, 1-20.

Are Valued Craftsmen as Important as Prestige Goods

Ideas about Itinerant Craftsmanship in the Nordic Bronze Age

Heide Wrobel Nørgaard

Introduction

Since the beginning of the 20th century, the distribution of metal artefacts has stimulated debates about the organisation of metal crafting. Within this topic, this paper will focus on itinerant craftsman.

Childe's theory about the organisation of metalworking in prehistory (Childe 1930; 1952) is one of the most cited and discussed theories in archaeology (Trigger 1980; Pigott 1965; Rowlands 1971). Childe concludes that Bronze Age metalworkers were highly specialised, full-time craftsmen, and, due to the technical demands of their work, were also accorded high social status (Childe 1930, 4). The organisation of craftsmen into guilds and the possibility that these metalworkers were winnowed out into a "detribalised" class was, for him, very likely (Childe 1930, 30). According to his model, socially independent itinerant craftsmen were the primary means of organising metalworking in prehistory. (Childe 1952, 78) For that reason, mobility was a premise for creativity, due to the fact that craftsmen spread knowledge and developed technical processes in various ways.

> *"But if they were detribalized they were* ipso facto *liberated from the bonds of local customs and enjoyed freedom to travel and settle where they could find markets for their products and skill"* (Childe 1940, 163).

New methods can be applied to Bronze Age material which contrast with Childe's theory about the organisation of metalworking. In McNairn's opinion, the mobile craftsman was employed to explain the "rapid development of the European bronze industry" (McNairn 1980, 42).[1] Theoretical and investigative developments over the past two decades have proved his model unlikely. Ethnographic sources in particular do not support the fundamental pillars of his model, such as that of full-time[2] craftsman (Rowlands 1971, 213-214; Neipert 2006, 51-73). Even if ethnographic examples cannot be caulked directly onto Bronze Age society, they should be taken seriously when discussing the organisation of metalworking.

However, far too little attention has been paid to bronze and bronze working material culture. Is it possible to identify the individual smith through the traces he/she has left on specific bronze objects? What kind of material culture or which kind of material culture traces could be used to identify this rarely-mentioned itinerant craftsman? While this method has already been proposed (Rowlands 1971, 215), it has never been exercised on the material. In this paper, the new crafting methods documented on ornaments from Germany and Scandinavia will be presented and suggestions will be made as to the means by which the metalwork could have been organised. This is possible due to intense observation and technological background knowledge through which individual craftsman's traces can be revealed. New conclusions about crafting and the crafting process resulting from these close observations are presented along with further theoretical contructs concerning the possible ways and means of craftsman exchange.

Variability in Craftsmanship During the Bronze Age in Northern Europe

Before discussing the organisation of metalworking in prehistoric societies, it is necessary to define the different craft directions and processes that are implied by the use of the term of 'metalwork'. In today's world, 'metalwork' encompasses everything from mining, smelting and the extraction of metals to the tool-making process, toreutics[3] and the creation of highly developed models. The variety of metalworking activities is easily illustrated through a study of the ethnography. The Awka smiths of Nigeria, for example, demonstrate a general skill repertoire. They deal with iron forging as well as lost-wax casting and toreutics (Neaher 1979, 358). In Katanga (a southern province of the Republic of Congo), the mining and smelting of copper is carried out by village people under the direction of the chief during the three-month dry season (Rowlands 1971, 212). The actual working of the metal is done only by certain individuals. At the Swamimalei Hereditary Bronze Manufacture in Tamil Nadu, India, employees are solely concerned with a single step within the production process of their bronze figurines: the embedding of the wax model in the clay of the casting mould (Levy *et al.* 2008, 62).

The ethnographic examples described above are of great help in identifying the different crafting duties a metalworker might undertake. They are also necessary for the identification of the diverse products that these craftsmen could contribute to society. The repertoire of a smith consisted of more than just the creation of tools and weapons. It also included tableware or personal ornaments as well as status symbols and religious items. Figuratively, the ability of the individual craftsman might have been the decisive factor for specialisation. Therefore, it might be assumed that tool smiths, fine smiths and all-round smiths co-existed. Hence, the term 'smith' would automatically have included the activities of casting, melting and alloying, even if each denomination of the practice utilised its own terms to describe these activities. Mining and the extraction of metal[4] should be seen as a separate, specialised activity (Primas 2008, 135).

Furthermore, we must concern ourselves not merely with the repertoires of metal craftsmen, but also with the time-span in which crafting was executed. Is it possible that Bronze Age smiths could carry out their activities in tandem with their other duties, or was it already possible that theirs was full-time work by this point in time? How does the itinerant craftsman fit into this topic? An examination of the necessary economic factors required for the existence of each of the described ways of carrying out crafting activities and a subsequent correlation of these with the given possibilities in Bronze Age Europe might allow us to answer this question.

It is only in surplus economies that the community is able to provide for other members' food and living in exchange for specialised work (Rowlands 1971, 212). The ethnographic record, however, suggests additional possibilities for the existence of full-time specialists. The majority of published research on this issue has shown that full-time craftsmanship is commonly related to privileged minorities, or, in other words, elites (Rowlands 1971; 1980; Brumfiel and Earle 1987; Peregrine 1991). Ethnographic research also describes cases in which the metalworker was excluded from work in the fields for religious reasons and was therefore forced to carry out various craft activities. These activities might have been full-time, but they were not necessarily concentrated around a single profession. Ergo, the rate of specialisation is very low. West African Margi and Dogon smiths, for example, perform various wood working activities and are often used for special social duties in addition to their metalworking (Neipert 2006, 69). Their social group supplies them with the goods they require in exchange for labour and expertise.

Ethnographic reports generally agree about the participation of general craftsmen in the common economy of their social unit. These craftsmen perform their various crafting activities part-time. Ethnographic examples, such as that of the Celebres in Indonesia (Marschall 1968, 143), record special kinds of part-time metalworkers who are particularly required before or after the harvest. During this period, customers come with broken or worn tools which are in need of repair. In this instance, their otherwise part-time work is greatly in demand and can be carried out seasonally as a full-time profession (Rowlands 1971, 212).

It might be that this kind of village-dependent, on-demand metalworker was highly likely in the Bronze Age, especially in the case of tool-making craftsmen. In such an instance, the active metalwork-

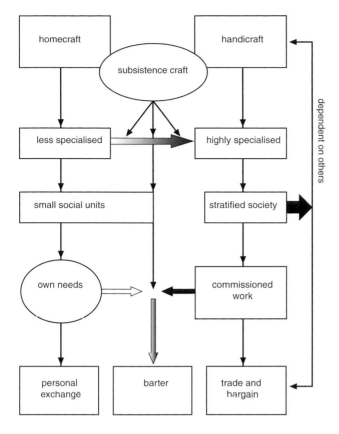

Figure 1. The diagram shows the different categories of craftsmanship explained in the text – based on Schlesier 1981.

er provided special skills and was therefore needed during special periods. Less specialised metalworkers producing a wider range of products could be considered "subsistence craftsmen" (Schlesier 1981, 13). The term "subsistence crafting" was first used by Schlesier to describe this intermediate step between producing for one's own household (homecraft) and a wider, more extensive production for trade. In this latter instance, the products produced would have been crafted on-demand and would generally be exchanged (Schlesier 1981, 13). On the other hand, it might be possible that craftsmen with special skills went beyond the borders of subsistence crafting (Fig. 1) to produce special objects or tools intended for sale (as commodities), while simultaneously participating in the normal economy.

This interrelation between the repertoire and the timing of metalcrafting activities now inevitably raises the questions of specialisation and specialists. 'Specialisation' is mainly used in terms of the repertoire of the smith and his or her product range. By contrast, a 'specialist' does not need to be specialised in one type of object or object group. Rather, he or she shows extraordinary skills and a high dexterity within the profession. The step from a specialised metalworker to a specialist is therefore a matter of quantity and crafting experience.

Specialisation might be possible even within the production of extraordinary bronze ornaments, such as is exemplified by specially skilled workers who concentrate purely on the production of clay casting moulds (Levy *et al.* 2008, 62). M. Primas suggests that, when a high degree of specialisation existed, such craftsmen would only be able to work part-time for their own subsistence (Primas 2008, 87).

It follows to wonder at how such a significant specialist presence in Northern Europe in the Early and Middle Bronze Age could best be explained. Again, the presence of a full-time metalworker might only be possible within a surplus society. This is due to the time and practical knowledge required in the specialisation process as well as the requisite raw materials. Similar conditions would also have been necessary for the existence of the independent craftsman described by Childe (1952). This was rarely possible in pre-industrial societies. Additional ethnographic studies nearly exclude the possibility for socially independent craftwork (see Neipert 2006).

A widespread archaeological theory discusses specialists who depended on a patron who was "typically either a social elite or a governing institution" (Brumfiel and Earle 1987, 5; Vandkilde 1996, Kristiansen 1987; Kristiansen and Larsson 2005; Rowlands, 1971). Such individuals performed their profession as full-time workers with better results. Such elite connections are a potential means by which itinerant craftsman could have organised themselves within the Northern European Bronze Age. Furthermore, the evidence at present supports a clear diversity in the organisation of metalcrafting (Primas 2008; Nørgaard 2011b).

The Connection between Elites and Specialised Craftsmen

The nature of the connection between qualitatively extraordinary handicrafts and the wealthier parts of Bronze Age society is unclear at present. However, a direct link between social influence and a higher quality of craftsmanship has been supported (Kristiansen 1987; Kristiansen and Larsson 2005; Rowlands 1971) or at least considered (Kienlin 2007; Levy, 1991; Primas, 2008) by many renowned Bronze Age researchers. The degree to which archaeological material – especially prestige weapons and ornaments – is connected to social elites is still a matter of debate. A portion of the evidence supports their direct association, suggesting that the rise of powerful elites was tied to the presence of the attached specialists needed to produce those symbols of power displayed by the elites in the first place (Brumfiel and Earle 1987, 5; Vandkilde 1996). The presence of such a symbiosis has two main areas of support. Firstly, a specialist produced goods for others and therefore needed a system of exchange (Rowlands 1971, 219). Secondly, elites required unique, highly visible symbols and ornaments to display their position (Earle 1987, 89). According to Peregrine, elites employed their own specialists as a means of developing their authority (Peregrine 1991, 1). By supporting craftsmen and controlling production facilities, elites maintained their dominance (Peregrine 1991, 3). Controlling these items was a political strategy for the legitimatization of political authority. According to Peregrine, craft activity was, in this way, a political activity rather than an artistic one (Peregrine 1991, 8). He further declared that a society in which the power and authority of higher status groups was based on specific personal ornaments could be referred to as a prestige goods system. In such a system, ornaments were equivalent to wealth and could be used as payment in socio-economic situations, such as bride gifting (Peregrine 1991, 3).

However, what if not the *goods* but the *craftsmen* able to produce such high quality work were exchanged? Such extraordinary handicrafts had the power to strengthen alliances between social groups due to the fact that they were exchanged as part of a gift exchange system (Mauss, 1990) and could unite people through the visible presentation of similar symbols of power (Rowlands 1980). In this case, might it not also be conceivable that the craftsmen themselves were involved in such exchanges?

The Itinerant Craftsman in a New Light

At present, there are but a few instances known in which itinerant smiths travel free from social bonds (Rowlands 1971, 214). Many ethnographic examples of metalworkers who move for their profession demonstrate tight social connections including socio-

economic duties between the smith and the social unit to which they are connected (Neipert 2006, 75-102). The reasons behind this rather cumbersome way to execute one's profession are manifold. Of particular importance here is the kind of mobility that was taking place. Most applicable to Bronze Age society is the "regular craftworking movement" model in which itinerant workers had "diverse seasonal dwellings" (Torbert 1988, 220). Such a model can be easily envisaged in sparcely populated areas where every village could not afford a metalworker. Ethnographic work in Nigeria shows that small-scale settlements often depend on outsiders for the supply of metal wares (Neaher 1979, 357).

Also worthy of consideration is the possibility that "the number of smiths available would outstrip the needs of a local community", making it necessary for some some craftsmen to move to another area (Rowlands 1971, 218). These different patterns of irregular mobility were principally caused by exogenous factors and were probably oriented along established social structures (Cameron 2000) rather than being socially independent, as suggested by Childe (Childe 1940, 163).

The importance of specialised crafts to the exchange system between palace economies in the Near East (around 1000 BC) was presented by Zaccagnini through an examination of written sources (Zaccagnini 1983). The possibility that such an attached specialist exchange existed in the Bronze Age in Northern Europe, however, has yet to be considered. However, this hypothesis should be examined a little further, since the existence of elite structures in the Nordic Bronze Age and its connection to highly specialised crafts is often discussed in archaeological research.

Written sources from the Mari archive describe highly skilled and specialised full-time craftsmen who worked within the palace realm and were tightly bound to the administration which supplied them with food and materials (Zaccagnini 1983, 245). In his study, Zaccagnini distinguished between three different mobility patterns; his redistributive mobility pattern (Zaccagnini 1983, 247-249) occured only in the centralised and spatially-articulated economic structure of the palace. In such an environment, craftsmen were highly dependent on their patrons, and the process could, therefore, be seen as the exploitation of those craftsmen's professional capabilities. The mobility of these craftsmen, (themselves equal to prestige goods), occurred when no qualified workers were present in the kingdom. Within the reciprocate mobility pattern (Zaccagnini 1983, 250-254), the transfer of tightly bound specialists occurred between partners of different rank. "The exchange of qualified manpower between different palace organizations is patterned according to the rules of gift-exchanges" (Zaccagnini 1983, 250). Due to the fact that these specialists were seen as prestige-goods and were not, therefore, customary items sent with gift or tribute, they could be requested and/or refused or dispatched like gifts (Zaccagnini 1983, 251).

That exchange of people within such a network is nothing unusual; it is also confirmed by the existence of the so-called "foreign women". Between 1300 -1100 BC, burials in the vicinity of the Nordic Bronze Age (especially in the Lüneburg Heath and Southern Scandinavia) included characteristic costumes which originated far from their places of deposition (Bergerbrant, 2007); (Bergerbrant 2003, 119-123; Jockenhövel 1991; Wels-Weyrauch 1989). These predominantly female burials are seen as evidence for limited, voluntary female mobility enacted to secure networks and alliances between neighbouring social groups (Jockenhövel 1991).

Given Mauss's assumption that not individuals but rather collectives exchanged obligations and contracts (Mauss 1990, 5), alliances between neighbouring social units during the Northern European Middle Bronze Age might have been of great importance. In the same way that marriage alliances created a connection between social groups, similar personal ornaments (with the aim of distinguishing from the general public) might have been be a strong factor in connecting different social or hierarchical cadres. As mentioned by Rowlands "to gather and hold a warrior force, a ruler had to offer suitable rewards... symbolized by similarly exalted items of wealth" (Rowlands 1980). The exchange of specialist craftsmen between evenly allied partners could, therefore, be seen as an "act of politeness" and might form a small part of a "much more general and enduring contract" (Mauss 1990, 5) between social units at that time (Fig. 2).

The "reciprocative mobility pattern" (Zaccagnini 1983) cannot be directly transferred to the Nordic Bronze Age. It must be subjected to some changes due to significant deviations in the social and eco-

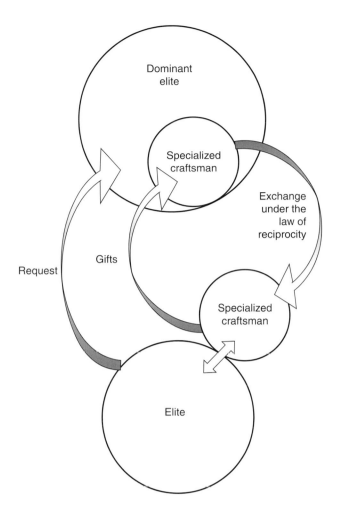

Figure 2. The visual representation of the "reciprocative mobility pattern" – after Zaccagnini 1983.

nomic structures of the time. In opposition to the highly structured society described in the documents from the Mari archives, we assume the Nordic Bronze played host to several more or less equal social elites (Kristiansen and Larsson 2005; Vandkilde 1996). Accordingly, a model must be created based on exchange relationships between equal partners. There might also have been an exchange of these prestige items separate from regular exchange. Finally, the possibility remains that there were two different types of "reciprocative mobility patterns" for specialists within this area. An unequal exchange might have existed in which specialists were exchanged for prestige objects with the expectation that the specialist remained at their new destination (Fig. 3). By contrast, an equal exchange might have existed in which specialists of different kinds were exchanged in relation to the type of work that needed to be done (Fig. 4). Both systems might have operated under the law of reciprocity (Mauss 1990, 13).

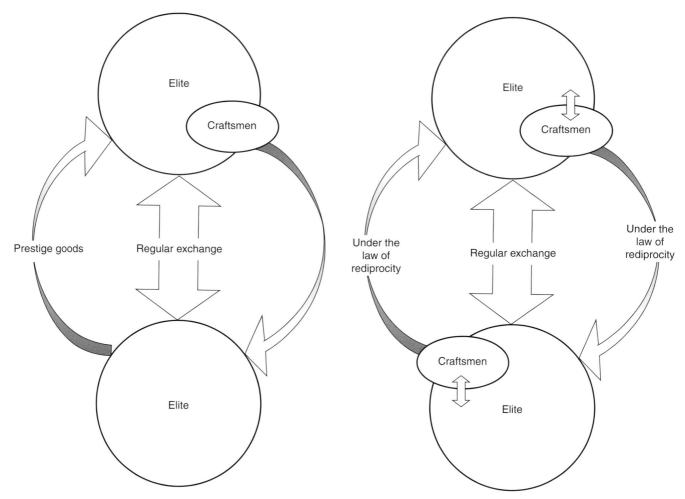

Figure 3. The "unequal exchange model" in which specialized craftsman are exchanged at a prestige goods level in addition to regular exchange – after Zaccagnini 1983.

Figure 4. The "equal exchange model" in which specialized craftsman are exchanged for each other in relation to lack of work.

Finding the Itinerant Craftsman in Material Culture

In contrast to the Middle East, material culture is the only available source for the investigation of the organisation of crafting in the Nordic Bronze Age. How is it possible to detect the movement of attached specialists in societies without written sources? Assuming that the magnificent decorated objects in question had an important and exclusive position in the Bronze Age assemblage, it follows that the same objects could have been used as an indication of social position or wealth (Primas 2008, 159; Sørensen 1997). Furthermore, these objects were made to be seen and, therefore, were likely to have been thought to present their owners in the best possible way. Customised objects can only be achieved through direct contact between craftsman and customer.

The material culture of the Nordic Bronze Age is rich in forms that were not subjected to great stylistic change over wide areas. Suppose, therefore, that the meaning of these objects was in the visual demonstration of social class rather than the representation of the individual partners who formed an alliance. As a result of these requirements, exchange must have taken place separately from normal trading activities. Such a disseminated picture of prestige objects could have been caused by the presence of mobile craftsmen (assuming a direct contact between craftsman and customer would have been necessary) whose mobility was part of a dependent relationship. In this case, the attached specialist could have become an itinerant specialist.

The determination of the craftsman, or the "hand that crafted"[5] in archaeological material is only possible through the intensive investigation of crafting traces on the objects themselves. To do this, it is necessary to be aware of the fact that certain physical apply just as well to the prehistoric world as to the current one. Therefore, it is possible to reveal working steps by detecting the traces left by the tools or even those distinct patterns that appeared during the working process. When objects show similar traces or similar underlying patterns in their construction, than there is a high possibility that they were crafted by the same hand.

New research on crafting traces in the area of the Northern European Bronze Age could reveal different individual markers on objects crafted through the lost-wax method. The fact that the final forms of objects crafted via the lost-wax method are already set in the model suggests that similarities in crafting traces must be clear evidence for their origin from the same craftsman/workshop. Some newly identified individual markers which could help to identify the itinerant craftsman in future research were recently documented on neck collars and belt-discs from Mecklenburg, Germany (Nørgaard 2011b).

Among other things, it was noted that the neck collars from Lubmin[6] and Sarmstorf[7] demonstrated wave-like changes in the rib notches. More intensive investigation suggested that these changes were caused by the spread of surplus material on the cut edges of the rib decoration during the incision of said ribs into the soft wax model (Fig. 5). The result was an accumulation of material on the top of the ribs.

Another example of individual markers that could definitely help to identify a particular craftsman (even over long distances) was documented on two Weitgendorf type pins.

In this case, a visible connection of ornament parts in the form of small notches (indicating a later spreading of material to connect two model parts) could be documented. As malleable material was required for this operation, it can be assumed that these objects were crafted as cast models via the lost wax method (Fig. 6). Furthermore, it was possible to determine multiple percussion tracks (as indicated by multiple points of light on bulges). These tracks suggest that up to three strikes were necessary to give the desired depth to the decorative bosses on the pins from Sparow[8] and Heinrichswalde.[9] Despite the fact that the production techniques of this period did not allow for identical reproduction, it is exactly these kinds of individual signs which allow for the recognition of a single craftsman.

Figure 5. Wave-like changes in the rib notches documented on the neck collar from Lubmin, Kr. Ostvorpommern (ALM 1994/3/1) and the collar from Sarnstorf, Kr. Güstrow (ALM Br. 93) in Mecklenburg – Photo: H.W. Nørgaard with permission from the Archäologisches Landesmuseum Mecklenburg.

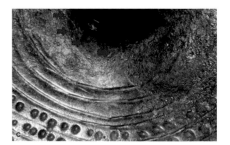

Figure 6. Small notches indicate a subsequent spreading of material connecting two model parts documented on the Weitgendorf type pin from Karbow, Kr. Parchim (ALM Br. 88) and Weisin, Kr. Lübz (ALM 2195) and on the belt disc from Dabel, Kr, Sternberg – Photo: H.W. Nørgaard with permission from the Archäologisches Landesmuseum Mecklenburg.

The Krasmose Neck Collars: An Itinerant Craftsman Case Study

To verify the theoretical models presented in the previous section, a material group was selected which is characterised both by particularly high crafting quality as well as a wide distribution area. Krasmose-type collars are classified as smooth neck collars. Their decoration is comprised of a double spiral row framed by head- and triangle-ornaments. Between the two related spiral rows is an undecorated space. Like the spiral rows, it is framed by triangle-, line-, and head-ornaments. The endpoints of the open space frame point in the direction of the spirals. The final design of the spirals and the ornament combinations on the end-plates vary from piece to piece. A total number of eleven collars, of this type, whose distribution was limited to Scandinavia during Bronze Age Periods II and III, were collected (Nørgaard 2011a, 80-83). Of particular interest to this study is the dispersion of archaeological sites which contained Krasmose neck collars. The main dissemination area of this collar type appears to be in Jutland. Seven collars were recovered from archaeological sites on the mainland in depositions and burials which were dated to Period II (Aner and Kersten 1977) due to the objects which accompanied them. Of the three pieces found on Bornholm, one was recovered as a single find, another in a grave, and the last from a hoard context. Of special interest here is the chronological context in which the Bornholm pieces were discovered; it was different from those in Jutland. In the Krasmose hoard, a metal vessel was found next to bracelets, fibulae and sickles which date from Period III. With regards to this information and the questionable Period II date of the burial from Jomfrugård (using undecorated spiral rings), the Bornholm neck collars shall be placed in late Period II to Period III. This is supported by the date of the Bornhom-type fibula in the Krasmose hoard.

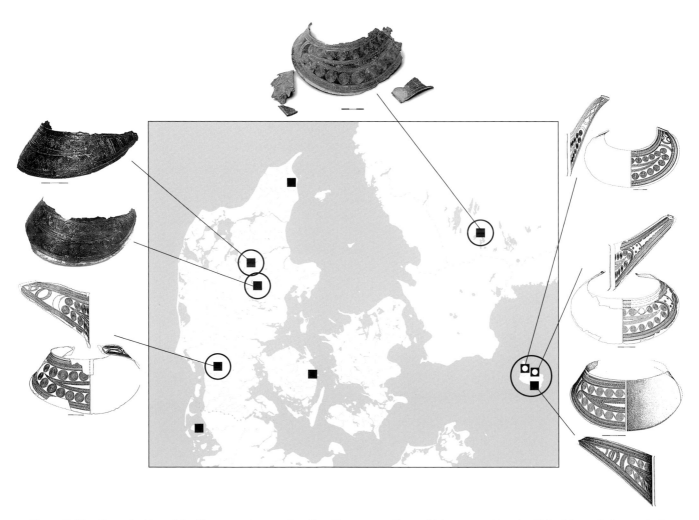

Figure 7. The dissemination of the Krasmose type neck collar. The seven collars which are considered within this study in particular are highlighted – after Nørgaard 2011.

The last piece was found in a rich hoard in Stock-hult, Skåne. Oldeberg dated this hoard to Period II based on the weaponry (Oldeberg 1974). In addition to the Krasmose-type neck collar, this hoard contained two other collars with spiral decoration. These two collars were decorated with three spiral rows in the same style as were the Krasmose collars. The Stockhult-type neck collar, however, appeared only in southern Sweden in late Period II and Period III.

The decoration on each Krasmose neck collar is slightly different. However, in total, their decorative differences are so small that they can easily be combined into one type group, as seven of the eleven pieces are very similar in appearance. They will be considered in particular in this study (Fig. 7). However, these pieces also differ from each other in terms of their decoration.

It is precisely these subtle nuances of difference that are a decisive criterion for origin studies.

The neck collars from Goting,[10] Rosilde,[11] Slud-strup,[12] and the second collar found at Vorup[13] will be only secondarily involved in this investigation. Although they are similar in formal appearance (i.e. they meet overall criteria), the differences in their decoration indicate that these items were more probably copies of the original collars.

Analysis of the Decorative Elements

Within the Nordic Bronze Age, a variety of decorative elements occur which are often in unique combinations. The fact that these single ornamental details can be combined in unique ways which are themselves indicative of a special local area was revealed by Ronne's study of the Danish islands (Rønne, 1987; see also Aner 1962). This phenomenon has been interpreted as representative of the diverse interests of different communities and the dissemination of their style within an area of influence. Accordingly, it can be hypothesised that the combination of certain decorative elements acted as a social marker. When inverted, this specific combination of ornamental details will enable a researcher to determine its place of origin.

The most commonly used basic elements within the investigated ornaments are bands of parallel lines (Fig. 8, 4) and strips of hanging and standing triangles (Fig. 8, 1). Indeed, the majority of the Krasmose-type neck collars show these decorative elements.

A combination of the two described main decoration strips form a frame around the spirals on

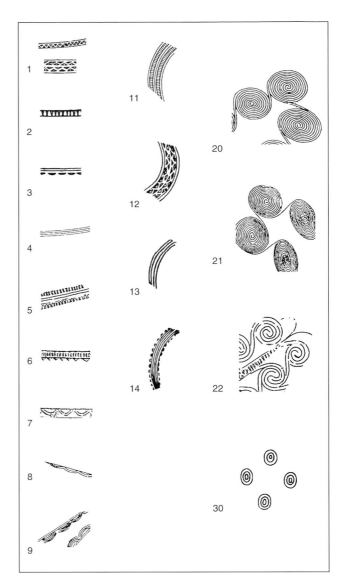

Figure 8. List of the single decorative elements found on the chosen bronze objects. These elements create the basis for the investigation on decoration.

the Bornholm[14] collar as well as the collars from Jomfrugård,[15] Krasmose,[16] Stockhult[17] and Vorup.[18] Another frequent decorative element comprises a series of hanging or standing triangles which tend to appear in the centre of the collar with their tips pointing towards each other. These decorative elements as well as the ones described above can be noted on the collar from Vammen.[19]

The main decorative design of two spiral lines on the front differs from collar to collar. The spirals are of high quality, meaning that they consist of several turns and are uniformly round. The connection between the individual spirals can be constructed as a single or double line, or even as the vertical end of a double spiral. However, only three different variants of the coupling of the two spiral rows were found (Fig. 8, 20-22). On the collars of Hverrehus,[20] Stockhult (Scania) and Jomfrugård (Bornholm), the spirals were not connected at their ends. The last spiral of every line is framed by an ornamental ribbon which begins outside the object field and creates an arc in which the spiral is placed. The second version can be seen on the collars from Bornholm and Krasmose, in which a spiral connects the two rows resulting in a triangular shape. Only the neck collar from Vorup (Ribe) has vertically-merged spirals.

However, there is a marked similarity in the use of the decorative elements despite their scattered distribution. The crafting technique employed for the production of the neck collars is the *cire perdue* method (Rønne 1989; Drescher 1953). However, differences in the ornamentation indicate that we can exclude the possibility that these objects were cast from the same mould.[21]

Nevertheless, the neck collars from Jomfrugård (Bornholm) and Stockhult (Scania) are so similar that they might have been designed by the same craftsman or at least have originated from the same place. The collars from Bornholm and the piece in Krasmose (Bornholm) give evidence for a similar origin. These two differ from the others only in the connection of the spiral rows and in a few extra decorative elements on the end plates. The neck collar from Vorup (Ribe) has the same basic elements, but differs in its spiral decoration. Fundamentally different ornamental ribbons can be found on the neck collars from Hverrehus and Vammen. The former is almost exclusively decorated with hourglass punch ribbons and its lower spiral band is formed of double spirals. The piece from Vammen is adorned with a combination of head-bands and triangular bands as well as a section decorated with double arches bordered by lines.

The three pieces found in Jutland differ in terms of their formal appearances. The collar found in Vorup (Ribe) has the most in common with those pieces from Bornholm and Scania. The probability that the neck collar from Vorup is linked with those of the more eastern regions increases due to its location within a west-to-east contact zone between Jutland and Scania (Nørgaard 2011a, 116). The consideration of the other bronze objects in the assemblage confirms the supposition that the collars originated in Jutland. The inventory of the hoard from Hverrehus (Aner and Kersten 2008) is evident as a local product because of its formal appearance and decoration. Although bracelets with spiral ends often appear in west Zealand, they are also known in Jutland. Accordingly, L8-type swords have a dispersal on Zealand as well. However, Ottenjann observed that the looped eye sword (*Schlingenbandwürfelaugen*) spread accross Zealand and into central Jutland (Ottenjann 1969). Bronze looped motif combs were found in Vammen (Viborg) and Hverrehus (Viborg). These pieces confirm that only objects which originated in Jutland were found at this archaeological site.

The objects from the sites on Bornholm seem to be indigenous, as in two cases the collars were found in assiciation with Bornholm-type fibulae. The hoard from Stockhult[22] in Scania had a different pattern

	Vorup B6622a	Krasmose B647	Bornholm B2884	Jomfrugaard B16577	Gjedsted B13259	*Stockhult* *SHM 11217*	Roskilde B10240	Sludstrup B298	Vorup B6622b
Weight	266 g	124 g	165 g				(16.4 g)	54.6 g	(5.6 g)
Height cm	10.23	9.54	6.60				(3.66)	5.4	(3.72)
Diameter T	12	11	12				–	10.84	–
Diameter B	15	21	19				–	12	–
Spiral size	1.75	1.6	1.1			?	0.68	1	5.4
Spiral coil	12	12	12			5-7	4	4-6	3-4
Spiral middle	D2c	D2b/c	D2c			?	D2a	D2b	D2a
Spiral number	22	23	22			21	(10)	26	(6)
Spiral direction	left	left	right			(left)	left	left	left
Triangle ribbon	yes	yes	yes				no	no	yes
Parallel line	yes	yes	yes				yes	yes	yes
Headband	yes	yes	yes				no	yes	yes
Arrow ribbon	no	no	no				yes	no	no
Hourglass punch	no	no	no				no	yes	yes

* The information is taken from Herner 1987.

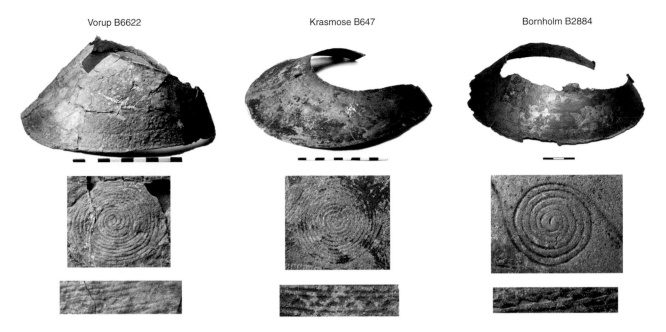

Vorup B6622   Krasmose B647   Bornholm B2884

Figure 9. The figure shows the three large collars described from Vorup (B6622), Krasmose (B647) and Bornholm (B2884). The similarities concerning the size of the collars are clearly visible as well as the differences in the spiral construction (especially in terms of the first and last piece) – Photo: H.W. Nørgaard with permission from the Nationalmuseet København.

(Oldeberg 1974, 68). This rich deposit contained a selection of the most representative pieces from Period II. Because of the placement of the hoard, academic discussion centres around it being a craftsman's deposit (Stenberger 1964, 202). The heavy axes with hemispherical neck knobs are known from Halland and north Jutland. Spearheads of the Ullerslev type (Jacob-Friesen 1967, 143) appear in Scania, on the Danish islands and in central Jutland. In Holland, they occur in northern Jutland and on Zealand. Like most objects in this hoard, the male figurines bear clear evidence of long-distance symbolic relations to the west and southeast (Kristiansen and Larsson 2005, 313).

Based on the individual combination of single decorative elements, an area of origin for the vast majority of Krasmose-type collars could be mapped. Interestingly, some of the pieces with a strong similarity in decorative structure and other formal criteria show significant local elements.

Analysis of Production Marks and the Crafting Process

In order to make valid statements about craftsmen, however, this investigation needs to go far beyond the use of individual decorative elements, as these are not individual-specific but, rather, socio-cultural in nature. The traces which allow for the identification of the artisans must therefore be of a technical nature, i. e characteristic of individual production.

Assuming that the basic steps of the crafting process are similar when completed by the same hand, then similar traces can reveal the ' hand that crafted'. The completion of repetive or similar working habits happens unconsciously and therefore part of the craftsman because of his or her internalised working steps (i.e. the use of counter-clockwise spirals) or the craftsman's own taste and style. Formal attributes (such as the height and weight of an object) are similar when produced by the same person insofar as these pieces should fulfill the same criteria. When analysed comparatively, the ornaments under investigation should be similar in height, weight, diameter, direction, size, orientation and centre (see Table 1). The overall orientation of the various decorative elements should also be comparable. In addition, similar traces in crafting should indicate the existence of a relationship between the pieces under study.

An examination of six of the eleven collars and several additional objects (such as the belt discs from the Vorup burial) revealed extensive differences in technical details between the ornaments. In the following section, it was possible to separate the collars from

B647

B6622

Figure 10. The spirals from the neck collar from Krasmose (B647) and those from the collar of Vorup (B6622) – Photo: H.W. Nørgaard with permission from the Nationalmuseet København.

B647

B6622

Figure 11. The single, decorative ribbons are attached to each other in a similar way. Both pictures show the decoration on the end plates – Photo: H.W. Nørgaard with permission from the Nationalmuseet København.

Rosilde, Sludstrup and Vorup II from the larger ones from Vorup I, Krasmose and Bornholm. The latter pieces show similarities in weight,[23] formal appearance and ornamental details. Concerning spirals, however, the piece from Bornholm[24] differs in the size and, most importantly, in the clockwise turning direction of the spiral it bears (Fig. 9).

The similarities between the technical details of the collars from Vorup and Krasmose are remarkable. The spirals are similar in terms of the coils, the connecting lines (Fig. 10), and even (in some instances) in size. The same method of combining single decorative elements is used on both collars (Fig. 11). Perhaps due to its poor preservation, the Vorup collar displays no visible evidence of hammering like that found on the collar from Krasmose (Fig. 12).

By contrast, the collars from Rosilde, Sludstrup and Göting reveal spirals which were constructed in an entirely different manner. On the Rosilde collar, the space between the single grooves of the spiral differs, making the spiral of lesser quality than those described above. A similarly constructed spiral with varying spaces between the grooves and a different kind of connection between the spirals was included on the Sludstrup collar. Additionally placed vertical connective lines give the piece a unique appearance. Interestingly, additional ornaments in the Sludstrup grave show similarly marked lines and connective junctures between spirals (Fig. 13). In summary, it can be concluded that the technical differences between the objects presented here – at least concerning the spirals – were significant.

Figure 12. Hammer traces on the end roll and the back of the collar from Krasmose. In addition to the fact that these traces prove reworking after the casting process was completed, they can also be a tool to trace the "hand that crafted" – Photo: H.W. Nørgaard with permission from the Nationalmuseet København.

Figure 13, The ornaments in the Sludstrup grave show similar connection points between the spirals as well as similar marks in the lines itself – Photo: H.W. Nørgaard with permission from the Nationalmuseet København.

Prestige Objects Travel? Trading Goods or Proof of the Itinerant Craftsmen

Ongoing investigation of the Krasmose neck collar group shows the potential of detailed examination of archaeological material. The evaluation of the decorative analysis based on established theories supports the idea that there was an active movement of people in the Nordic Bronze Age. Preliminary results show that the Krasmose collars seem to have originated in central Jutland.[25] The basic similarity of the three collars from Hverrehus, Vammen and Vorup could reveal a regional grouping by which the female upper class identified itself. Despite the small amount of ornamental differences, the formal appearance of the

neck collars could be the result of these collars' production in the same workshop. This is also partially supported by the technical analyses. The similarities between the collars from Vorup and Krasmose are so great that they can be interpreted as being crafted by the same hand.

In comparison, the crafting differences in the neck collars from Sludstrup, Rosilde and Göting might be considered to be reworking. It is quite possible that the pieces were crafted based on verbal descriptions or that they represent copies produced from memory. A personal interpretation of a basic pattern is clearly evident in all pieces described.

However, it might be possible that the remains from Rosilde are those of a stranger. This assumption is based on the similarities in the ornamental details with the collar from Gjedsted "Hverrehus".[26] However, the only other piece in the grave which could be used to support the idea of the woman being foreign was a tutulus fragment with remains of a star-shaped arch motif. These kinds of motifs occur on sword hilts in the Early Bronze Age in central Jutland. Nontheless, tutuli with star-bow ornaments are known mainly from northwest Zealand (Rønne 1987, 92) and other parts of Denmark. In the case of the Rosilde burial it is not possible to draw a definitive conclusion connecting the neck collar to those originating in Jutland.

A possible interpretation of the Krasmose-type neck collars would revolve around the use of trade goods or barter objects and would include the presence of moving craftsmen. The possibility that the ornaments travelled as comodities cannot be excluded. The collar from the Stockhult hoard might be one such an example. However, in the case of the Krasmose collars, one must consider that a personal ornament of this quality might be crafted on-demand. Individual additional decorative elements (such as on the collars from Bornholm) suppport this hypothesis. Given that the temporal mobility of specialised craftsman is an established fact in pre-industrial societies, it could be possible that, due to individual changes, the craftsman moved rather than the items he or she produced.

It can be assumed that the first piece which appeared on Bornholm (the collar from Jomfrugård, Period II) was made by the same person who crafted the Vorup collar. Despite slight variations in ornamentation, the other pieces seem to have been created by the same craftsman. Minimal changes and the additional local ornamentation details support the assumption that the craftsman moved from Jutland to Bornholm. The possibility remains that a Bronze Age specialist was 'lent out' to create extraordinary metalwork for the upper class of the neighbouring community. It is also possible that these data patterns represent the movement of a smaller social unit such as a family. The uniformity of the collars described above can be seen to support the connection of the craftsman to a stable social group. In this case, outside influences would not rapidly take root, as there would be no direct need to assimilate.

The detection of itinerant craftsmen in the material culture of the Nordic Bronze Age has yet to be conclusively proven. Nonetheless, the case study of the Krasmose-type collars shows that the dissemination of prestige items needs to be investigated in terms of the similarities of their technical appearance. Only the combination of individual craftsmen's traces and local elements or developments of technical characteristics can prove the existence of itinerants in the Bronze Age. The case study clearly shows the potential of this kind of investigation. While thinking about the organisation of metalcraft in the Nordic Bronze Age, one needs to consider more than one possibility. The ethnographic examples described earlier show that metalcraft can be organised in various ways and that craftsman might be much more mobile (especially in terms of small-scale movements) than was originally expected. A final supporting fact for this thesis might be seen in the low demand for stationary tools. A skilled metalworker can produce any tool required from a simply-constructed fireplace. However, these fireplaces are not easily discernable in the archaeological record. A great quantity of tools are needed to produce wax models (i.e. out of materials such as wood, hair and/or other plant fibres). In light of this, it is easy to imagine that the presence of a itinerant metalworker might not be visible on archaeological sites but rather in the material itself.

Acknowledgements

The research leading to these results has received funding from the European Union Seventh Framework Program (FP7/2007-2013) under Grant Agreement no. 212402. Additional special thanks go to the Archäologisches Landesmuseum Mecklenburg and the National Museum in Copenhagen for supporting my research by allowing me access to the objects. I also wish to thank Samantha Reiter for correcting the English version of this paper and Helle Vandkilde and Svend Hansen for many inspiring discussions.

Notes

1. A summary of Childe´s model of the organization of metalwork in prehistory, critical opinions concerning the itinerant craftsmen and the use of ethnological data to underline this theory can be found in Neipert (NEIPERT 2006, 9-14).
2. "Hence it is not surprising that in the earliest historical societies, as among contemporary barbarians, metallurgists are always specialists…The operations of mining and smelting and casting are too elaborate and demand too continuous attention to be normally conducted in the intervals of tilling fields or minding cattle. Metallurgy is a full-time job. " (Childe 1952, 77).
3. 'Toreutics' refers a metal crafting process in which the metal is formed by hammer and anvil or engraving in order to create a three-dimensional relief.
4. However, there are exceptions. M. Primas (among others) posits that there was an organized approach and specialized knowledge behind the targeted exploration of ores (Primas 2008, 135). Rowlands lists several ethnographic examples in which ores were not exploited by the same people who work metal (Rowlands 1971, 212).
5. The term 'hand' is often used to describe the workshop (or artisan) which produced a series of pieces (Neipert 2006, 26; Driehaus 1983, 50; Driehaus 1961, 22; Biel 1985, 89).
6. Lubmin, Kr. Ostvorpommern; cremation burial in a mound, Period III, five additional goods (ALM 1994/3/1).
7. Sarmstorf, Kr. Güstrow; cremation burial in a mound, Period III, one additional grave good (ALM Br. 93).
8. Sparow, Kr. Waren; burial in a mound, Period II, 41 additional grave goods (ALM LII Z1g1).
9. Heinrichswalde, Kr. Neubrandenburg; closed hoard in wetland, Period II, eight additional finds (ALM 7236b).
10. Goting, Wyk, Föhr; female burial, Period II (Wyk G 65).
11. Rosilde, Vindinge herred, Svendborg amt; closed female burial in a mound, Period II, four additional grave goods (NM B 10239-42).
12. Sludstrup, Kjærum sogn, Hjørning amt; closed female burial in a mound, Period II, three additional grave goods (NM B 298).
13. Vorup, Vejen herred, Ribe amt; closed hoard deposit in a burial mound, Period II, four additional finds (NM 6622).
14. Bornholm amt, unknown place; probably from a burial mound, Period III, unknown additional goods (NM 2884).
15. Jomfrugård, Bornholm amt; closed female burial, Period II (?), two additional goods (NM).
16. Krasmose, Klemensker sogn, Bornholm amt; closed hoard, Period III, 14 additional goods (NM B 647).
17. Stockhult, Schonen; closed hoard, Period II, 48 additional goods (SHM 11217).
18. Vorup, Vejen herred, Ribe amt; closed hoard (?) depos-

ited in a burial mound, Period II, four additional goods (NM 6622).

19. Vammen (sogn), Viborg amt; burial, Period II, one additional good (VSM 2364).

20. Gjedsted sogn (Hverrehus), Viborg amt; probably hoard, Period II, 81 additional goods (NM B 13259).

21. Neck collars are cast using the *cire perdue* method (lost wax casting). A wax model is formed and placed in fine clay. After the form is dry and the wax is rendered out of the form, the liquid bronze will be poured into the mould. The mould is destroyed through the removal of the cast object and therefore cannot be re-used. Nonetheless, the cast collar can be used as a model for further collars, although subsequent results will differ from the original in size and detail.

22. The items in this hoard were integrated in the investigation following after a critical examination because of this hoard's special position in Bronze Age research.

23. The weight of the collar B6622a from Vorup was affected by oxidation.

24. Bornholm amt, unknown location; probably burial mound, Period III, unknown additional goods (NM 2884).

25. This is supported by the chronological data (Aner and Kersten 1997; 2008). The collars cannot have originated on Bornholm because most of them can be dated to Period III.

26. To date, only the collar from Rosilde could be investigated. However, it shows no direct similarities to the collars from Krasmose or Vorup in whose group the Gjedsted collar should belong. Further investigation is necessary in this area.

Bibliography

Aner, E. 1962: Die frühen Tüllenbeile des Nordischen Kreises. *Acta Archaeologica* 33, 165-217.

Aner, E. & K. Kersten 1977: *Die Funde der älteren Bronzezeit des nordischen Kreises in Dänemark, Schleswig-Holstein und Niedersachsen.* III. Bornholms, Maribo, Odense und Svendborg Amter. Neumünster.

Aner, E. & K. Kersten 2008: *Die Funde der älteren Bronzezeit des nordischen Kreises in Dänemark, Schleswig-Holstein und Niedersachsen.* XII. Viborg Amt. Neumünster.

Bergerbrant, S. 2003: Fremde Frau eller i lånade fjädrar? Interaktion mellan Sydskandinavien och norra Europa under period I och II. In: Golhahn, J. (ed.): *Mellan sten till järn. Rapport från det 9:e Nordiska bronsålderssymposiet, Göteborg oktober 2003-10-09/12.* Gotarc Serie C. Arkeologiska skrifter No. 59. Göteborg, 229-240.

Bergerbrant, S. 2007: *Bronze Age Identities. Costume, Conflict and Contact in Northern Europe 1600-1300 BC.* Stockholm Studies in Archaeology 43. Lindome.

Brumfiel, E.M. & T.K. Earle 1987: *Specialization, Exchange and Complex Societies.* Cambridge

Cameron, C.M. 2000: Comment on: Burmeister, Archaeology and Migration. 2000. *Current Anthropology* 41, 555-556.

Childe, V.G. 1930: *The Bronze Age.* Cambridge.

Childe, V.G. 1940: *Prehistoric Communities of the British Isles.* London.

Childe, V.G. 1952: *What happened in History.* Harmondsworth.

Drescher, H. 1953: Eine technische Betrachtung bronzezeitlicher Halskragen. *Offa* 12, 67-72.

Earle, T.K. 1987: Specialization and the production of wealth: Hawaiian chiefdoms and the Inka empire. In: Brumfiel, E.M. & T.K. Earle (eds.): *Specialization, Exchange and Complex Societies.* Cambridge, 64-75.

Jacob-Friesen, G. 1967: *Bronzezeitliche Lanzenspitzen Norddeutschlands und Skandinaviens.* Hildesheim.

Jockenhövel, A. 1991: Räumliche Mobilität von Personen in der mittleren Bronzezeit des westlichen Mitteleuropa. *Germania* 69, 49-62.

Kienlin, T.L. 2007: From the forging of the axes: On the preparation and adaptation of metallurgical knowledge in course of Early Bronze Age. *Praehistorische Zeitschrift* 82, 1-22.

Kristiansen, K. 1987: From stone to bronze. The evolution of social complexity in Northern Europe 2300-1200 BC. In: Brumfiel, E.M. & T.K. Earle (eds.): *Specialization, Exchange and Complex Societies.* Cambridge, 30-52.

Kristiansen, K. & T.B. Larsson 2005: *The Rise of Bronze Age Society. Travels, Transmissions and Transformations.* Cambridge.

Kuijpers, M.H.G. 2012: The sound of fire, taste of copper, feel of bronze, and colours of the cast - sensory aspects of metalworking technology. In: Sørensen, M.L.S. (ed.): *Embodied knowledge. Perspectives on belief and technology.* Cambridge, 137-150.

Levy, J.E. 1991: Metalworking, Technology and Craft Specialization in Bronze Age Denmark. *Archeomaterials* 5, 55-74.

Levy, T.E., A.M. Levy, D.R. Sthapathy, D.S. Sthapathy & D.S. Sthapathy 2008: *Masters of Fire. Hereditary Bronze Casters of South India.* Bochum.

Marschall, W. 1968: *Metallurgie und frühe Besiedlung Indonesiens.* Köln.

Mauss, M. 1990: *The Gift. The form and reason for exchange in archaic societies,* London

Mcnairn, B. 1980: *The Method and Theory of V. Gordon Childe Economic, Social and Cultural Interpretations of Prehistory.* Edinburgh.

Neaher, N.C. 1979: Awka Who Travel. Itinerant metalsmiths of southern Nigeria. *Africa: Journal of the International African Institute* 49, 352-366.

Neipert, M. 2006: *Der Wanderhandwerker.* Rahden/Westf.

Nørgaard, H.W. 2011a: *Die Halskragen der Bronzezeit im nördlichen Mitteleuropa und Südskandinavien.* Bonn.

Nørgaard, H.W. 2011b: Workshops in Mecklenburg. In: Hauptmann, A., D. Modarressi-Therani & M. Prange (eds.): *Archaeometallurgy in Europe III. Abstracts.* 4. Sonderheft. Bochum, 248-249.

Oldeberg, A. 1974: *Die ältere Metallzeit in Schweden.* Stockholm.

Ottenjann, H. 1969: *Die nordischen Vollgriffschwerter der älteren und mittleren Bronzezeit.* Berlin.

Peregrine, P. 1991: Some political aspects of craft specialization. *World Archaeology* 23, 1-11.

Pigott, S. 1965: *Ancient Europe from the Beginnings of Agriculture to Classical Antiquity: A Survey.* Edinburgh.

Primas, M. 2008: *Bronzezeit zwischen Elbe und Po. Strukturwandel in Zentraleuropa 2200-800 v. Chr.* Bonn.

Rowlands, M.J. 1971: Archaeological Interpretation of Prehistoric Metalworking. *World Archaeology* 3, 210-224.

Rowlands, M.J. 1980: Kinship, alliance and exchange in the European Bronze Age. In: Barret, J. & R. Bradley (eds.): *Settlement and Society in the British Later Bronze Age.* BAR International Series 83, 15-57.

Rønne, P. 1987: Stilvariationer i ældre bronzealder. Undersøgelser over lokalforskelle i brug af ornamenter og oldsager i ældre bronzealders anden periode. *Aarbøger for nordisk Oldkyndighed og Historie* 1986, 71-124.

Rønne, P. 1989: Early Bronze Age Spiral Ornament -the technical Background. *Journal of Danish Archaeology* 8, 126-143.

Schlesier, E. 1981: Ethnologische Aspekte zu den Begriffen Handwerk und Handwerker. In: Jankuhn, H., W. Janssen, R. Schmidt-Wiegand & H. Tiefenbach (eds.): *Das Handwerk in vor- und frühgeschichtlicher Zeit.* Göttingen, 9-36.

Stenberger, M. 1964: *Det fortida Svergie.* Uppsala

Sørensen, M.L.S. 1997: Reading Dress. The construction of social categories and identities in bronze age Europe. *Journal of European Archaeology* 5, 1, 93-115.

Torbert, N. 1988: *The Ethnoarchaeology of the Zaghawa of Darfur (Sudan). Settlement and Transcience.* Cambridge.

Trigger, B.G. 1980: *Gordon Childe. Revolutions in Archaeology.* London.

Vandkilde, H. 1996: *From Stone to Bronze. The Metalwork of the Late Neolithic and Earliest Bronze Age in Denmark.* Aarhus.

Wels-Weyrauch, U. 1989: „Fremder Mann". *Germania* 67, 162-168.

Zaccagnini, C. 1983: Patterns of Mobility among Ancient Near Eastern Craftsmen. *Journal of Near Eastern Studies* 42, 245-264.

Materiality and Mobility in the Late Neolithic and Early Bronze Age of Southern Scandinavia

A Comparative Study of Danish Flint and Bronze Daggers

Karin Johannesen

Introduction

Although the European Bronze Age began in the second half of the third millennium BC, bronze did not impact the Danish area until the middle of the second millennium BC. Indeed, other technologies and resources were vital to both economy and society until the Late Neolithic (henceforth abbreviated as LN) of this area (Vandkilde 1996, 295, 298; Kristiansen and Larsson 2005, 112f.). Nonetheless, flint and bronze existed simultaneously in the area of what would become modern day Denmark from the beginning of the LN and were likewise used in a similar fashion (Vandkilde 1996). Bronze eventually gained the upper hand, while flint was relegated to the practical sphere (Eriksen 2010). Flint and bronze are two very different materials, although they were used for some of the same objects. The properties and features of an artefact are important factors in the choices involved in producing material culture. The visual and practical characteristics of bronze were favoured over flint and were thus important to the development of European Bronze Age societies.

In order to shed light on the relations which existed between metal and flint artefacts and the changes exemplified by them during the LN/Early Bronze Age transition, this article makes a comparative analysis of flint and bronze daggers focussing on the features and characteristics of each material as well as the production and depositional practices with which each group of artefacts was associated. The complex relationship between flint and bronze is inserted into a framework of artefact materiality and the different types of networks comprised thereof (including both humans and objects). This analysis will examine the area of what is now Denmark in accordance with the core-periphery model, in which Southern Scandinavia was considered to have been peripheral to the Central European core (Vandkilde 1996, 299; Shennan 1986, 140f.). However, before approaching this topic, we must first begin by examining the nature and interpretation of material culture.

Materiality and Material Culture

The empirical material for archaeological studies is made up of the material culture left behind by past peoples. In modern archaeology, this material is used to outline past society and culture. Certain assumptions are made in these formulations (namely, that artefacts are representative of the ideology of the society to which they belong) (e.g. Hodder 1985; Childe 1956). One of the aspects of artefacts examined in such a fashion is the context in which they occur. However, context can be a tricky thing to define. Paradoxically, context must necessarily be the society which produced a particular artefact as well as the subject being researched by the examination of material culture in the first place. Of course, there are often other objects from approximately the same period which can pro-

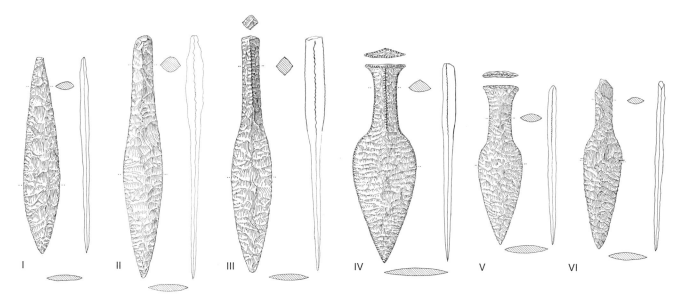

Figure 1. Types of flint daggers – after Lomborg 1973.

	Lomborg 1973		Madsen 1979			Vandkilde 1996	
1400							
1500		VI				EBA	
1600							VI, V A
1700					VI	LN II	
1800		V					I B, IV
1900	LN C	IV	LN C	IV	V	LN I	
2000					III		
2100		III	LN B		II		I, II, III
2200	LN B	II	LN A	I			
2300	LN A	I					
2400							

Figure 2. Chronological periods and flint dagger types.

vide a context for any hypothetical artefact (just as they, in turn, provide context for others). Therefore, one must consider as many artefacts as possible in order to delineate the various aspects of any given society as accurately as possible. To define context, one must view any artefact in light of its social, temporal and cultural present (Robb 2004, 133).

As mentioned above, some assumptions are made in the creation of context. One assumes that material culture is the transformation of ideas and values into physical reality (DeMarrais 2004, 11, 13). One also assumes that objects are used reflectively to signal certain affiliations to (or dissociations from) diverse sections of society (van der Leeuw 2008, 223; Wiessner 1983, 256; Wobst 1977, 319f.; Sackett 1977, 370).

Since the material of which an artefact is made also represents certain characteristics of the artefact itself (Ingold 2007), it is important to take note of the material from which an artefact is comprised (Scarre 2004). This is of import not merely due to functionality, but also because different raw materials required different production methods and had diverse connotations associated with them. In other words, material reflects not just the purpose of an object, but also the pathway of its production (i.e. the decisions that were made during the transformation of raw flint or metal ore into a final end product).

The difficulty for archaeologists stems from the fact that they mostly study material culture in retrospect. The archaeologist's subject material is at the end of a long and complex line of creation, use, loss or deposition and various and sundry formation processes. In order to elucidate meaning from that material, the archaeologist must think backwards (van der Leeuw 2008, 218). By contrast, when considering the characteristics of a specific material in relation to a specific artefact, one must think forwards instead.

The finished artefact has a multitude of expressions, not just in terms of its functionality and design, but also with regard to the connotations conferred by both maker and user. All of these expressions and impressions can be considered to contain a certain kind of information. The most obvious categorisations for such information involve status, provenance or ethnicity. However, we cannot forget that artefacts are simultaneously also objects which can be perceived and used in various ways. Therefore, an object has many layers of information. Materiality is one of those layers. The cultural framework surrounding a particular object (or type of object) is a construction of many elements, the craftsman among them (Högberg 2010, 63). The material from which an object is made can be chosen by necessity and/or it can be used deliberately. Interestingly, this choice is not always practical; there are often cases of less-than-ideal materials being used in place of their more utilitarian fellows. Therefore, any single object exemplifies the range of overlapping choices which define it. These choices interact in different ways, aesthetics counterbalancing usability just as symbolism acts as the counterweight to practicality.

Mobility

Mobility is not limited to the movement of the physical artefact alone. It can also be applied to the movement and transfer of the *idea* of an artefact. Subsequently, this idea can be locally interpreted in another form or material, just as an artefact does not always travel alone but can also carry ideas and symbolism along with it (Urry 2007, 5). Although these ideas can be replicated exactly, they can also be fashioned into versions of the original concept. Alternatively, the original work can be moulded to fit pre-existing traditions. These two types of mobility (i.e. the actual artefact and the connotations carried by it) can of course also be combined in various ways. This can make it difficult to determine the proportion of local to foreign when analysing local innovations with the potential for inter-regional inspiration (Kristiansen and Larsson 2005, 11f, 14). Since materials and ideas were exchanged between different areas and groups of people, this exchange acted to create and shape human relationships, at least in part. Those same relationships were concomitantly one of the factors deciding both which exchanges took place as well as the route or tone said exchanges took in the first place.

Relations and Exchange

Two theories about the interaction between different areas are of note here: the peer polity interaction model (Renfrew 1986) and the core periphery model (Shennan 1994; Sherratt 1994b). The peer polity model considers polities in relation to other polities. These polities are defined as human groups that showed territorial behaviour, regardless of whether they were formally defined in territorial terms (Renfrew 1986, 4). In short, peer polity interactions explain the presence of shared elements within a civilisation; these changes are neither entirely autonomous nor entirely due to external influences; they rather emerge from an assemblage of interacting polities (Renfrew 1986, 6).

The core periphery model was based on the foundations laid by Wallerstein's work (1974) on changes in the modern world and the relations between different social systems within an overarching world system. This model can be adapted for use with prehistoric societies (Sherratt 1994b, 4). In the adapted core periphery model, societies were smaller, and relations were of shorter duration (Sherratt 1994b, 5). The areas involved were linked by flows of materials which structured the relationships between them. According to Wallerstein (1974), flows were based on the exchange of prime value for added value, i.e. the exchange of raw materials for processed commodities. This implied the presence of a technically asymmetrical relationship, which is, in turn, one of the characteristics of a core-periphery structure (Sherratt 1994b, 4). Aside from the fact that Bronze Age groups in Northern and Central Europe formed pre-state societies, it is likely that there were nonetheless organisational differences between these two regions. Such differences would fit admirably with the core periphery relationship between urban consumption and manufacturing centres and their politically and economically less-developed peripheral areas (Sherratt 1994b, 4).

Both models can be said to be versions of diffusion theory (e.g. Childe 1956), albeit with certain variations. They seem to agree that changes within a society occurred as a result of both external influences and internal continuity (Renfrew 1986, 5; Shennan 1994, 60). The peer polity model does, however, seem to imply that technologically-influential polities were more advanced and civilised, while recipient polities were less developed, despite the fact that both groups were of equal status (Renfrew 1986, 8). The core periphery model has the same distinction (albeit in more general terms, since it implies that the core areas were superior to the peripheral ones) (Wallerstein 1974, 349, 350; Rowlands 1987, 5; Shennan 1994, 62; Sherratt 1994a, 337; Sherratt 1994b, 4).

Despite the fact that these models can be useful in the analysis of the European Bronze Age, the core periphery model seems more appropriate for these types of relations, insofar as some areas were clearly more resourceful and structurally-organised than others (Sherratt 1994b, 4). On the other hand, the theory of peer polity was more suitable for the application to prehistoric societies, as it did not emphasize the inequalities of the different polities involved (Renfrew 1986, 3f.).

When Wallerstein's theory is placed into its historical context, we must ask whether the core-periphery model was not actually based on an imperialistic and evolutionist world view (Rowlands 1987 8), in which less-developed marginal societies were somehow delayed on their path towards becoming like more developed core societies. However, if we focus on the more material aspects of this theory (such as the exchange of goods and the availability of resources), it might prove useful in describing the relations between the Bronze Age societies of Northern Europe and the ways in which their interactions affected local material culture.

Flint and Bronze

The advantages of bronze compared to flint are numerous; bronze is less likely than flint to break while in use, metal tools can be re-sharpened when they dull, and broken or unwanted bronze artefacts can be re-melted to form other objects. Re-melting might be an important aspect of the exchange system of bronze, as bronze can be altered according to cultural context. Flint artefacts, by contrast, are more difficult to alter post-production. Thus, a flint dagger can hardly be turned into an axe without a great degree of reduction in size and a concomitant potential reduction in value (Sherratt 1994b, 13).

However, flint also has its own advantages. Some aspects of flint technology are more easily accessible; knapping does not necessarily require specialist knowledge or tools (Högberg 2010, 67f.; van Gijn 2010, 47f.), although the production of some artefacts (such as daggers and swords) necessitates specialists (Eriksen 2010, 90f; Högberg 2010, 76; van Gijn 2010, 51; Apel 2001, 42f.). Flint can also be reused when a tool becomes too worn or breaks. It needs merely be converted into a smaller shape or different type of object (Eriksen 2010, 90; Eriksen 2000, 83; Lindeman 1988, 122). This process is often neglected in the analysis of the distribution and find contexts of flint. This last is aptly demonstrated by the flint-edged swords of the Danish period (which are mostly found in set-tlements). Said swords often consist of fragments of whole swords (Rønne 1987, 88) which could indicate that the broken edges of the sword were reused as different objects related to everyday tools. It is, therefore, debatable whether these finds can truly be defined as flint swords and thus be included in sword analyses.

As two materials, flint and bronze have very different appearances and features. Naturally, this means that humans perceive them in very different ways. Bronze is golden and exudes a different kind of indestructibility in comparison to more fragile flint. Although bronze is one of the softer metal alloys, it is harder than both gold and copper, which were the other most common metals used in the Bronze Age (Tylecote 1976, 3-10.; Vandkilde 1996, 182; Kristiansen and Larsson 2005, 121f.). The combination of the thin shape and the glass-like character of flint meant that flint daggers were quite brittle. In this respect, flint was an impractical material for for stabbing weapons for example. Wear analysis of Danish flint daggers from the Netherlands shows traces of polishing achieved by some kind of plant material. This type of polish is not thought to have come from active use wear but rather from the repeated removal and reinsertion of the daggers from their sheaths (van Gijn 2010, 52; Lindeman 1988, 124). Finally, bronze was not a natural resource within the confines of Southern Scandinavia and was certainly not available to all. It must have been imported, and was, therefore, not just exotic in material, but might also have embodied non-local shapes and types.

The Gathering of Flint and Bronze and the Production of Artefacts

Even though flint and bronze can be used for the same types of artefacts (axes, daggers, arrowheads, spear-heads, sickles and swords), both the finished tools and processes by which they were produced were quite different. The production process was not defined by the technological possibilities and limitations of both material and craftsman alone. One must also take into account the cognitive processes behind production and the stylistic considerations (including both conscious reflection and the unconscious influences of society).

The extraction, raw processing and the smelting and casting of bronze require specialist knowledge of such varied phenomena as oxidation processes, smelting temperatures, casting and cold-working (Tylecote 1976). Furthermore, the raw material was available from limited geographical locations in Europe and was, therefore, not directly accessible by all. Flint and flint-like materials, by contrast, are available from various parts of Europe from both primary and/or secondary sources (Weisgerber 1981). These characteristics must be emphasized in any comparison of bronze and flint production.

However, there are multiple layers in flint production, as some flint artefacts required specialist knowledge (Stafford 1998, 347; Apel 2001, 42), while others were produced as *ad hoc* tools (Eriksen 2010; van Gijn 2010, 46). The production of flint artefacts such as fish tail daggers, sickles and swords needed expert skill. Creating such tools necessitated a fixed idea of the end project as well as great knowledge of the material (Stafford 1998, Eriksen 2000, 75). Furthermore, the raw material for these objects had to be of a particular size and quality. Finds from flint mines (Eriksen 2000, 75; Becker 1993, 112, 118) and specialist flint-knapping locations (Glob 1951, 29) seem to support the idea that there was a certain degree of institutionalisation at this time.

The production of flint tools required knowledge which had been possessed by mankind to a greater or lesser degree for millennia. Metal technology, by contrast, was probably present from LN I. However, there is no clear evidence for metallurgy before LN II. The first metal tools produced in Scandinavia were mainly flanged axes, and it was not until Bronze Age IB that that repertoire was expanded. It is also in this period that the quantity of metal dramatically increased (Vandkilde 1989, 32; Vandkilde 1996, 263f., fig. 279).

The production process might be an important element in the perception of the finished artefacts for several reasons. First of all, the materials from which bronze was comprised were not mined in Southern Scandinavia. Flint, by contrast, was easily available from within what would become Denmark, as it was accessible both from mines as well as secondary occurrences, like surface collection (Fig. 3; Becker 1993, 125f.). Flint was also a material from which many people could produce everyday tools, whereas bronze was only mastered by a select few. Therefore, the consumer of a bronze artefact must have been aware of the fact that they themselves did not possess the knowledge to rework such material.

The Context and Distribution of Flint and Bronze Daggers

In order to shed light on the role that flint and bronze daggers played in the societies of prehistoric Denmark and the changes which might have taken place during the transition between LN and the beginning of the Bronze Age, this paper will next briefly go through the different contexts associated with daggers and the ways in which these contexts changed over time.

Flint Daggers

The distribution of early flint daggers (types I-II) in the Danish Late Neolithic corresponds to the geographical distribution of flint resources which were centred on the Limfjord area and southeast Denmark (Rasmussen 1990, 33; Vandkilde 1996, 281; Thomsen 2000; Fig. 3). Later types of flint daggers (types III-VI) were more evenly distributed (Rasmussen 1990, 33). Flint dagger typology is also chronologically conditioned, although it seems that type I (with the exception of subtype ID) is of western origin, while types ID and II are of eastern origin (Madsen 1978, 55; Rasmussen 1990, 33). The periods by which the LN is divided are based on the chronology of flint daggers so that types I, II and III belong to LN I, type IV and VB to LN II and type VA and VI to the Early Bronze Age (Vandkilde 1996, 13f.). However, when considering the total amount of flint daggers in relation to the respective lengths of each period, a rather surprising picture emerges. Most daggers were produced in LN I, as expected. This amount decreased in LN II. Surprisingly, there was an increase in the number of flint daggers in period I of the Early Bronze Age (Fig. 4). While it is, of course, possible that this increase reflected greater production of flint daggers in spite of the increasing amount of bronze objects, this anomaly nevertheless gives cause for chronological revision. However, said chronological study is beyond the scope of this paper.

The distribution of flint daggers in hoards and grave deposits followed the general downward tendency of deposits in hoards from LN I to the first period of the Early Bronze Age (Vandkilde 1996, 263, Fig. 6-7). Deposits in graves seem to have remained relatively constant, although they were more common in LN I than in other periods (Fig. 5). However, the total amount of flint daggers found in graves decreased

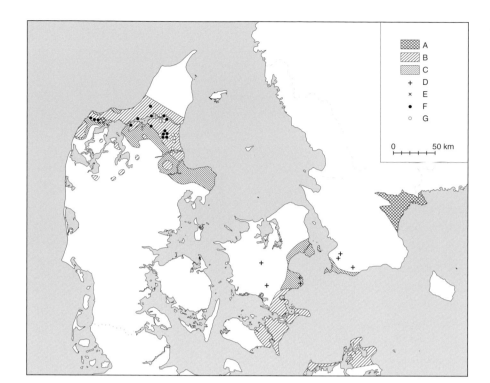

Figure 3. Flint resources in Southern Scandinavia – after Becker 1973.

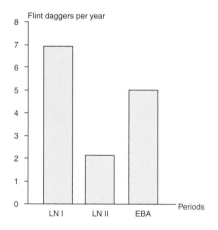

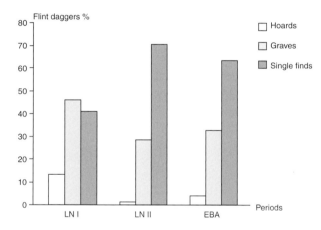

Figure 4. Number of flint daggers per year.   *Figure 5. Find context of flint daggers in relation to period.*

greatly in the aftermath of type I (Fig. 6). Single flint dagger finds reached a maximum in LN II, but this group generally constituted a large part of the total finds, especially in LN II and the Early Bronze Age. In LN II, the amount of single dagger finds was relatively greater than the combined amount from hoards and graves (Fig. 5).

Find circumstances changed due to the fact that dagger types III, IV, V and VI were more commonly found as single finds than earlier types (Fig. 6; Lomborg 1973, fig. 25-28). This was not the result of different find circumstances for individual types, but, rather, was due to their original deposition (which could

signify that the daggers where originally deposited as single items). However, the possibility remains that they could have belonged to destroyed graves or smaller hoards scattered by modern ploughing or subsequent activities.

Type I is by far the best-represented, with a total of 1,964 examples. Type Ix is particularly prevalent, making up almost half of the total amount. Half of the recorded examples of this type were found in graves (App. 1). Type Ix is characterised by sharpening or re-working. Therefore, its deposition in graves is indicative of little or no distinction between practical tools and ritual objects. Type VI is the second most

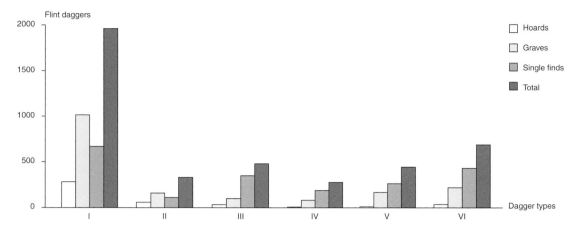

Figure 6. Find context of flint daggers in relation to type.

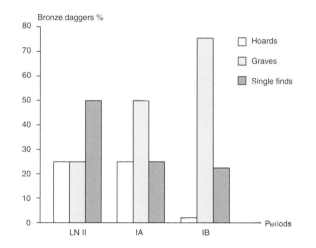

Figure 7. Find context of bronze daggers in relation to period.

common dagger, although this type was not as common in graves as type I, due to its large quantity of single finds. The practice of depositing flint daggers in graves seemed to regain popularity during the first part of the Early Bronze Age (Fig. 5-6). This is in line with an overall pattern in which there was increased production of flint daggers in the first periods of the Early Bronze Age (Fig. 4).

Type I (excepting subtype Id) was principally found in the west, whereas ID and II can primarily be associated with the eastern part of Denmark (Rasmussen 1990, 33). This means that the burial practice in the western part of Denmark LNI involved flint daggers to a greater degree than in the east. This supports the hypothesis that flint daggers were initially a translation of traditions from the western Bell Beaker Complex (Lomborg 1973, 87; Apel 2001, 249f.). Furthermore, it acts as an example of meaning shift: the connotations of one type of artefact were transferred to another.

Bronze Daggers

The first bronze daggers date from LN II. A grand total of eight daggers have been found thus far, four each from LN II and Early Bronze Age Period IA (Vandkilde 1996, 192-214). These few examples are hardly a representative quantity for analysis and/or interpretation. However, the bronze daggers from each period are distributed between hoards, graves and single finds.

Forty-nine bronze daggers or dagger blades from Early Bronze Age Period IB have been recovered (Vandkilde 1996, 224-240). During this period, finds came predominantly from graves or single finds, with hoard finds constituting a very small portion of the total (Fig. 7). When compared to the general pattern of deposits, bronze daggers do not largely differ. In this respect, this group of artefacts followed a general tendency in which metal became increasingly common in burials (Vandkilde 1996, fig. 262, 298).

To a minor extent, bronze artefacts were probably already produced in Southern Scandinavia in LN I (Vandkilde 1996, 263). However, the first local artefacts consisted mostly of flanged axes. This tendency continued until Early Bronze Age Period IB, at which point production was slightly more varied (Vandkilde 1996, 264). Both the increased amount of metal and the growing local production of bronze artefacts illustrate the ways in which bronze became more incorporated into Southern Scandinavian society. This was also demonstrated by an increase in the amount of metal artefacts in graves at the cost of flint daggers in Bronze Age Periods IA and IB (Fig. 6). The increasing amount of bronze and the different applications of this material might indicate a change in its perception. It might have been viewed as somehow less exotic and more of a commodity, just as the foreign places from which the material originated also became more familiar (Shennan 1994, 62).

The amount of bronze daggers in graves during the Early Bronze Age never matched the number of flint daggers deposited in graves in the LN (Vandkilde 1996, fig. 215, 267). Although the symbolism of flint daggers was transferred to those made of bronze, there was a change in the general perception of the dagger as an object. It lost importance in comparison to the other types of metal objects which were present in the Early Bronze Age. It is of course important to note that the variety of types increased in Bronze Age Period IB (Vandkilde 1996, 264).

The Relation of Flint and Bronze

Flint and bronze are transformed, both in terms of turning raw materials into usable items and as regards the life cycle of the finished artefact. In both production processes, material must be extracted and prepared before the completion of a finished artefact. However, the extraction of flint occurred locally and had been undertaken for centuries (Becker 1958, 82; Becker 1993, 112, 114). Bronze, by contrast, was imported as a finished material, product and (eventually) as ingots. The production technologies associated with that alloy were new to the Danish area (Vandkilde 1996, 295). These circumstances alone must have influenced the perception of the material. Bronze, aside from being a little-known material unavailable to the majority of the population, was also technologically unavailable. By contrast, most people were likely to be acquainted with flint and flint production. This must have been one of the factors which influenced the 'status' of bronze over flint.

The life cycles of finished artefacts also diverged. If a flint object broke or became worn, the only methods for its conversion were reductive: re-sharpening or its complete transformation into a different object. In the latter case, the object might move from one context to another (Lindeman 1988, 122). Bronze artefacts can also be re-sharpened, but they also have the additional ability to be re-melted. Re-melting is not a reductive method, thus the value of the material is not necessarily diminished. In other words, metal as a material maintains its value whereas flint (when curated or re-cycled) can never be restored to its original value. This tendency is also illustrated by the numerous hoards dating from the Danish Bronze Age which resemble scrap metal stashes rather than ritual hoards (Levy 1982, fig. 3-1, 24-44).

The amount of flint daggers produced in the LN and the Early Bronze Age was not reflected in the production of bronze daggers. The latter remained rare objects both in the Danish LN and Early Bronze Age. When the amount of flint and bronze daggers in different contexts were analysed, they actually seem to show continuity in their use in graves (Fig. 5, 7). Therefore, it is possible that the daggers maintained the same symbolic value regardless of the material from which they were made.

Flint daggers of type Ix are the most numerous, and are characterised by re-sharpened or reworking (Lomborg 1973, 44), probably as a result of use damage. The Ix type is just as numerous in graves as were types which were not reworked and appeared in a larger absolute quantity than any other type (App. 1). This would indicate that this kind of dagger had both a functional and symbolic value. The same was the case with the earliest metal artefacts from the Danish area. While the tools could be used for practical purposes, they also clearly had a symbolic function as well (Vandkilde 1993, 56). This dual functionality of flint and metal daggers implied a similar perception of the artefacts in question in spite of the different materials from which they were produced.

Even though flint daggers were produced and distributed in the region of prehistoric Denmark in great numbers, bronze daggers did not become the preferred product until metalcraft finally reached Southern Scandinavia. It seems, therefore, that it was not only flint daggers which decreased in importance, but rather that the concept of the dagger as a whole did not maintain the same popularity (Vandkilde 1996, fig. 345). This development was probably due to the increasing variation within artefact types in Early Bronze Age Period IB (Vandkilde 1996, 264). However, in this period deposition traditions seem to have changed.

Flint daggers are perceived as imitations of metal templates, implying that the concept of the dagger travelled through Eastern, Western and Central Europe to Southern Scandinavia. The concept of the dagger doubtless had certain connotations depending on the area in which it was found. Even though the shape was similar, the connotations that it carried may not have been uniform over the vast area of its dispersion. Rather it could be viewed as the local translation of a foreign concept, just as the Scandinavian flint daggers can be regarded as metal daggers translated into another material.

The Development of Core-Periphery Relationships in Southern Scandinavia

The earliest Danish flint daggers were influenced by Western European dagger types (Lomborg 1973, 91; Vandkilde 1989, 30, 38). These influences were seen not only through the emerging tradition of depositing daggers in graves as status symbols (a custom also seen in western Bell Beaker Complexes) (Butler and van der Waals 1967, App. I; Lomborg 1977, 23), but also through other metal items, such as the LN flanged axes which originated in the British Isles and Dutch Bell Beaker metallic traditions (Vandkilde 1996, 177; 1989, 38).

Danish flint dagger types were also found outside of Denmark (i.e. in Northern and Central Europe) (Apel 2001, 278). The distribution of flint daggers in these areas spreads over all periods; type I is of course also the most numerous in this context, just as type VI comprises a substantial part of exported daggers. Type III is almost at the same level as type VI. This last is surprising, as this amount does not echo the number found in the Danish area (Fig. 5, 7). Perhaps this reflects different functions for certain dagger types. Likewise, it is also worth noting that type III is most often found as a single find, which could also be indicative of a distinct kind of use.

Most daggers travelled north to the areas of prehistoric Norway and Sweden as finished products (Apel 2001, 228). Danish flint daggers, however, were also found in both Western and Central Europe. The amount of daggers which went north in the LN and Early Bronze Age was greater than in other areas, although material from Central Europe was represented in all periods. The movement of flint daggers to Norway and Sweden was most intensive in LN I, although it continued into the Early Bronze Age as well (Fig. 9b).

The largest amounts of Danish flint daggers found in the south include types I, III and VI, meaning that most dagger traffic took place during LN I. This corresponds with our idea of Early Bronze Age Central Europe as an area in which bronze production was not yet entirely consolidated and whose exchange networks with Southern Scandinavia had yet to be firmly established. The fact that 130 type I daggers were found in Thüringen-Saxony (more than twice as many as all other types put together) implies that flint artefacts were still considered to be valuable. This could be due to the relatively small amount of metal in circulation in this period, but it is also possible that flint remained the primary material in some areas for other reasons (e.g. tradition). This occurrence of flint daggers illustrates the possibility that other factors influenced the perception of material culture and the materiality of the artefacts.

The changes which occurred in Central Europe in the third millennium BC due to new subsistence strategies and metal extraction technologies resulted

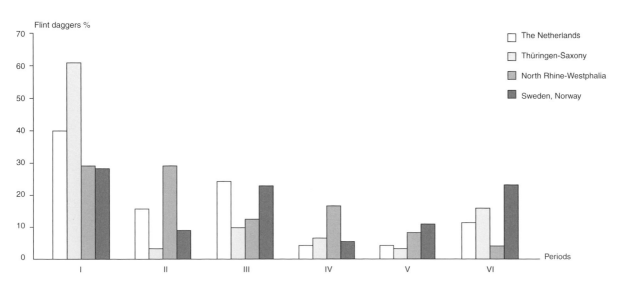

Figure 8. Distribution of Danish flint daggers in Europe – after Apel 2001.

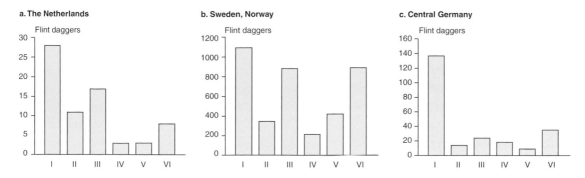

Figure 9. Chronological distribution of Danish flint daggers in Europe – after Apel 2001.

in an increasingly differentiated society (Shennan 1986; 1994, Kristiansen and Larsson 2005; Vandkilde 2007). Although these changes affected Southern Scandinavia, it was not in the same fashion. The relations between Central and Northern Europe can be considered to be a core-periphery relationship in which Northern Europe was peripheral to metal-producing areas (Shennan 1994, 61-62). In this instance, the core-periphery relationship was based on the core area's possession of those raw materials coveted by the periphery. This probably resulted in differing perceptions of the material, as metal ranged from a status item in the periphery to a commodity in the core (Shennan 1994, 62-63). Metal can be considered to have two kinds of value. In the periphery, it had value as a rare and exotic material primarily used to symbolise status. In the core area, by contrast, metal was valued for its function as a commodity or perhaps almost as a currency (Shennan 1994, 62). In other words, metal was valued for being metal in the core area, whereas in the periphery, it was objectified to a greater degree.

If the core-periphery principle is followed according to Shennan (1994) and Sherratt (1994a) in terms of the actual materials in use, then the core area for bronze was Central Europe with Southern Scandinavia as periphery, whereas the core area of flint was Northern Europe, particularly Denmark (Sherratt 1976, 564). Sherratt specifically states that "...the Early Bronze Age...saw the formation of small-scale regional asymmetries based on access to copper and tin" (Sherratt 1994b, 18).

The relationship between these areas appears to be more complex, as the areas seemed to compete. The metals of Central Europe were already influencing Northern Europe when the flint mines were in use. This situation complicates the use of the core-periph-

ery model, since the flint dagger example positions the periphery (Southern Scandinavia) in a superior position to the core, even though this is the case in only one respect (i.e. the exchange of materials). During the LN, Southern Scandinavia was technologically very advanced in certain areas (such as flint production). The area had vast resources of flint which were both exported to the north (Becker 1993, 126, 128) and simultaneously used as a means of establishing long-distance connections with metal-producing regions (van Gijn 2010, 55; Rassmann 2001, 26).

If Bourdieu's theory of symbolic capital (Bourdieu 1980, 203-207) is adapted to the knowledge of materials in these different areas and some of the conclusions of Apel's study are followed through in relation to the craftsmanship of flint daggers (Apel 2001), then the craftsmanship of flint and bronze should be roughly comparable. In LN I, the crafting of flint still possessed some symbolic capital. In LN II, however, the crafting of bronze slowly gained more power and outflanked the crafting of flint. In this way, it pushed Southern Scandinavia into the background necessitating that the inhabitants of that region. This shift in the prestige of different crafts was due both to technologically more advanced extraction methods (which could satisfy an increased demand for bronze) as well as the material characteristics of bronze (i.e. its practical and symbolic advantages over flint).

Conclusion

In archaeology, artefacts are usually evaluated according to two main criteria. The first of these is utilitarian effectiveness. If practical usability is not apparent, then the artefact in question is usually thought to have had another kind of value (often symbolic, ritualistic or aesthetic). However, a single feature cannot rule out the others. By changing the material of an object, this relation between usability and other properties was also changed. The characteristics of the material must be considered when analysing the distribution, transformation, and methods behind any particular distribution. One very important aspect of this is the availability of the material both in terms of resources and technology. These are the basic preconditions for producing an artefact in a certain material. In the case of Southern Scandinavia, the lack of metal resources was an obvious reason for the production of lithic tools, especially in the locally-abundant flint.

Because we regard prehistory in retrospect, the change from stone to metal seems natural. However, this might not have been the case for the Late Neolithic individual. In his or her experience, flint had been one of the most common materials for both tools and prestige items and was made with a popularly-available technology which had been utilised for thousands of years. Metal may, therefore, not have been thought to posses all the practical advantages that we acknowledge today, but could perhaps rather have obtained its acceptance due to other factors (such as the exoticism of the material itself and/or the connotations associated with it).

In many cases, the same objects made in flint or bronze seem to carry the same ideas and connotations, so the concept of the dagger as a shape and type does seem to have been translated across materials. It seems as if objectification happened independently of the material. Concrete materiality was, therefore, not necessarily important for the symbolic or ritual use of artefacts. An awareness of the differences of the material must still have been present, since the appearance, production processes and life cycles of the two material types were very dissimilar. As soon as the amount of metal was sufficient in Southern Scandinavia, that substance seems to have been preferred over flint. Flint remained an important resource in the daily sphere, although it gradually lost importance in economic and political development as well as in interregional relations.

Humans and material culture interact. On the one hand, humans create artefacts and infuse them with meaning, ideas and associations. On the other, humans are influenced by the objects they produce. Concepts such as specific material forms are developed by humans and are constantly changing in both similar and varying contexts. At the same time, these concepts impose continuity due to the mean-

ings inherent within them. Material can be a decisive factor in human choice, but it can also be transcended in order to fit into desired ideologies (as was the case with the early Danish flint dagger). When technologically feasible and with adequate resource availability, the choice of material became more important. The preference for a certain material became as important a factor in the development of Southern Scandinavian societies as the desire for bronze. Developments in Central Europe resulted in the creation of a core-periphery relationship between these two areas (again, with Southern Scandinavia at the periphery).

Future work would do well to expand this comparative study into other groups of the material culture from this period. Certainly, in this respect, a revised typology and chronology of flint daggers would be relevant. Furthermore, it could be interesting to extend this analysis, spreading it over a broader societal perspective by including production processes and sites in order to shed light on how the production of both flint and bronze was affected by other aspects of society as well as being affected by them in their turn.

Bibliography

Apel, J. 2001: *Dagger, Knowledge & Power*. Uppsala.

Becker, C.J. 1958: 4000-årig minedrift i Thy. *Nationalmuseets Arbejdsmark*, 73-82.

Becker, C.J. 1993: Flintminer og flintdistribution ved Limfjorden. In: Lund, J. & J. Ringtved (eds.): *Kort- og råstofstudier omkring Limfjorden. Rapport fra seminarer afholdt 7.-8. nov. 1991 i Bovbjerg samt 23.-24. april 1992 i Aalborg.* Aarhus, 111-134.

Bourdieu, P. 1980: *Le sens practique*. Paris.

Butler J.J. & J.D. van der Waals 1967: Bell Beaker and Early Metal-working in the Netherlands. *Palaeohistoria* XII, 1966, 41-139.

Childe, V.G. 1956: *Piecing Together the Past*. London.

DeMarrais, E. 2004: The Materialization of Culture. In: DeMarrais, E., C. Gosden & C. Renfrew (eds.): *Rethinking materiality. The engagement of mind with the material world.* Cambridge, 11-22.

Dobres, M.-A. & J.E. Robb 2000: Agency in archaeology – Paradigm or platitude? In: Dobres, M.-A. & J.E. Robb (eds.): *Agency in Archaeology*. London, 259-263.

Eriksen, B.V. 2010: Flint working in the Danish Bronze Age: The decline and fall of a master craft. In: Eriksen, B.V. (ed.): *Lithic technology in metal using societies. Proceedings of a UISPP Workshop, Lisbon, September 2006.* Aarhus, 81-93.

Eriksen, B.V. 2000: "Chaîne opèratoire" – den operative proces og kunsten at tænke som en flinthugger. In: Eriksen, B.V. (ed.): *Flintstudier. En håndbog i systematiske analyser af flintinventarer.* Aarhus, 37-50.

Glob, P.V. 1951: En flintsmedie på Forsnæs. *Kuml*, 23-39.

Hodder, I. 1985: Postprocessual Archaeology. *Advances in Archaeological Methods and Theory* 8, 1-26.

Högberg, A. 2010: Two traditions and a hybrid? South Scandinavian Late Bronze Age Flint. In: Eriksen, B.V. (ed.): *Lithic technology in metal using societies. Proceedings of a UISPP Workshop, Lisbon, September 2006.* Aarhus, 61-80.

Ingold, T. 2007: Materials against materiality. *Archaeological Dialogues* 14, 1, 1-16.

Jones, A. 2007: *Memory and Material Culture.* Cambridge.

Kristiansen, K. & T.B. Larsson 2005: *The Rise of Bronze Age Society. Travels, Transmissions and Transformations.* Cambridge.

Levy, J.E. 1982: *Social and Religious Organization in Bronze Age Denmark. An Analysis of Ritual Hoard Finds.* BAR International Series 124. Oxford.

Lomborg, E. 1973: D*ie Flintdolche Dänemarks. Studien über Chronologie und Kulturbeziehungen des südskandinavischen Spätneolithikums.* Nordiske Fortidsminder Serie B, 1. København.

Lomborg, E. 1977: Klokkebæger- og senere Beaker-indflydelser i Danmark. Et bidrag til Enkeltgravskulturen datering. *Aarbøger for Nordisk Oldkyndighed og Historie* 1975, 20-41.

Madsen, T. 1978: Perioder og periodeovergange i neolitikum. *Hikuin* 4, 51-60.

Rasmussen, L.W. 1990: Dolkproduktion og -distribution i senneolitikum. *Hikuin* 16, 31-42.

Rassmann, K. 2001: Die Nutzung baltischen Feuersteins an der Schwelle zur Bronzezeit. Krise oder Konjunktur der Feuersteinverarbeitung. *Bericht der Römisch-Germanischen Kommission, 81,* 2000, 5-36.

Renfrew, C. 1986: Introduction: peer polity interaction and socio-political change. In: Renfrew, C. & J.F. Cherry (eds.): *Peer Polity Interaction and Socio-political Change.* Cambridge, 1-18.

Robb, J. 2004: The Extended Artefact and the Monumental Economy: a Methodology for Material Agency. In: DeMarrais, E., C. Gosden & C. Renfrew (eds.): *Rethinking materiality. The engagement of mind with the material world.* Cambridge, 23-32.

Rowlands, M. 1987: Centre and periphery: a review of a concept. In: Rowlands, M., M. Larsen & K. Kristiansen (eds.): *Centre and Periphery in the Ancient World.* Cambridge, 214-235.

Rønne, P. 1988: Flintægsværd fra bronzealderen. *Aarbøger for Nordisk Oldkyndighed og Historie* 1987, 85-96.

Sackett, J.R. 1977: The Meaning of Style in Archaeology. *American Antiquity* 42, 3, 369-380.

Scarre, C. 2004: Displaying Stones: The Materiality of 'Megalithic' Monuments. In: DeMarrais, E., C. Gosden & C. Renfrew (eds.): *Rethinking materiality. The engagement of mind with the material world.* Cambridge, 141-152.

Shennan, S. 1986: Central Europe in the Third Millennium B. C. *Journal of Anthropological Archaeology* 5, 115-146.

Shennan, S. 1994: Commodities, transactions, and growth in the central European Bronze Age. *Journal of European Archaeology* 1, 2, 1993, 59-73.

Sherratt, A. 1976: Resources, technology and trade in early European metallurgy. In: Sieveking, G. de G., I.H. Longworth & K.E. Wilson (eds.): *Problems in Economic and Social Archaeology.* London, 557-581.

Sherratt, A. 1994a: Core, Periphery and Margin: Perspectives on the Bronze Age. In: Mathers, C. & S. Stoddart (eds.): *Development and Decline in the Mediterranean Bronze Age.* Sheffield, 335-345.

Sherratt, A. 1994b: What would a Bronze-Age world system look like? Relations between temperate Europe and the Mediterranean in later prehistory. *Journal of European Archaeology* 1, 2, 1993, 1-56.

Stafford, M. 1998: In search of Hindsgavl. *Antiquity* 72, 338-349.

Thomsen, E. 2000: Flintens geologi og mineralogi. In: Eriksen, B.V. (ed.): *Flintstudier. En håndbog i systematiske analyser af flintinventarer.* Aarhus, 17-36.

Tylecote, R.F. 1976: *A History of Metallurgy.* London.

Urry, J. 2007: *Mobilities.* Cambridge.

van der Leeuw, J.E. 2008: Agency, Networks, Past and Future. In: Knappett, C. & L. Malafouris (eds.): *Material Agency: Towards a Non-Anthropocentric Approach.* New York, 217-247.

Van Gijn, A. 2010: Not at all obsolete! The use of flint in the Bronze Age Netherlands. In: Eriksen, B.V. (ed.): *Lithic technology in metal using societies. Proceedings of a UISPP Workshop, Lisbon, September 2006.* Aarhus, 45-60.

Vandkilde, H. 1989: Det ældste metalmiljø i Danmark. In: Poulsen, J. (ed.): *Regionale forhold i Nordisk Bronzealder. 5. symposium for Bronzealderforskning på Sandbjerg Slot 1987.* Aarhus, 29-46.

Vandkilde, H. 1993: Aspekter af teknologi og samfund i overgangstiden mellem sten- og bronzealder i Danmark. In: Forsberg, L. & T.B. Larsson (eds.): *Ekonomi och näringsformer i nordisk Bronsålder.* Studia Archaeologica Universitatis Umensis 3, Umeå, 53-69.

Vandkilde, H. 1996: *From Stone to Bronze. The Metalwork of the Late Neolithic and Earliest Bronze Age in Denmark.* Aarhus.

Vandkilde, H. 2007: *Culture and Change in Central European Prehistory 6th to 1st Millennium BC.* Aarhus.

Wallerstein, I. 1974: *The Modern World-system,* I. London

Weisgerber, G. 1981: *5000 Jahre Feuersteinbergbau. Die Suche nach dem Stahl der Steinzeit.* Bochum.

Wiesner, P. 1983: Style and social information in Kalahari San projectile points. *American Antiquity* 48, 2, 253-276.

Wobst, H.M. 1977: Stylistic Behaviour and Information Exchange. In: Cleland, C.E. (ed.): *For the Director. Research Essays in Honour of James B. Griffin.* Michigan, 317-342.

The Transmission of Spiral Ornamentation through Bronze Age Europe

Disa Lundsgård Simonsen

Introduction

In 1600 BC, a whole new world of ornamentation and artefacts appeared in the area which would become modern-day Denmark. The most prominent of these were spiral decorations and the sword. The spiral was quickly incorporated into Danish metalworking communities, but said ornament was not an autochthonous innovation; the Danish design derived instead from new and increased contact with the continent. However, in what way did the spiral travel to Southern Scandinavia and how was it transferred? Did the sword (which arrived in the Danish region at the same time as the spiral) act as a "carrier", or was its transmission effected by other means? In this article I analyze spiral ornamentation found on swords and look at other kinds of objects and materials on which this decorative element appeared. In so doing, I hope to achieve a better understanding of the transfer and potential status change of the spiral upon its arrival into new cultural zones. Georg Karo's descriptions of the spiral (Karo 1930-33) are employed in these analyses, as they include thorough clarifications of all spiral ornamentation types which appear in the material from the Mycenaean Shaft Graves.

Research History

Study of the ancient connection between the Mediterranean and Southern Scandinavia by means of the transmission of the spiral is somewhat new. It has been suggested that the spiral is proof of an extant exchange between Southern Scandinavia and the Carpathian Basin as well as between the latter area with the Bronze Age Mediterranean. It is interesting, therefore, to investigate whether these Bronze Age trade links could be viewed, not as a tripartite line, but rather as a triangle, thereby providing a direct link between Southern Scandinavia and the sunny Mediterranean.

While his methods were not necessarily revolutionary to the field, Lomborg's suggestion that the spirals on Danish bronze swords indicated a connection between that northern region and the Carpathian Basin (Lomborg 1965) was the first instance of archaeological interest in and engagement with the spiral question. Naturally, this was not the last paper, nor the last word on the subject. Penner (1998) posited that wavy band and spiral decoration came to the Carpathian Basin not from the Mediterranean, but rather from the Orient (Penner 1998, 211-215). Wolfgang David (2001) disagreed, at least in part. He acceded that while some wavy band decoration originated in the Orient, many wavy band decorative elements (as well as the spiral) must have been transmitted into the Carpathian region via the Mediterranean (David 2001). Unfortunately, these three crucial papers leave us with more questions than they answer. It is on these very questions as well as several other important investigations – which themselves touch upon the spiral debate (Harding 1984; Bouzek 1985; Kristiansen 1998; Vandkilde 1996; 2007) – that the Nordic-Mediterranean focus of this paper is founded.

A Theoretical Approach to Long-Distance Exchange

The data used in this paper derive from several locations throughout Europe (Denmark, Hungary, Romania and Greece) and are all dated to the period around 1600 BC. This leaves the impression that the transmission of the spiral occurred over long distances in a very short period of time. One may wonder, therefore, how this transmission manifested with such rapidity.

Mădălina Nicolaescu states that "globalization is conceived of largely in terms of a cultural translation" (Nicolaescu 2004, 75). Cultural transmission and translation can occur by means of text or object. In good textual translation, the message remains the same, while the letters and words which make it up are changed in order to be locally comprehensible. In this way, the English 'hello' and the French 'bonjour' both convey the sense of a friendly salutation, despite the fact that the words which communicate this are vastly different. The translation of objects, however, undergoes a very different sort of transmutation. In that instance, 'translation' refers to the recreation of a foreign object by a host culture into a version with a feasible means of construction and locally-comprehensible form. Such a recreation usually necessitates some changes from the original. Because of this, items found in a hypothetical Area A will not necessarily have the exact same form, material or symbolic meaning as those in Area B. On a local/global level Nicolaescu views this exchange as a necessity:

> "…[T]he import of practices or of consumer products cannot be devoid of the hermeneutic dimension of interpretation and translation. The local use of global products or practices always involves a process of creating meanings." (Nicolaescu 2004, 81).

In order for a culture to fully grasp an innovation from another culture, the host must create a hybrid form of new and old. By giving an innovation a meaning comprehensible to the local community, the admission of the innovation into said community will be more rapid.

This translation could also function as a means of determining whether an outside admission actually took place, since the acceptance of new technology is always a social decision (Johannsen 2010, 61). Indeed, it could be argued that translation might therefore have been a prerequisite for the acceptance of a new technology or object. Once the translation had occurred, both translation and original coexisted. According to Nicolaescu (2004), the translation would normally obtain a higher status. This does not necessarily mean that the value of the original would then decrease: "translations involve an accretion in the value and meanings of the original, with the latter

reaching a superior stage" (Nicolaescu 2004, 76). She finds support in the writings of Andrzej Pydyn (1999):

> "When physical things travel long distances, knowledge about them tends to become partially contradictory and differentiated. This knowledge, or rather lack of knowledge, creates their value and very often gives them a special symbolic character, used to establish and maintain power in prestige-goods societies." (Pydyn 1999, 10).

The value of an imported object might, therefore, withstand or even increase when one chose to exchange with distant cultures rather than with neighbors or kinsmen.

One should be wary an assumption that admission took place, based solely on the observation that no visible versions similar to the original exist within a specific material culture set. Naturally, it is also risky to think that the first area in which an object is found is the area from which it originates; an object recovered in Area B may look exactly like the original from Area A without being the original object.

The Spiral in Denmark

The spiral made its Danish debut in the Valsømagle hoard at the beginning of 16th century BC (Period IB) (Lomborg 1960, 83; Vandkilde 1996, 314) with an appearance on a magnificent spearhead (Broholm 1944, 40f.). The Valsømagle ornamental style consisted mainly of spirals and concentric circles, but, as is apparent in the case of the aforementioned spearhead (Fig. 1), this particular style also contains local ornamental elements such as the illustration of a fish (Vandkilde 1996, 233f.). During Period IB (1600-1500 BC), extant ornamental styles could be divided into one of two groups: the traditional Period IB style with predominantly linear geometric decoration and the new Valsømagle style. Both, it would seem, have a background in the geometric decoration and spiral hooks of Carpathian bronzes (Vandkilde 1996, 256).

As we know, the spiral was not alone upon its arrival in Danish territory. It made its first appearance around 1600 BC with the sword (Vandkilde 1996, 314), an object which would become the single most important piece of warrior equipment throughout the rest of the greater Bronze Age. The value given such items was made evident early on, as evidenced by the finds of the magnificent swords from Stensgård (Fig. 2) and Torupgårde on the island of Lolland. These swords were of the Hajdúsámson-Apa type and

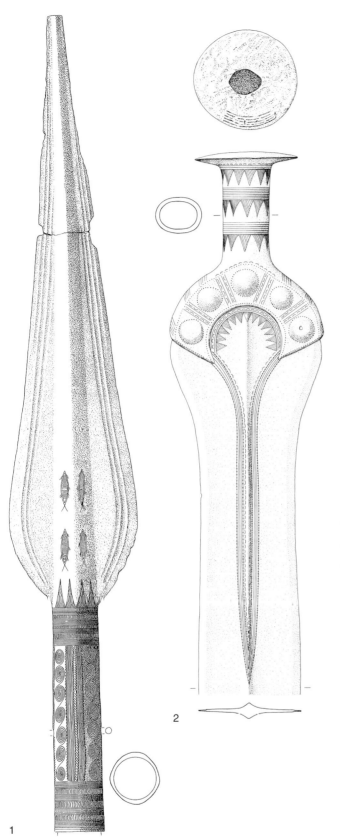

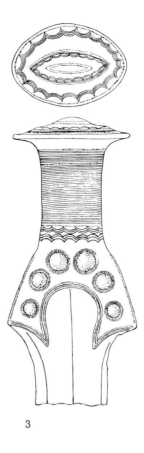

Figure 1. The Valsømagle spearhead – after Vandkilde 1996, 232.

Figure 2. Sword from Stensgård – after Lomborg 1960, 97.

Figure 3. Sword from the Valsømagle hoard – after Lomborg 1960, 97.

were imported from the Carpathian Basin, specifically from areas which today belong to Hungary and
Romania (Lomborg 1960, 72; Vandkilde 1996, 224f.).
While singular in archaeological import, these finds
were not unique within the record. The beautiful

spiral spearhead from Valsømagle was also recovered
in the company of an Au/Valsømagle sword typologically associated with (and influenced by) a number of
Central European swords from Simontornya (Hungary), Zaita (Hungary), Au (Austria) and Spatzenhausen

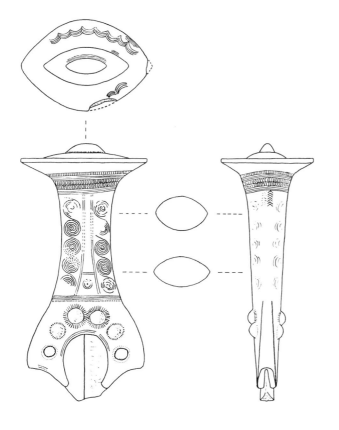

Figure 4. Au/Valsømagle type swords. The sword on the left was found at Riiskov on Funen, the sword on the right was found at Vejle on the Jutland peninsula – after Lomborg 1960, 86-89.

(Germany) (Lomborg 1960, 76; Vandkilde 1996, 236f.). Lomborg is skeptical about the latter being a region of influence upon the early Danish metalworkers, as the swords from this region were chronologically too early (Lomborg 1965, 231).

While the spiral made its first archaeologically-known appearance with the spearhead from Valsømagle, that decorative element does not appear on the sword which accompanied it (Fig. 3) (Lomborg 1960, 97). The spiral must have first been transferred to swords as part of the Danish metalworking tradition. The swords analyzed by Lomborg and Vandkilde appear to have all been produced in Denmark (Lomborg 1960; Vandkilde 1996). In the beginning of the 16th century BC, the spiral only occurred on Valsømagle-type objects (Vandkilde 1996, 314). However, as time went on and the new ornamental elements were adopted by Danish metalworkers, a fusion of different style elements ensued.

This latter coming together is clearly demonstrated by the transfer of the spiral onto Valsømagle/Au type swords. The decoration on the sword hilt from Vejle (Fig. 4, on right) consists of two wavy bands and one spiral. The upper band is a double wavy band in which the lines encircle concentric circles. The overall effect is one of a continuous, strictly composed figure which almost encloses the sword hilt twice. The

middle decoration also contains concentric circles connected by a double band. The last portion of the hilt ornamentation consists of a simple double-lined spiral encircling the hilt. This latter has been classified as a 'false spiral' because of the fact that its circle is not closed (Lomborg 1965, 224) but is rather formed by the inclusion of the outer band and the open empty space in the middle. Lomborg (1965) has doubtlessly borrowed his terminology from Georg Karo (Karo 1930-33, 267). According to Lomborg, the closest parallels to the lower spiral ornament on the Vejle sword hilt are found in Hungary and Romania (Lomborg 1965, 231).

By contrast, the sword hilt from Riiskov (Fig. 4, on left) demonstrates a "true spiral hook" (Karo 1930-33, 273), as is also known from the Valsømagle spearhead. Lomborg suggests that this element has also been transferred from the modern day areas of Hungary and Romania (Lomborg 1965, 230f.), where it appears in the Cófalva hoard at Tufalau (Fig. 5). This will be further discussed in the next section.

A possible detractor from the direct association between spirals and 16th century BC Valsømagle type objects is the metal-hilted Hajdúsámson-Apa sword found at Stølstrupgård (Fig. 6). Although difficult to make out, it is possible see the spiral ornamentation inside the circle on the blade of this sword. The

Figure 5. The gold disk from Tufalau – after Bouzek 1985, 65.

Figure 6. Local copy of a Hajdúsámson-Apa type sword found at Stølstrupgård, Sorø on Zealand – after Vandkilde 1996, 225.

decoration consists of a four-jointed true spiral hook from which the lines continue to run the length of the blade. In this instance, the spiral appears on a sword type which is not normally associated with it, neither in its original context, nor in a Danish one. The Stølstrupgård sword was first dated to Period IB, but further investigation by Randsborg and Christensen suggests that this sword was in fact from early Period II (towards the close of the 16th century BC) and is thus too young to have any influence on the transmission of the spiral into Denmark (Randsborg and Christensen 2007, 97).

A more satisfactory interpretation of this artefact would be as an example of style fusion (Vandkilde 1996, 224f.). It would seem that such a meld is not uncommon among the local interpretations of Hajdúsámson-Apa swords and daggers found in Denmark. According to their shape, ornamentation and the techniques by which they were cast, only the swords from Stensgård and Torupgårde could be considered real imports from the Carpathian Basin (Vandkilde 1996, 225).

It appears that there is little evidence to support the hypothesis that the cradle of the spiral – and of the sword – was located in the area which today belongs to Hungary and Romania (Lomborg 1965, 230). This conclusion is further amplified by Lomborg's other investigations (reviewed in the next section). Thus far, it would seem that the transfer of the spiral was not dependent upon the transfer of the sword. Both decoration and weapon originated from the same region and entered the Danish region at the same time, but they did so independently of each other.

The Carpathian Basin

As evidenced by the objects mentioned above, the origin of the new styles and objects is to be found in the Carpathian Basin, more precisely in Hungary and Romania. In earlier times, the Únětice groups of central Germany acted as the metal distributors for Central and Northern Europe as well as Southern Scandinavia. However, following the spread of hill settlement sites from the Carpathian Basin northwest into central Germany circa 1700 BC, the Únetician core collapsed (Vandkilde 1996, 307). These hill settlement sites came from parts of Hungary, Romania and Moravia in which the Otomani Culture had taken hold (Kristiansen 1998, 370). A rich bronze-producing society emerged from these ashes boasting contacts across the Black Sea (David 2001, 73). These new settlements became new nodal points in a wide-ranging distribution net of many items, including tin-bronze (Szeverényi 2004, 28; Vandkilde 1996, 307).

During the 16th century BC, significant changes occurred over a wide geographical area. Within a very short amount of time, a new culture emerged in western Central Europe which embraced a new variety of funerary ritual: interment in barrows. These earthen mounds often included the burial of members of the most prominent families with spectacular weapons and jewelry (Kristiansen 1998, 377). The

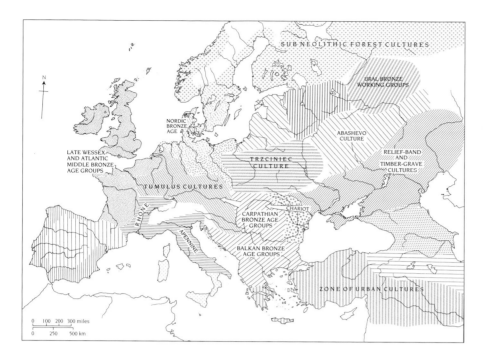

Figure 7. The general Bronze Age settings after the formation of the Tumulus culture – after Sherratt 1998, 247.

new culture was named after the novel funerary ritual: Tumulus. The Tumulus Culture's beliefs, material culture and social behavior probably originated in Transylvania (Romania), and may then have spread to Europe through the exchange network among the rival elites at the fortified settlements (Fig. 7). The culture flourished in the 16th century BC, this *flourit* concomitant with the decline of the Otomani Culture (Vandkilde 2007, 129).

At this point in prehistory, European societies were very much subject to an unequal division of wealth and status. Those individuals which Kristiansen and Reményi believe were the elite of the Tumulus Culture (Kristiansen 2008, 368; Reményi 2005, 7) used prestigious weapons and other riches to mark their status in the tomb. This clear demonstration of wealth was very much in contrast to earlier practices in which valuables were not placed in the graves, but were rather used as part of enormous depositions (Vandkilde 2007, 108). The establishment of a more individual burial custom in which the leaders of prominent families demonstrated their power and riches had begun.

It has been suggested that contact with the Tumulus Culture was the means by which the spiral was delivered to Southern Scandinavia (Hachmann 1957, 142). Lomborg, however, disagrees. He argues that the Central European specimens were too young and did not greatly resemble the Nordic examples (Lomborg 1965, 231). The idea that the spiral came from modern day Hungary or Romania has recently gained support (e.g. Kristiansen 2008, 374; Vandkilde 2007, 129).

In the Carpathian Basin, spiral design differed from region to region. A review of Carpathian objects demonstrates a predominance of the type of spirals with which we are already familiar in Hungary and Romania as well as the dominance of wavy band decoration in Turkey, Serbia and the Czech Republic (Bouzek 1985, 60-68). Naturally, these decorative homelands do not have absolute borders. Wavy band decoration is found in Hungary and Romania, just as spirals have also been recovered from Anatolia, Serbia and Bohemia. However, the potential areas of origin mentioned here seem to reflect general areas of greater spiral predominance.

There are spiral decorative elements which closely resemble Nordic spirals within the Otomani Culture. A gold plate found with the Cófalva hoard from Tufalau, Romania demonstrates true running spiral hook decoration exactly like that on the sword hilt from Riiskov (Lomborg 1965, 230). In Hungary, a bronze belt (broken in three places) decorated with a true spiral hook (both as running and single motif) was found in a grave at Chotín (Mozsolics 1973, 140) (Fig. 8). Unfortunately, the exact circumstances of the find are unknown, so it is, therefore, impossible to pinpoint its chronological origin. However, the similarities between this spiral and the ones on the Riiskov hilt and the Valsømagle spearhead are so strong that it is easy to be convinced by Lomborg's hypothesis (i.e.

Figure 8. Bronze belt found at Chotín – after Mozsolics 1973, 254.

that the Otomani Culture was the means of the spiral's arrival in the North (Lomborg 1965, 230).

Metal, however, is not the only material associated with spirals. Indeed, that decorative element appears on many different materials, the most popular of which was bone (Vandkilde 2007, 125; David 2001, 57). Spiral-decorated bone horse gear is frequently recovered from Carpathian tells and hilltop settlements (Vandkilde 2007, 125f.). However, gold, bronze and ceramics were also embossed with spirals (Bouzek 1985, 60). David views this material diversity as a clear indication of Mycenaean influence (David 2001, 57), since the spiral is equally present on multitudinous materials (bone, gold, rock, and glass) in that region. He finds it likely that the Mycenaeans were the ones to first introduce the spiral to the cultures of the Carpathian Basin.

Let us return to that secondary subject of the sword, which made its first appearance in eastern Hungary and Romania around 1600 BC (Harding 1984, 153; Vandkilde 2007, 125). At that time, there were many finely decorated metal-hilted swords with elaborate spiral decoration (Lomborg 1960, 74) such as are exemplified by the swords from the hoards of Hajdúsámson and Apa (Fig. 9). The decoration on the sword from the Hajdúsámson hoard consists of line bundles, dotted lines, triangles, arches and spiral hooks. However, this ornamentation differs greatly from the Danish spiral hooks. The sword from the hoard at Au, by contrast, does not contain spiral decorations at all. In addition to the fact that the swords from Stensgård and Torupgårde do not have spirals (Fig. 2), one can again conclude that it was not by means of Carpathian swords that the spiral was first introduced to the Nordic region.

When examining the material discussed in this paper, it is evident that it was through the Otomani that Denmark first gained contact with the spiral and the sword. In the Carpathian Basin, the design of the spiral differed greatly, and it is those spirals that occur in Otomani areas that most closely resemble the Danish spiral. Moreover, the sword made its first appearance in eastern Hungary and Romania around 1600 BC. Since the sword appeared in the Danish region at almost the same time (or at least very soon thereafter), it is tempting to assume that the means of delivering both the spiral decoration and the sword took the form of Otomani traders.

The arrival of the sword in the Carpathian region can be notably connected with the early Mycenaean

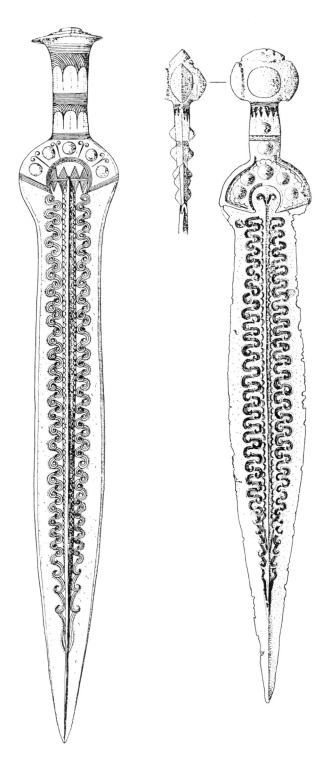

Figure 9. Swords from the Carpathian Basin. The sword on the left was found in the Hajdúsámson hoard, the sword on the right was found in the Apa hoard – after Lomborg 1960, 73-75.

swords which first emerged around 1800 BC (Vandkilde 2007, 126). In combination with the spirals of the Otomani Culture, the sword has given rise to the assumption that it was the Mycenaeans that introduced the spiral to the Carpathian Basin.

Why did the Mycenaeans bring the spiral to the Carpathian Basin in the first place? As mentioned earlier, different spirals were distributed across the Carpathian Basin. This may have resulted in an instance in which the Mycenaeans, having noted the popularity of local spirals, introduced their own version, perhaps in the hopes of improving trade. However, this is merely speculation.

The Origin of the Carpathian Spiral

Connections between Mycenae and the Danubian-Carpathian region have been the springboard for much discussion (Harding 1984, 4-11). Spirals have been employed both to support and detract from the direct connection hypothesis (Vandkilde 2007, 126). The question as to whether Carpathian crafts and their spiral ornamentation can be used as evidence for contact with the early Mycenaean kingdoms has often been raised. Several researchers emphasize the fact that the spirals on Carpathian material were designed by compass and cannot, therefore, be compared with Mycenaean spirals (Harding 1984, 199; Bouzek 1985, 60). Furthermore, it is argued that there are almost no Aegean imports among the Carpathian material and that many decorations found in the Carpathian region are incomparable to those from the Aegean (Bouzek 1985, 60). Bouzek, however, confesses that there are too many resemblances between the two regions for them to be coincidental (Bouzek 1985, 60). It must also be emphasized that in the 16th century BC, the Carpathian Basin was also influenced by other foreign practices, such as those stemming from the Orient and Russia (David 2001, 62), which themselves may have had an impact on the use of the spiral coming from Mycenae.

The appearance of the spiral on horse gear (among other objects) gave rise to the assumption that the spiral might have originated in the Orient and was brought to the Carpathian Basin by invading forces in horse-pulled wagons (Penner 1998, 161f.). However, after a thorough investigation of wavy band decoration, it is clear that only a minor proportion of the decorations examined could truly be qualified as Oriental (David 2001, 72).

Im Donau-Karpatenraum, aus der Peloponnes, in Anatolien und in der Amuq-Ebene kommt somit jeweils nicht nur die gleiche in Motiven und Komposition unverwechselbare Wellenbandornamentik vor, sondern es lassen auch die bloßen Formen der als Träger dieser typischen Verzierung in Erscheinung tretenden Pferdegeschirrteile, Scheiben und pyxiden- oder griffartigen zylindrischen Gegenstände unmittelbare Verknüpfungen zwischen den genannten Räumen zu. [...]handelt es sich bei den Vergleichmöglichkeiten nicht lediglich um vereinzelte oder allgemeine Analogien, sondern es lassen sich jeweils mehrere Motive und Motivgruppen miteinander verknüpfen.1 (David 2001, 64).

David goes so far as to claim that the ornamental and morphological similarities between some of the Danubian pieces and Mycenaean or Anatolian examples are so great as to be impossible *sans* direct contact (David 2001, 69). Since the Orient mainly distributed a certain kind of wavy band decoration to the Carpathian region (David 2001, 62f.), the next step in the clarification of the movement of the spiral is to turn towards Mycenae.

Mycenaean Shaft Graves

The political and economic *floruit* in the Aegean during the early 2nd millennium BC was due to a long-distance trading network for copper, silver, tin and textiles in the eastern Mediterranean and the Near East (Kristiansen 1998, 359). On the island of Crete, the first palace-organized states emerged around 2000 BC. On the Greek mainland, they did so two centuries later (Vandkilde 2007, 96). According to Kristiansen, this trade network served as the basis for the rise of the Mycenaeans, who took over the western edge of Near Eastern commercial networks in the 17th century BC and then further developed those connections (Kristiansen 1998, 359f.). However, it was probably not before the middle of the 1st millennium BC that "the contact became more formalized and Central Europe became a periphery to a core cluster of early city-states in the Mediterranean region" (Vandkilde 2007, 117).

The wealth of the Mycenaeans is clearly demonstrated by the six Shaft Graves (Karo 1930-33, 15). The apogee of Mycenaean Shaft Grave construction occurred in 1600 BC (Vandkilde 2007, 126). The graves contained some 1, 000 items (Karo 1930-33, 166) ranging from pottery to swords and from stone to gold. The majority of the grave goods were found in graves IV and V (Karo 1930-33a, 71-154). The Shaft Graves additionally contain several different spirals, both single and double (Karo 1930-33, 272-281). A spiral that is also present in the Carpathian Basin and the

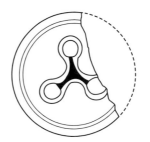

Figure 10. Trefoil wavy band decoration. The disk on the left was found at Sălacea, the disk on the right was found in Mycenaean Shaft Grave IV – redrafted after David 2001, 59.

Nordic region is the true running spiral hook, which we see included on several different objects and materials, such as swords and daggers from graves IV and V (Karo 1930-33, LXXXII and LXXXV), as well as grave stones (Karo 1930-33, V-X) and the silver jugs recovered from grave V (Karo 1930-33, CXXXIV). In addition, the inclusion of specific wavy band decoration indicates an Otomani connection. A direct comparison (in terms of decoration, size and shape) can be made between the trefoil wavy band ornamentation on a bone disc from the Otomani settlement of Sălacea and several gold-plated double buttons (Fig. 10) found in graves IV and V (David 2001, 58).

If we take a closer look at swords 402 and 404 (Fig. 11) from grave IV (Karo 1930-33, LXXXV), we see two completely different styles of spiral. The spiral on sword 404 is the well-known true spiral hook, while sword 402 demonstrates spiral ornamentation which is similar to the spirals present on the Hajdúsámson and Apa swords.

Another interesting fact that helps bolster the spiral-via-Mycenae hypothesis is the vast amount of amber found in the Shaft Graves dated to c. 1600 BC (Vandkilde 2007, 127). This may indicate a close (or even a direct) connection between the Nordic region (from whence the amber is likely to have originated) and Mycenae. This also illustrates how quickly the transmission took place. All these examples seem to indicate that Europe's ornamental world radically changed around 1600 BC through close contact with the Mycenaeans.

Several items from the Mycenaean Shaft Graves clearly support the association between Mycenae and the arrival of the spiral in the North by means of the Carpathian Basin. The presence of amber in the Shaft Graves seems to indicate that an almost direct connection existed between Mycenaean trad-

Conclusion

Although the spiral and the sword seem to have travelled together through Europe, the sword did not act as a carrier of one specific type of spiral. When the swords included in this paper were examined, it became clear that a change in decorative style was present in each new region. If other objects such as disks, buttons etc. were included as well, we see clear evidence that the true running spiral hook travelled from the Mediterranean to Southern Scandinavia in an almost unchanged form. Thus, it can be concluded that, when travelling across Europe, the spiral was reproduced and transmitted by means of many different objects. The similarities of the true running spiral in the Danish region with those found in the Carpathian Basin and Mycenae are too strong to have been the result of incorporated memory – it is only through a physical model that one could achieve such similar results. In this instance, therefore, there is a clear example of the admission of an idea from one culture into another. In this case, the form of the idea remained constant, while its mode was altered. In other words, the design of the spiral remained the same, but the materials on which it appeared varied according to the needs and whims of the host culture. This type of transfer is highly reminiscent of Nicolaescu's ideas (2004). A "translation" of the spiral in both the Carpathian Basin and the Danish region is what lead the Mycenaean spiral through Europe, which could also explain the rapid pace at which the spiral was transferred and admitted into new cultures. By utilizing the spiral on locally-known objects, its acceptance occurred more quickly than if the culture was required to accept both a new design as well as a new object.

In Mycenae and the Carpathian Basin, the spiral appeared on different objects and materials than it did in the North (where the spiral first appeared on weapons and only in bronze). Therefore, one might be inclined to think that the spiral first achieved a high status with its transfer to the Nordic region. Nevertheless, one must not forget in which contexts the spiral was found in other regions; it seems to have been of equally high status in the Carpathian Basin and Mycenae, since it appears on objects found mainly in the hill settlements inhabited by Otomani elites and within the rich Mycenaean Shaft Graves. One may, therefore, conclude that the spiral decoration had a high status throughout Europe which reached a climax upon its admission to the North.

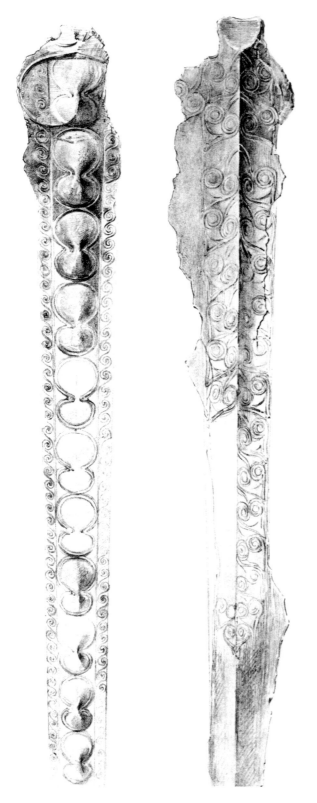

Figure 11. Swords from the Mycenaean Shaft Grave IV – after Karo 1930-33b, LXXXV.

ers and those from the Nordic regions, most likely through meetings in the Carpathian Basin. The fact that the arrival of the true running spiral in the North occurred at almost the same time (around 1600 BC) lends further support to this conclusion.

Note

1. "In the Danube-Carpathian region, the Peloponnese, Anatolia and in the Amuq Plain, it is not merely the same motifs and compositions of the distinctive wave band ornamentation which appear, but also the same forms which carry this ornamentation, such as horse harnesses, disks and pyxides- or handle-like cylindrical objects, which can be seen as a direct connection between the areas described. […] the several possible comparisons suggest that it is not only about single or general analogs, but a connection of several motifs and motif groups. "(David 2004, 64, author's translation).

Bibliography

Bouzek, J. 1985: *The Aegean, Anatolia and Europe. Cultural inter- relations in the second millennium B. C.* Gothenburg.

Broholm, H.C. 1944: *Danmarks Bronzealder. Andet Bind. Kultur og folk i den Ældre Bronzealder.* København.

David, W. 2001: Zu den Beziehungen zwischen Donau- Karpatenraum, osteuropäischen Steppengebieten und ägäisch-anatolischem Raum zur Zeit der mykenischen Schachtgräber unter Berücksichtigung neuerer Funde aus Südbayern. *Anodos. Studies of the Ancient World 1,* 51-80.

Hachmann, R. 1957: *Die frühe Bronzezeit im westlichen Ost- seegebiet und ihre mittel- und südosteuropäischen Beziehun- gen. Chronologische Untersuchungen.* Beiheft zum Atlas der Urgeschichte, 6. Hamburg.

Harding, A.F. 1984: *The Mycenaeans and Europe.* London.

Johannsen, N. 2010: Technological Conceptualization: Cogni- tion on the Shoulders of History. In: Malafouris, L. & C. Renfrew (eds.): *The Cognitive Life of Things. Recasting the Boundaries of the Mind.* Cambridge, 59-69.

Kilian, G. 1999 22: *Die Schachtgräber von Mykenai.* München.

Kirstiansen, K. 1998: *Europe before History.* Cambridge.

Lomborg, E. 1960: Donauländische Kulturbeziehungen und die relative Chronologie der frühen nordischen Bronzezeit. *Acta Archaeologica* 30, 1959, 51-146.

Lomborg, E. 1965: Valsømagle und die frühe nordische Spi- ralornamentik. *Acta Archaeologica* 36, 223-232.

Moszsolics, A. 1973: *Bronze- und Goldfunde des Karpatenbeck- ens. Depotfundhorizonte von Forró und Opályi.* Budapest.

Nicolaescu, M. 2004: Circulating Images: The Translation of the Global into the Local. In: Vainovski-Mihai, I. (ed.): *New European College GE-NEC Program 2000-2002.* Bucharest, 75-114.

Penner, S. 1998: *Schliemanns Schachtgräberrund und der europäi- sche Nordosten.* Saarbrücker Beiträge zur Altertum- skunde 60. Bonn.

Pydyn, A. 1999: *Exchange and Cultural Interactions. A study of long-distance trade and cross cultural contacts in the Late Bronze Age and Early Iron Age in Central and Eastern Europe.* Oxford.

Randsborg, K. & K. Christensen 2007: Bronze Age Oak- Coffin Graves. Archaeology and Dendro- Dating. *Acta Archaeologica* 77, 1-246.

Reményi, L. 2005: The golden Age of the Carpathian basin and the Beautiful Warrior. In: Hjørungdal, T. (ed.): *Gen- der, Locales and Local Genders in Archaeaology.* BAR Inter- national Series 1425. Oxford, 1-11.

Sherratt, A. 1998: The Emergence of Élites. Earlier Bronze Age Europe, 2500-1300 BC. In: Cunliffe, B. (ed.): *Prehisto- ric Europe. An illustrated history.* Oxford, 244-276.

Szeverényi, V. 2004: The Early and Middle Bronze Ages in Central Europe. In: Bogucki, P. & P.J. Crabtree (eds.): *Ancient Europe, 8000 BC to AD 1000. Encyclopedia of the Barbarian World. II. Bronze Age to Early Middle Ages (3000 BC – AD 1000).* New York, 20-30.

Vandkilde, H. 1996: *From Stone to Bronze. The Metalwork of the Late Neolithic and Earliest Bronze Age in Denmark.* Aarhus.

Vandkilde, H. 2007: *Culture and Change in Central European Prehistory 6th to 1st Millennium BC.* Aarhus.

The Fårdrup-type Shaft-hole Axes
Material Hybridity in Bronze Age Europe c. 1600 BC

Zsófia Kölcze

"Spirit is what we are; matter is what we do."
Adapted from Philip Pullman's *His Dark Materials* series

Introduction

It is difficult to discuss the movement of artefacts and ideas without touching upon the concepts of transmission and reception. As is mentioned by other papers in this volume, the material manifestations of these concepts may occur in several forms dependent on such diverse factors as economy, technological advancement, socio-cultural setting and political and ideological flows. Common to all kinds of transmission and reception, however, is the fact that they occur in the space between sender and receiver. They are thus the means by which archaeology is able to contribute new knowledge about the nature of the interactions between these two forces.

In archaeology and anthropology, it is important to discuss not only the movement or exchange of artefacts and ideas, but also their transmission and reception (Nicolaescu 2002, 75-114; Kristiansen and Larsson 2005, 4-31). By discussing 'transmission' rather than 'movement', we acknowledge the possibility that artefacts and ideas moved either separately or together from one socio-cultural sphere to another without said spheres being reduced to cultural entities void of social, ethical, aesthetical and/or ideological values. Quite to the contrary, the traditions and practices of distinct socio-cultural groups may have a profound impact on the way objects and ideas are transmitted between them. In turn, this makes notions of the reception of these objects and ideas highly interesting and relevant. The various ways in which an artefact or an idea is transmitted between socio-cultural entities may provide information not just about those societies which send or receive, but

also about the complexity of the relationships which existed between the various senders and receivers.

In light of this, an examination of modes of reception is of crucial importance in illuminating the transition of impulses (be they material or immaterial) from one socio-cultural sphere to another. As discussed by Reiter (this volume), reception is understood here to indicate any means by which these impulses might be met, absorbed or incorporated into an existing society with its own pre-defined traditions. A theoretical understanding of the modes and processes of transmission and reception is important not only because these terms add a new dimension to our approach to archaeological data, but also because they may reveal information about inter-cultural interaction which is difficult to access through traditional archaeological analyses.

Special attention is paid in this paper to the phenomenon of material hybridity, as this is one of the most prominent and most easily traceable manifestations of the transmission and reception of ideas in archaeological data. In light of this, the first section of this text gives an overview of the use of the term in general as well as in specifically archaeological contexts. This is followed by a case study of the Scandinavian Early Bronze Age Fårdrup-type shaft-hole axes in order to illustrate how some of the characteristics of hybridity can be recognized in archaeological data. In this sense, this paper utilises Fårdrup-type shaft-hole axes to elucidate the various ways in which humans interact with their material surroundings, to highlight the advantages and shortcomings of the concept of hybridity in archaeology, and to explore transmission and reception in Bronze Age Europe.

Hybridity: A Theoretical Outline

Whereas the concept of hybridity has been employed in biology, the social sciences and art history for several decades, it is a relative newcomer to archaeological thought. According to the *Oxford Dictionary*, a hybrid is an "animal or plant that has parents of different species or varieties" or a "thing made by combining two different elements" (Hornby 1990, 611). Indeed, the Latin word for hybrid (*hibrida*) was originally used as a collective name for the offspring of a domestic sow and a wild boar, and was thus a purely biological term. In modern biology, the use of the word has been broadened to include the faunal or floral progeny of two different – but related – species (Kapchan and Strong 1999, 239-253).

In general, a hybrid is understood to be a creature which is possessed of a unique form which simultaneously shows the biological traits of both of its parents. This is aptly illustrated by the mule, which is the offspring of a stallion and a female ass. Another characteristic of the hybrid is an irregular reproduction pattern; it always takes a stallion and an ass to produce a mule as mules are infertile. These characteristics (i.e. the admixture of two 'parents' of diverse character and the rarity of independent reproduction) are vital to understanding the way in which the term hybrid is used in the humanities and social sciences.

When transferred from biology to the humanities, the hybridity phenomenon is broadly understood as a mixture of socio-cultural traditions, norms and aesthetics which often manifests materially. An apt illustration of this concept would be an electric bike, a hybrid between a traditional bicycle and a moped. As is the case in biology, it is still possible to speak metaphorically about the 'parents' of the hybrid (Stross 1999, 254-267) when actually referring to a meeting of distinct socio-cultural traditions or spheres.

At this point, it is crucial to address the challenge of defining what comprises a distinct socio-cultural tradition in the first place, as most social phenomena are the end products of the admixture between the totality of economic, social and ideological processes over a specific time period. If all societies are in a constant state of flux, whether or not one can accurately pin down socio-cultural parentage is debatable. In this sense, the concept of hybridity may be said to be related to syncretism, creolization (Kapchan and Strong 1999, 239-253), Lévi-Strauss' 'bricolage' (Lévi-Strauss 1966, 16-36) or Derrida's 'bricure' (Derrida 1980, 202-232).

Hybridity has often been described in sociology as well as art history and material culture studies, and like many other ambiguous terms, it has been understood in very different ways. The social sciences speak broadly about cultural hybridity. This type of hybridity has often been connected with racism in the sense that it advocates an acceptance of the concepts of 'pure' and 'mixed' or 'contaminated' cultures. According to Frello, by contrast, cultural hybridity results from the questioning of pre-existent norms and categories rather than any admixture of cultures (Frello 2006, 1-11). She posits that there are two perceptions of the nature of hybridity: either it is a consequence of cultural interaction and the exchange of cultural elements or an expression of ever-changing ideas of purity. Therefore, hybridity is closely linked to ideas of transgression understood as "the 'mixture' or 'blending' of cultural forms" (Frello 2006, 7).

In the social sciences, hybridity is often linked to the notion of identity and the negotiation of power relations, an important aspect in understanding hybridity in material culture studies. One of the first persons to introduce the term of hybridity to the humanities field was art historian Homi K. Bhabha. In contrast to other scholars who viewed the concept of hybridity as a mixture of traditions or cultures (see below), Bhabha described hybridity in terms of what he referred to as a "third space" where traditions, trends and impulses were confronted and negotiated (Bhabha 1994, 28-56; Bhabha 1996, 307-322). To Bhabha, hybridity is most evident in postcolonial and postmodern art with its constant negotiation between past and present and different cultural backgrounds or subcultures. According to him, the phenomenon of hybridity is closely linked to the concept of identity as it acts as a platform on which identities can be expressed, refuted or negotiated.

Much in the same fashion, Feldman argues that visual hybridity (traditionally called 'international style' in art history) is a material means of expressing the negotiations of power, identity and/or wealth which occurred between diverse diplomatically related cultural groups (Feldman 2006, 23-71). According to Feldman, artefacts displaying visual hybridity

Focal point	Information about
The hybrid itself and its qualities	Heterogeneity, hybrid vigour
The parents of the hybrid and qualities	Homogenety, purity, boundaries
The relations between the hybrid and its parents	Ancestry, belonging, mediation
The relations between the hybrid and its environment/context	Environmental facilitators, context, hybrid vigour
The hybridization process and the mechanisms by which hybrids are created	Hybridizing mechanisms, invention, borrowing, learning
The cycle of hybridity/the development of the hybrid	Refinement, adaption, contrast with other categories

Figure 1. Focal points of hybridity – adapted from Stross 1999, 256, Table 1.

should not be interpreted as the products of random experimentation or artistic creativity, but rather as deliberately- and systematically-crafted objects with the specific intent of materially bridging social, political and cultural gaps between diverse societies, communities or cultures (Feldman 2006, 59-71). This view of hybridity brings about another challenge regarding the nature of hybrid artefacts. In her studies of ancient Near Eastern luxury objects dated to 1400-1200 BC, Feldman perceives hybridity as something deliberately crafted for a specific effect or function. However, hybridity may also be understood as the unintended result of the mixture or diffusion of ideas and traditions as was pointed out by semiotician Bakhtin in his work with conscious and unconscious forms of linguistic hybridity (Bakhtin 1981, 358-366). While conscious hybridity describes the deliberate manipulation of language in order to create parody or another disjuncture between meaning and intent, unconscious hybridity refers to the natural process of language development or change.

In much the same line as Bakhtin, Young makes a distinction between organic and intentional hybridity; the former produces hegemony, new spaces and structure, while the latter spreads as a kind of translation or transformation (Young 1995, 1-28). Although most scholars agree on distinguishing between intentional and unintentional forms of hybridity, this categorisation does little or nothing to facilitate the practical employment of the term. That being said, it does, however, increase awareness of the complexity of the concept in terms of its many cognitive aspects and its use as an analytical tool.

Stross is one of the few scholars who has put forth a possible analytical system for the analysis and interpretation of hybrid phenomena. He takes his departure from the characteristics of biological hybridity. According to him, both biological and cultural hybridity consist of a number of aspects or characteristics which make them distinct from non-hybrid phenom-

ena (Stross 1999, 254-267). These characteristics can be observed through examination of at least six aspects of the hybrid (material or immaterial). Firstly, one can focus on the hybrid itself, shedding light on topics like heterogeneity and hybrid vigour. Hybrid vigour (or heterosis) refers to the phenomenon in which the hybrid often displays more growth capacity than either its parents or non-hybrids within its cohort (Stross 1999, 257). Secondly, one can investigate the parents of the hybrid from which one may glean information about homogeneity and boundaries. Thirdly, the relationship between the hybrid and its parent(s) can provide information on ancestry, belonging and mediation. Study of the relations between the hybrid and its surroundings/context can yield information about those environmental facilitators which enabled the hybrid to emerge. A focus on the hybridisation process, by contrast, may shed light on hybridisation mechanisms such as invention, borrowing and learning. Last but not least, concentration on what Stross calls the "cycle of hybridity" can place the hybrid into a wider temporal and spatial context (Stross 1999, 256). Fig. 1 provides an overview of the analytical focal points mentioned above as well as those topics illuminated by them.

In spite of a somewhat simplistic view of the relationship between the concepts of biological and cultural hybridity, Stross' paper offers a rather clear analytical approach to the phenomenon which begs for concrete application. In the following section, this approach will be applied to the Fårdrup-type shaft-hole axes due to the clear signs of material hybridity they demonstrate.

The Fårdrup-type Axes

The massive Fårdrup-type bronze axe heads date to Period IB of the early Nordic Bronze Age, ca. 1600 BC (Vandkilde 1996, 227-228). They are typically found either as single finds or in single-type deposits, and appear only rarely in connection with other types

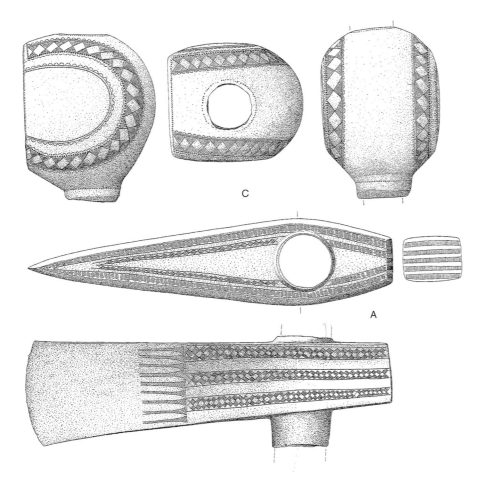

Figure 2. The large axe and mace head from the Fårdrup hoard, Denmark – after Aner & Kersten 1976, nr. 1178.

of objects (with the exception of the eponymous Fårdrup hoard in which two axes were found with a massive bronze mace head – see Fig. 2). So far, 118 Fårdrup-type shaft-hole axes have been found, all of them in the Nordic area, (i.e. Denmark, Norway, Sweden and northern Germany) with concentrations in northern Jutland and on the islands of Zealand and Funen (Malmer 1987, 19-27). They can rightfully be regarded as a characteristic South Scandinavian artefact type (Fig. 3).

All of the Fårdrup-type axes are shaft-hole axes and have presumably had an organic (wooden) shaft, although to the author's knowledge, no preserved Fårdrup axe shafts have yet been recovered. As has been previously noted, these axes bear a striking resemblance to Neolithic stone shaft-hole axes (Montelius 1917, 32; Brøndsted 1931, 111-116). Interestingly, 52 of the 118 (44,1 %) known Fårdrup-type axes are decorated with geometric motifs (Malmer 1987, 19-27), an aesthetic phenomenon which is only very rarely observed on stone Nordic shaft-hole axes. Geometric ornamentation was considered an important decorative element in South Scandinavia around 1600 BC (i.e. in the second half of Nordic Bronze Age Period I), possibly in connection with a dramatic increase in

metal production at that time (Vandkilde 1996, 262, Fig. 279).

Studies of the form and decoration of the Fårdrup axes have resulted in several diverse interpretations of their function, which range from their use as ceremonial weapons in connection with religious rituals (Brøndsted 1931, 111-116) to being measuring units in a Bronze Age weight system (Malmer 1992, 377-388). The Nordic Fårdrup axes emerged during a dynamic period of technological, social and cultural flow and were produced and circulated between ca. 1600 and 1500 BC (Vandkilde 1996, 259-308). Both their material appearance and their production methods show clear signs of various craft traditions from different cultural areas. In analysing the Fårdrup axes, several material and non-material characteristic elements are available for consideration. The elements studied here include form, decoration, material and production techniques. These might be called constitutional attributes, as they are the components which define the artefacts and render them comprehensible by the human mind.

The form of the Fårdrup axes is generally very homogenous; they are all massive shaft-hole axes with vertical cutting edges, flat or slightly convex broadsides and a flat butt. Some of the axes, however,

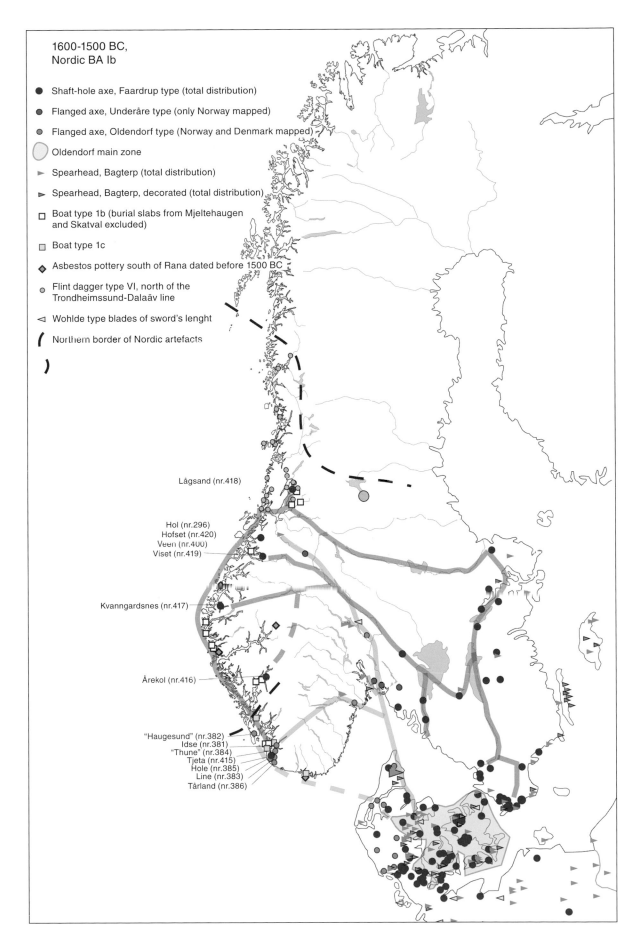

Lågsand (nr.418)

Hol (nr.296)
Hofset (nr.420)
Veen (nr.400)
Viset (nr.419)

Kvanngardsnes (nr.417)

Årekol (nr.416)

"Haugesund" (nr.382)
Idse (nr.381)
"Thune" (nr.384)
Tjeta (nr.415)
Hole (nr.385)
Line (nr.383)
Tårland (nr.386)

Figure 3. The distribution of Fårdrup-type axes – after Engedal 2010, Map 11.

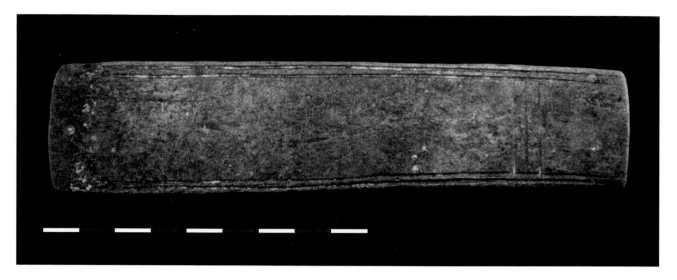

Figure 4. Fårdrup axe from Northern Jutland, Denmark. VHM 13780 – photo by the author, courtesy of Vendsyssel Historiske Museum.

have vertically-facetted broadsides at the shaft-hole or plastically formed rivet-like markers along the course of the shaft hole. The large axe (NM B11671) from the eponymous Fårdrup hoard (Fig. 2) has a metal support for the shaft which was cast in a single piece with the axe head. A similar axe was found near Fellingsbro in Sweden (Malmer 1987, 19-27). The weight of the axes generally ranges between 1000 to 2000 grams. In this instance as well, the large axe from Fårdrup is an exception; weighing 3172.1 g, it measures double the weight of the average Fårdrup axe. It is only matched by the 3237.1 g weight of the Fårdrup mace head. On the other end of the weight scale, we find a well-preserved shaft-hole axe (VHM 13780) from northern Jutland which, while formed like a Fårdrup axe, is more slender and much smaller, weighing in at only 752.0 g (Fig. 4).

As has already been pointed out, the shape of the Fårdrup axes follows the Nordic tradition of shaft-hole axes. Their massive and compact form mirrors that of Middle- and Late Neolithic stone battle axes with vertical cutting edges and shaft holes placed close to the butt. Flint axes and stone shaft-hole axes were both used throughout the Neolithic-Bronze age transition as well as the Bronze Age. This is demonstrated by their occasional appearance in Neolithic burial contexts and Bronze Age settlement layers (Lekberg 2002, 80-86). Stone shaft-hole axes were also common in the Finnish area during the Bronze Age (Meinander 1954, 67-84), indicating their strong connection to the Nordic axe producing tradition.

Fifty-two of the 118 known Fårdrup axes are deco-rated, all with geometric patterns. This decoration shows a huge variation from simple lines to complex ornaments covering most of the surface. Generally, the ornamentation of the shaft-hole axes is dominated by a vast amount of different (and, in most cases, unique) patterning consisting of various combinations of only a few geometrical features, such as lines, curves, triangles and zigzags. However, some of the features which appear on the axes (such as a characteristic dagger- or fish-shaped element) have a semi-figurative quality to them which is regularly but rather tentatively discussed in the archaeological literature (Kristiansen and Larsson 2005, 186-212; Jockenhövel 2005, 601-619; Vandkilde, *forthcoming*). A list of the geometrical features appearing on the Fårdrup axes can be seen in Fig. 5.

The possibility of applying fine ornamentation on the Nordic shaft-hole axes went hand-in-hand with the technology employed in the production of these artefacts. Obviously, it is difficult or impossible to decorate stone axes with the same kind of detailed geometrical patterns as are characteristic of the Fårdrup-type axes.[1] Therefore, it may be assumed that an implementation of the Southeast- and Central European decorative tradition occurred secondarily to the spread of metallurgy in South Scandinavia. Although the very first examples of metalworking came from western Bell Beaker cultures, later connections between Scandinavia and Central Europe might have played a crucial role in the exchange of knowledge. This was likely linked to the production of tin-bronze, as shown by early metal hoards from

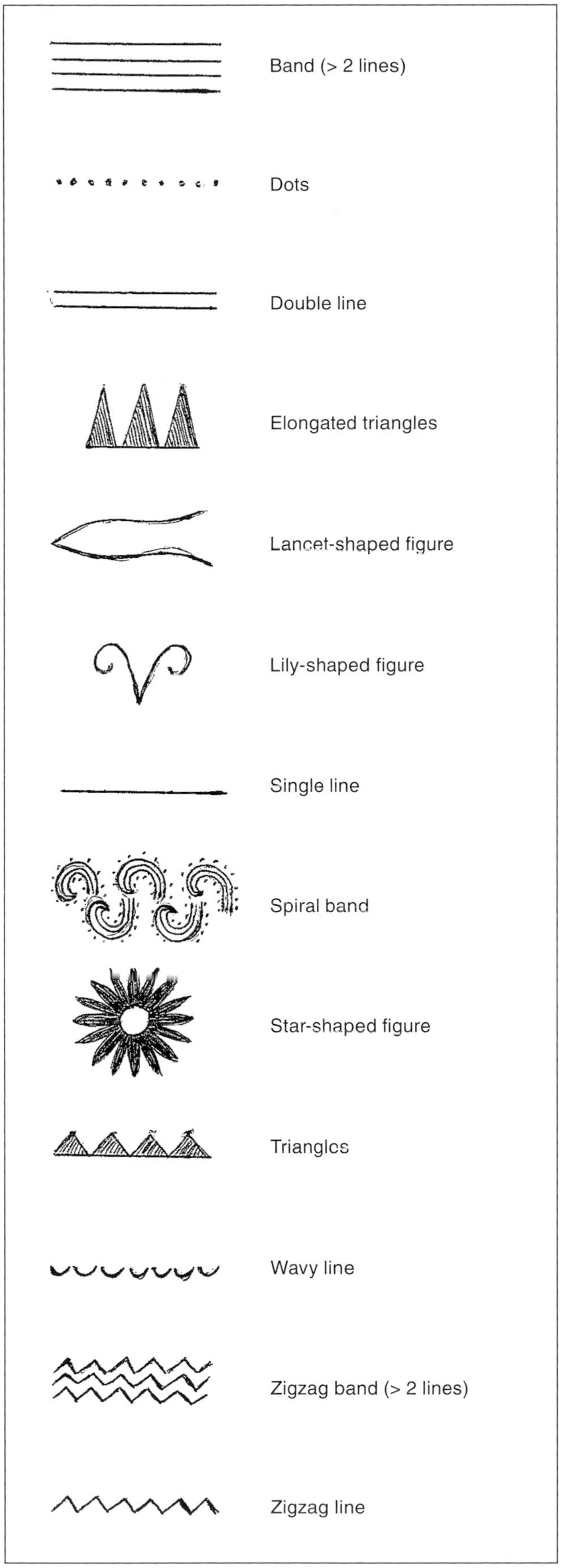

≡≡≡	Band (> 2 lines)
· · · · · · · ·	Dots
═══	Double line
▲▲▲	Elongated triangles
⌐───	Lancet-shaped figure
∿	Lily-shaped figure
───	Single line
୧୧୧	Spiral band
✺	Star-shaped figure
▲▲▲▲	Triangles
∪∪∪∪∪∪	Wavy line
⋀⋁⋀⋁	Zigzag band (> 2 lines)
∧∨∧∨	Zigzag line

Figure 5. Ornamental elements on Hajdúsámson-Apa-related metalwork, c. 1600 BC – after Kölcze 2010.

Skeldal (Zealand) and Pile (Scania) (Vandkilde 1996, 259-308; Vandkilde 2007, 91-120).

One intensively-discussed issue is the techniques by which the Fårdrup axes were produced. Their massive and often crude shape has often been thought to be indicative of the use of open moulds in the casting process (Brøndsted 1931, 111-116; Malmer 1957, 19-27). However, their decoration suggests that these axes – like most ornamented Early Bronze Age metalwork – were produced via the lost wax (*cire perdue*) technique widely employed among the earliest Nordic metal casters (Rønne 1993, 71-92). Thus, it becomes highly probable that the hybridised Southeast European-style of decoration on the Fårdrup-type axes was introduced to Scandinavia in combination with tin-bronze as a raw material and was empowered by the *cire perdue* casting technique.

Hybridity and the Fårdrup-type Axes

If an analysis of the Fårdrup-type shaft-hole axes is carried out in terms of Stross' theoretical hybridity paradigm (Stross 1999, 254-267), then there are even more indicators pointing towards the possibility that these axes were produced and perceived as veritable hybrids.

First, we have cases in which hybrid objects themselves display characteristics which mark them as clearly distinct from other types of axes. The massive shape and detailed decorations of the Fårdrup axes appear in connection with other types of Scandinavian objects; for instance many of the geometrical decorations known from the axes are also found on Bagterp-type spearheads and Hajdúsámson-Apa and Valsømagle-type swords. In addition, the characteristically massive form of the Fårdrup axes are to be found in the Nordic weapon tradition with the stone shaft-hole axes produced throughout the Neolithic and the Bronze Age. However, the combination of detailed decoration and massive shape occurs in for the first time on the Fårdrup-type axes.

Examining the *parentage* of the axes as well as *relationship between the Fårdrup axes and their parents* is more difficult. The Fårdrup-type axes were produced in a period when metalworking technology was advanced enough to create subtle and less metal-hungry designs, such as widely distributed flanged axes and Y-palstaves (Vandkilde 1996, 223-

257). Typologically, they belong more to a tradition of stone shaft-hole axes than to any of the new metal axe types. Whether the stone shaft-hole axes found in Bronze Age contexts reflect an unusually long circulation period for this specific type of object, or a continuously-reproduced and chronologically-coherent local tradition of axe production is debatable. In any case, the Fårdrup axes may be seen as revival or re-invention of this tradition within the confines of a new material (Hobsbawm 1983, 1-14), enhancing a locally-recognisable and possibly value-laden form. Also typologically linked to the Fårdrup-type shaft-hole axes are the five small amber axes recovered from Hørdum in Thy and which are dated to the Late Neolithic or Early Bronze Age (Brøndsted 1931, 111-116; Jensen 2000). Morphologically, these miniature shaft-hole axes are very like full-size Fårdrup-type axes or stone shaft-hole axes. One is even decorated with the simple lines typical of full-size Fårdrup axes.

Investigation of social *environment* or context offers an opportunity for a deep insight into the spread of the Fårdrup-type shaft-hole axes. What socio-cultural factors may have facilitated the development and production of these axes? As shown by archaeological evidence, the period around 1600 BC was an era of technological innovation and rapid social change, not only in Scandinavia, but throughout the whole of the European continent (Kristiansen and Larsson 2005, 118-132; Vandkilde 2007, 121-161). In Jutland and the Danish Isles, (where the Fårdrup-type axes are most highly concentrated) there was an increased focus on war and warriorhood which was associated with the adoption of new tin-bronze technology. The increased amount and variation of weapon finds like the Bagterp-type spearheads and the Valsømagle and Sögel-Wohlde metalwork show not only intensified social competition, but also the rise of high-ranking individuals and groups which expressed their identity, power and wealth through the use of bronze artefacts. In Europe, the period around 1600 BC witnessed the impact of the Santorini eruption (Manning *et al.* 2006, 565-569; Andersen 2007, 15-24), the gradual rise and expansion of the Tumulus Culture, and innovations in warfare (the use of swords, partial armour and horse-drawn chariots) and settlement patterns (hillforts along fluvial transport corridors) (Kristiansen and Larsson 2006, 120-130). Furthermore, there seems to have been some experimentation with new metalworking techniques, as shown by the famous sky-disc from Nebra-Sangerhausen

(Meller 2010, 23-73; Pernicka 2010, 719-734) and the drum-like artefacts from Balkåkra and Haschendorf (Knape and Nordström 1994). All in all, the archaeological evidence dated to c. 1600 BC indicates a rapidly changing society with strong technological, cultural, political and ideological dynamics. In short, it was an innovative period ideal for the development of material hybrids like the Fårdrup-type shaft-hole axes.

When focussing on the *hybridisation process* and *hybridity cycle* of the Fårdrup axes, it becomes clear that archaeological material does not provide much information. Although massive shaft-hole axes are known from earlier periods, it is difficult to point out exactly what might have triggered a production of massive metal axes. Obviously, the arrival of metal-casting technology in the north played a crucial role in the occurrence of this type as well as the spread of Southeast European decoration styles (Vandkilde 1996, 259-308). However, the rapidity and width of the spread of the Fårdrup axes suggests that they became exceedingly popular almost overnight not only in the southern parts of Scandinavia, but also further north in the areas of modern day Sweden and Norway (Fig. 3). At the same time, the circumstances of their sudden disappearance from the Nordic Bronze Age typological sequence remain obscure, especially in the light of the fact that stone shaft-hole axes were still being used and produced (Lekberg 2002, 80-86). Perhaps this rapid climb and fall was due to the huge amounts of raw material required for the production of each axe, or even the invention of new (and more economical) casting techniques. While both massive and heavy, the so-called ceremonial axes of later Bronze Age periods recovered from South Scandinavia (seen on many of the Swedish and Norwegian rock carvings) were often cast with a smaller width and a wider edge, thus reducing the amount of metal needed for the artefact, as is demonstrated by the two axes from Viby, Zealand (Kaul 2004: 338, Fig. 142). Another potential cause for the abandonment of Fårdrup-type shaft-hole axe production might have its roots in the new social, cultural and aesthetic trends which entered Nordic Bronze Age society alongside the influence of the Tumulus Culture around 1500 BC.

Discussion

The geometric patterns featured on the Fårdrup axes show a close kinship with the decorative traditions of Central and Southeast European Middle Bronze

Figure 6. The hoard from Hajdúsámson, Hungary – after Bóna 1993, 51.

Age metalwork, specifically the ornamentation of early Hajdúsámson-Apa-type swords and the Apa and Hajdúsámson-type disc-butted shaft-hole axes usually deposited in conjunction with the former in southeast Europe (Vulpe 1970, 66-67; Bóna 1993, 48-65). The spread of the Hajdúsámson-Apa-type swords and daggers, which are almost equally distributed between South Scandinavia and the Carpathian Basin, suggests that these artefacts were the material means by which the ornamental traditions of southeast European metalwork were brought to the Nordic area (Lomborg 1959, 51-146; Vandkide 1996, 259-308). The shifts between decorated and undecorated areas framed by single lines, dotted lines or bands occurring on all decorated Fårdrup axes are characteristic features of European Middle Bronze Age metalwork. However, some patterns characteristic of Southeast European metalwork are not found on the Fårdrup axes (e.g. the complex wave-like meander or spiral hook motif common on the Carpathian disc-butted axes and the early Hajdúsámson-Apa-type swords) (Fig. 6). This might indicate that a selection of patterns took place during the journey from one cultural sphere to the other, determined by either a conscious aesthetically-founded selection or by the underlying skills of Nordic craftsmen.

The Fårdrup axes are not the only examples of hybridity which date to the beginning of the Nordic Bronze Age. The production and design of flint-edged swords was also clearly influenced by the Hajdúsámson-Apa-type swords imported to South Scandinavia from the Carpathian Basin (Lomborg 1960, 146-183). These were joined by the Late Neolithic flint daggers which were mass-produced in the northern part of Jutland, crafted as local imitations of Aunjetitz triangular bronze daggers (Frieman 2010, 33-44). The swords and the daggers suggest that the phenomenon of hybridity was not uncommon in the Early Nordic Bronze Age.

As is shown by the Fårdrup-type axes and other hybrid artefacts, the ideas, materials, and technological knowledge crossing political, social and cultural boundaries are seldom passed on in their original form, nor are they necessarily accompanied by their original purpose or function. During their journey from one cultural sphere to another, one or more material and ideational aspects of an object might undergo several changes and replacements in order to be more easily adopted by the receiving society. Romanian anthropologist Nicolaescu has been working with the inter-cultural transmission of ideas and concepts as exemplified by a case study involving the consumption of American women's magazines and soap operas by Romanian society (Nicolaescu 2004, 75-114). Her studies show that a concept or idea is not simply passed on from one socio-cultural area to another, but is transformed by the needs and traditions of the area of reception. The transformation of an object, idea or concept is largely dictated by the demands of the receiving community (Nicolaescu 2004, 75-114). Thus, the adopted version of an object or an idea will often be a mixture of the characteristics of the original and the traditions of the receiving socio-cultural sphere.

In the case of the Fårdrup-type axes, this translation of foreign impulses manifests in the design and visual appearance of the artefacts insofar as there is an obvious combination of the traditional local form of the massive shaft-hole axe and the technological knowledge and aesthetic values conveyed by foreign southeast European Bronze Age metalwork. It is clear that there is more to the Fårdrup-type shaft-hole axes than a simple conversion of stone artefacts into bronze, as has been suggested for other Early Nordic Bronze Age artefacts (Frieman 2010, 33-44).

One wonders what the purpose of the above-mentioned combination of material traditions might have been in Nordic Bronze Age society. The material characteristics of the Fårdrup axes suggest that there is more to their appearance than a general passive diffusion of culture and tradition. For several decades,

diffusionist ideas were readily accepted as explanations of the convergence of different traditional traits in material culture (Trigger 1999, 211-313). However, these ideas do not account for the fact that some material and ideational elements were chosen over others (i.e. the abandonment of the spiral hook motif). In her study of luxury artwork from the ancient Near East, Feldman's definition of *international style* (Feldman 2006, 25-58) includes artwork and crafts which display an intentional fusion of two or more artistic/aesthetic traditions. In the ancient Near East, these objects are often found in the context of palace environments or other high status settlement areas (Feldman 2006, 1-22) and both their valuable materials and high-quality workmanship suggest that they were connected with those parts of society that were powerful and well-to-do.

Feldman (2006) interprets these luxury artefacts as objects of political negotiation and diplomacy. In other words, she suggests that they were pieces of material culture which expressed social cohesion among the social and political elites of disparate cultural groups (Feldman 2006, 103-156). At the same time, these artefacts were the material playground for the negotiation of identity, wealth and power. Just like the luxury objects of the ancient Near East, the Scandinavian Fårdrup-type axes supposedly played a special role in Bronze Age society. Malmer (1992) interpreted the Fårdrup axes as Bronze Age weight units (Malmer 1992, 377-388), but his explanation does not account for the amount of high-value bronze which went into each axe, the decoration of said artefacts nor their find contexts. The limited number as well as the massiveness and frequent high quality of the Fårdrup axes suggest that they should also be associated with the most prominent social classes of Nordic Bronze Age society (Vandkilde 1996, 259-308). Furthermore, the relative infrequency of the Fårdrup axes suggests that their primary function was not an everyday or utilitarian one. Moreover, the amount of raw material which went into each axe as well as the fine and exotic decoration present on many exemplars indicates that they were made by (or at least commissioned by) economically-resourceful individuals or groups.

The hybrid nature of the Nordic shaft-hole axes outlined above in conjunction with Feldman's theory on the purpose and function of hybrid luxury objects may very well point towards an understanding of the Fårdrup-type axes as artefacts which were not only actively employed to establish cross-cultural bonds, but were also used to negotiate social and political power and identity between the upper classes of South Scandinavia and southeast Europe. The form, decoration and material as well as the production techniques of the shaft-hole axes offered a platform for the exchange and transmission of aesthetics from one cultural sphere to another. At the same time, however, these negotiable elements may have presented a material platform for the mediation and transformation of knowledge and ideology.

Conclusion: From Matter to Spirit and Back Again

This paper stemmed from a desire to explore interactions between humans and artefacts in connection with archaeological material and the concept of hybridity. The aim here was to investigate the ways in which hybridity manifested materially and was thus archaeologically traceable in its role as Bronze Age societal mediator. To this end, the well-defined Fårdrup shaft-hole axes were chosen as case study because of their relatively small numbers, limited geographical spread and characteristic visual appearance.

Hybridity is a phenomenon which clearly manifests the fusion or exchange of ideas between two distinct sets of craft traditions, aesthetic values and/or cultural backgrounds, thus crossing geographical, social and cultural boundaries. As such, hybrid objects show clear traits from their parents. However, at the same time, they also maintain their own characteristics distinct from those of their progenitors as well as the other artefacts by which they were surrounded during their use.

Even from the small-scale study carried out in this paper, it has become quite clear that the phenomenon of hybridity was not a simple one in the case of the Fårdrup-type shaft-hole axes. Rather than being unpretentious metal copies of local stone axes, these axes display a wide variety of hybrid elements in their visual appearance as well as in their technical production and underlying ideas, not all of which are easily traced. Therefore, these locally-produced Nordic shaft-hole axes should be regarded as composite objects consciously designed and actively employed to fuse local and foreign craft traditions as well as

local and foreign technological ideas and knowledge. The highly sophisticated ways in which the Fårdrup axes merge Scandinavian axe production with southeast European technology and aesthetic traditions suggest that these artefacts played a significant role in the transmission and translation of ideas, knowledge and information between socially, culturally and (potentially) politically diverse societies like those which existed in South Scandinavia and Southeast Europe in 1600 BC. They may very well have been an important means of manifesting and negotiating concepts, ideas and traditions in a material form. Future research will hopefully provide a more detailed picture of the nature of ideas and information mediated through these peculiar objects.

Preliminary studies of the Fårdrup axes reveal that many of them were newly produced before their deposition, while others carried heavy traces of use and wear indicative of long circulation. This suggests that the perceived purpose or function of the axes might have changed over time. While a more detailed investigation of the temporal aspects of the Fårdrup-type axes is beyond the scope of this paper, it will hopefully be addressed in future studies.

Acknowledgements

My warm thanks go to Helle Vandkilde for supporting this publication with her good ideas and advice. I would like to thank Samantha Reiter, Constanze Rassmann and Heide Wrobel Nørgaard for their support and input as well as for our (probably neverending) discussions of material and materiality both in theory and practice. Last but not least, I would like to thank Moesgård's Forhistorisk Museum, Haderslev Museum, Horsens Museum, the Nationalmuseet København, Odense Bys Museer, Vendsyssel Historiske Museum, Vesthimmerlands Museum and Aalborg Museum for providing me with insight into the wondrous world of the Fårdrup axes.

Note

1. Stone axes may of course have been painted, which is difficult to document archaeologically. Some stone shaft-hole axes were decorated plastically in the form of engraved lines and concentric circles (Brøndested 1958, 259). However, rock as a raw material did not allow as detailed a decoration as was possible on metal artefacts.

Bibliography

Andersen, T. 2007: *Datering af fortiden. Om det første danske kulstof-14 laboratorium.* Aarhus.

Aner, E. & K. Kersten 1976: *Die Funde der älteren Bronzezeit des nordischen Kreises in Dänemark, Schleswig-Holstein und Niedersachsen. II. Holbæk, Sorø und Præstø Amter.* Neumünster.

Bakhtin, M. 1981: *The Dialogic Imagination.* Austin.

Bhabha, H. 1994: *The Location of Culture.* London & New York.

Bhabha, H. 1996: Postmodernism/Postcolonialism. In: Nelson, R.S. & R. Shiff (eds.): *Critical Terms for Art History.* Chicago & London, 307-322.

Bóna, I. 1993: Bronzeguss und Metallbearbeitung bis zum Ende der mittleren Bronzezeit. In: Meier-Arendt, W. (ed.): *Bronzezeit in Ungarn. Forschungen in Tell-Siedlungen an Donau und Theiss.* Frankfurt am Main, 48-65.

Brøndsted, J. 1931: An Early Bronze Age Hoard in the Danish National Museum. *Acta Archaeologica* II, 111-116.

Brøndsted, J. 1958: *Danmarks oldtid, II. Bronzealderen.* København.

Derrida, J. 1980: The Law of Genre. *Glyph* 7, 202-232.

Engedal, Ø. 2010: *The Bronze Age of Northwestern Scandinavia.* Dissertation for the degree of doctor philosophiae (dr. philos.) at the University of Bergen. Available: http://www.bronsereplika.no/2010b%20The%20Bronze%20Age%20of%20NW%20Scandinavia%20WEB.pdf [2014, 03/22].

Frello, B. 2006: *Cultural Hybridity. Contamination or Creative Transgression?* AMID Working Paper Series 54, Aalborg University, 1-11.

Frieman, C. 2010: Imitation, identity and communication: The presence and problems of skeuomorphs in the Metal Ages. In: Eriksen, B.V. (ed.): *Lithic technology in metal using societies. Proceedings of a UISPP Workshop, Lisbon, September 2006.* Aarhus, 33-44.

Feldman, M.H. 2006: *Diplomacy by Design. Luxury Arts and an "International Style" in the Ancient Near East, 1400-1200 BCE.* Chicago.

Hobsbawm, E. 1983: Introduction: Inventing Traditions. In: Hobsbawm, E. & T. Ranger (eds.): *The Invention of Tradition.* Cambridge, 1-14.

Hornby, A.S. 1990: *Oxford Advanced Learner's Dictionary of Current English.* 4th edition. Oxford.

Jensen, J. 2000: *Rav. Nordens guld.* København.

Jockenhövel, A. 2005: Bronzezeitliche Dolche und Schwerter als Bilder auf Objekten? – Zur Ikonographie einer Waffengattung. In: Spinei, V., C.-M. Lazarovici, D. Monah (eds.): *Scripta Praehistorica. Miscellanea in honorem nonagenarii magistri Mircea Petrescu-Dûmbovita oblata. Honoraria 1.* Iaşi, 601-619.

Kapchan, D.A. & P.T. Strong 1999: Theorizing the Hybrid. *The Journal of American Folklore* 112, 445, 239-253.

Kaul, F. 2004: *Bronzealderens religion. Studier af den nordiske bronzealders ikonografi.* København.

Knape, A. & H.-Å. Nordström 1994: *Der Kultgegenstand von Balkåkra.* Stockholm.

Kölcze, Z. 2010: *Design and Ideology. Early European Bronze Age Swords as Material Agents.* Unpublished MA-thesis, Aarhus University.

Kristiansen, K. & Larsson, T.B. 2005: *The Rise of Bronze Age Society. Travels, Transmissions and Transformations.* Cambridge.

Lekberg, P. 2002: *Yxors liv, Människors landskap. En studie av kulturlandskap och samhälle i Mellansveriges senneolitikum.* Uppsala.

Lévi-Strauss, C. 1966: *The Savage Mind (La Pensée Sauvage).* London.

Lomborg, E. 1959: Donauländische Kulturbeziehungen und die relative Chronologie der frühen Nordischen Bronzezeit. *Acta Archaeologica* XXX, 51-146.

Lomborg, E. 1960: Fladehuggede flintredskaber i gravfund fra Ældre Bronzealder. *Aarbøger for Nordisk Oldkyndighed og Historie* 1959, 146-183.

Malmer, M.P. 1987: Fårdrup-yxornas metrology och korologi – ett preliminärt meddelande. In: Poulsen, J. (ed.): *Regionale forhold i Nordisk Bronzealder. 5. Nordiske Symposium for Bronzealderforskning på Sandbjerg Slot.* Aarhus, 19-27.

Malmer, M.P. 1992: Weight systems in the Scandinavian Bronze Age. *Antiquity* 66, 377-388.

Manning, S.W. & C.B. Ramsey, W. Kutschera, T. Higham, B. Kromer, P. Steier, E.M. Wild 2006: Chronology for the Aegean Late Bronze Age 1700-1400 B.C. *Science* 312, 565-569.

Meinander, C.F. 1954: *Die Bronzezeit in Finnland.* Helsinki.

Meller, H. 2010: Nebra: Vom Logos zum Mythos – Biographie eines Himmelsbildes. In: Meller, H. & F. Bertemes (eds.): *Der Griff nach den Sternen. Wie Europas Eliten zu Macht und Reichtum kamen. Internationales Symposium in Halle (Saale) 16.-21. Februar 2005, 5/I.* Halle, 23-73.

Montelius, O. 1917: *Minnen från vår Forntid I: Stenåldern och Bronsåldern.* Stockholm.

Nicolaescu, M. 2004: Circulating Images: The Translation of the Global into the Local. In: Vainovski-Mihai, I. (ed.): *New European College GE-NEC Program 2000-2002,* Bucharest, 75-114.

Pernicka, E. 2010: Archäometallurgische Untersuchungen am und zum Hortfund von Nebra. In: Meller, H. & F. Bertemes (eds.): *Der Griff nach den Sternen. Wie Europas Eliten zu Macht und Reichtum kamen. Internationales Symposium in Halle (Saale) 16.-21. Februar 2005, 5/II.* Halle, 719-734.

Rønne, P. 1993: Problemer omkring bronzealderens metalhåndværkere. In: Forsberg, L. & T.B. Larsson (eds.): *Ekonomi och näringsformer i nordisk Bronsålder. Studia Archaeologica Universitatis Umensis 3.* Umeå, 71-92.

Stross, B. 1999: The Hybrid Metaphor. From Biology to Culture. *The Journal of American Folklore* 112, 445, 254-267.

Trigger, B.G. 1999: *A history of archaeological thought.* Cambridge.

Vandkilde, H. 1996: *From Stone to Bronze. The Metalwork of the Late Neolithic and Earliest Bronze Age in Denmark.* Aarhus.

Vandkilde, H. 2007: *Culture and Change in Central European Prehistory 6th to 1st Millenium BC.* Aarhus.

Vandkilde, H. 2013: Bronze Age Voyaging and Cosmologies in the Making: The Helmets from Viksö Revisited. In: Bergerbrant, S. & S. Sabatini (eds.): *Counterpoint: Essays in Archaeology and Heritage Studies in Honour of Professor Kristian Kristiansen.* BAR International Series 2508. Oxford, 165-177.

Vulpe, A. 1970: *Die Äxte und Beile in Rumänien I. Prähistorische Bronzefunde IX 2.* München

Young, R.J.C. 1995: *Colonial Desire. Hybridity in Theory, Culture and Race.* London & New York.

World in Motion

An Examination of the Skallerup Wheeled Cauldron and Conceptualisations of Mobility

Rannveig Marie Jørgensdotter Spliid

Introduction

The purpose of this text is to discuss perceptions of space and the body, distance and journeying in the Early Bronze Age of Scandinavia as reflected in the wheeled cauldron found in Trudshøj mound by Skallerup on the Danish island of Zealand in 1895. This discussion dovetails with earlier examinations of the container as a cognitive metaphor used in the European Neolithic structuring of time, distance and spatial affinities (Clausen 2011) and essentially points to a metaphorical connection between the container with the similarly-defined concepts of earth, birth, death, the body and ancestors.

The importance of the container to the formation and consolidation of Neolithic ontology and cognitive structures, together with the great stone monuments of the period, has been widely discussed in archaeological texts (e.g. Hodder 1990; Larsson 2009). Likewise, the cognitive ramifications of the Neolithic invention of wheeled transport are currently the subject of academic scrutiny (Johannsen, 2010a).

It seems reasonable that the metaphors which saturate Neolithic ontology would have proceeded to become part of the cognitive foundations on which later European Bronze Age societies' ontology and worldviews were based. In the wheeled cauldron, the metaphorical potential of the container was combined with that of the wheel, possibly transforming the meaning of both objects in various ways and reflecting and creating ontological changes for the persons who created the object in the first place. The intent of this paper is to investigate what ontological or cosmological concepts a wheeled cauldron could express and thereby tangentially approach the question of who might have been buried in such an extraordinary way.

Research History

As was mentioned above, the Skallerup wheeled cauldron was excavated as part of a mound burial in Trudshøj near Skallerup in 1895 (Blinkenberg 1895, 361-75; Aner and Kersten 1976, 177-178). It has been dated to circa 1300 BC in Nordic Bronze Age Period II (Johannsen 2010a, 161). The excavation story is somewhat dramatic, as the farmer who owned the land on which Trudshøj stood, wanted to demolish the site. Attempts from the National Museum in Copenhagen to protect Trudshøj were unsuccessful. Unfortunately, in spite of having reached a compromise in which the museum should receive ample warning before demolition, the mound was largely destroyed when archaeologists arrived on location. Naturally, the grave context had been greatly disturbed, so archaeologists made do by recording the location of finds in the grave from the landowner's memory and extrapolation from on-site examinations (Blinkenberg 1895, 362).

The wheeled cauldron (Fig. 1) is one of the more extraordinary finds of the Nordic Bronze Age. It is the only one of its kind in Denmark, and has therefore not only been exhibited at the National Museum in Copenhagen, but has also been the subject of much further study. The cauldron figures prominently in Aner and Kersten's catalogue (Aner and Kersten 1976, 177-178) of Bronze Age finds from Southern Scandinavia, and has traditionally been interpreted as a vessel used in the ceremonial consumption of beverages. This theory has been even extended to the modern day. One recent study even posited that the wheeled cauldron was the original cognitive prototype of contemporary European-style wine vessels (Rausing 1997). Two other, more conventional approaches to the wheeled cauldron include Thrane's study of Danish Early Bronze Age vessels (Thrane 1962) and

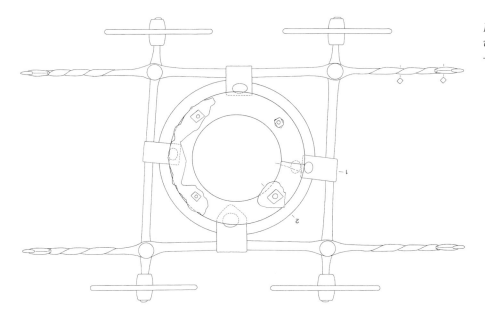

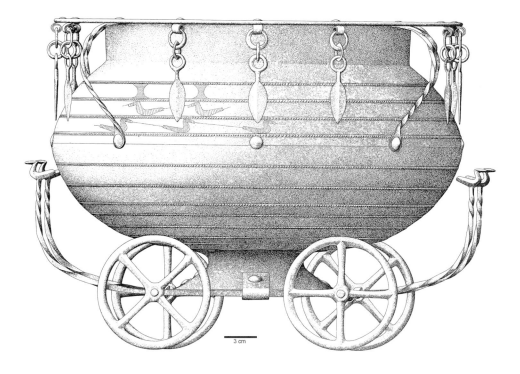

Figure 1. Reconstruction of the wheeled cauldrom from Skellerup – after Aner and Kersten 1976, 177f.

Treue's work on wheels and wagons (Treue 1965). It has also been mentioned in general works, such as Brøndsted's *Danmarks Oldtid* (Brøndsted 1939) as well as a short review by Jensen (Jensen 1984). Most recently, the wheeled cauldron was discussed by Randsborg (2006, 61) and by Johannsen, the latter in terms of his investigation of Bronze Age wheeled vehicles (Johannsen 2010b, 161). However, none of the studies mentioned above engaged with the wheeled cauldron as a primary subject, nor has it been the focus of any in-depth interpretation. While this article cannot entirely bridge this gap, it does neatly and effectively underscore the need for further study.

Theoretical Background

The context in which this text seeks to situate itself is the discourse of cognitive archaeology and anthropology, as discussed by Gamble (Gamble 2007) among others (see Johannsen 2010b; Henare *et al.* 2006). Furthermore, the goal is to link the discussion of cognition to discourse on network theory and mobility as exemplified by Urry (2007), Ingold (2008) and Helms (1988). In other words, this article examines the cognitive ramifications for the combination of container and vehicle which occurred with the Skallerup cauldron.

In his book on the prehistoric development of human cognitive modes, Gamble devotes a chapter to the organisation of space and time based around an *axis mundi* of the human body. The human *axis mundi* is experienced in two ways. It is both a container (for food, children and consciousness) as well as a being with limbs which both acts and inscribes (Gamble 2007, 104-106). The metaphorical potential of the container is rich in that it is not only cognitively associated with space and body, but also with time and memory. The concepts of time and memory appear often in linguistics, and are commonly associated with ideas of containment:

> "*Everyday activities take place in time and are often bounded by space. [...] Our bodies are not only containers that ingest and excrete substances, bear children and change as we grow and age. [...] The past is something that contains us and which we seek to contain*" (Gamble 2007, 70f.).

I have previously argued that Late Mesolithic and Neolithic ceramic vessels played a decisive role as metaphors in the ontological discourse of European neolithisation. In this way, they impacted and directed the construction and transformation of Neolithic ideology, cosmology and overall worldview:

> "*In [...] a contained cosmology, the 'dreamtime' of the hunter transforms into linear time, in which the relationship with ancestors and the dead – and thus with personal identity – is closely linked to particular localities. Home is no longer everywhere. Instead the landscape and the world are metaphorically contained in houses and monumental structures*" (Clausen 2011, author's translation).

In a similar vein, current research (Johannsen 2010b) focuses on the cognitive ramifications of the innovation of the wheel and the use of wheeled transport. Perhaps having been inspired by this paper, others have recently produced work discussing the wagon as cosmological metaphor within the funerary customs of the stone heap graves in the Jutish Single Grave Culture (Johannsen and Laursen 2010).

In *Mobilities* (2007), Urry argues for a paradigm shift in the study of sociological phenomena. He wants to move from processes of categorisation to the mapping of networks and relationships. The mapping of networks and relationships exists within a different cognitive mode than the one hitherto prevalent within Western academic writing. Urry illustrates the challenges of such a mode very aptly, firstly by positing that "the mobility turn is post-disciplinary" (Urry 2007, 6) but also in the multidimensional structure assumed by his own theoretical text. A similarly novel approach is apparent in Ingold's (2008) work, which makes use of a narrative mode to illuminate the writer's theoretical concerns. In this context, Mary Helms (1988) would seem to be ahead of her time. Helms' (1988) theoretical considerations pivot around the role of journey and distance in the construction of knowledge and social power.

Given that academic attention has often focussed on metaphor in Bronze Age mobility studies, the application of cognition as a theoretical tool is not without precedent. The cognitive approach considers the basic metaphorical nature and structure of human experience. The underlying assumption on which such a study is based holds that material culture continually shapes (and is shaped by) human cognitive processes. This phenomenon is the effect of a change in cognitive modus; the move from a subject/object division to a relational mode creates a direct interplay between archaeologist and artefact.

Methodology

The best means of examining the Skallerup wheel cauldron via the theoretical positions outlined above is through contextualisation with other contemporary symbolic and metaphorical expressions and discourse analysis. Questions of causality (i.e. the exact geographical origins of the wheeled cauldron) fall outside the scope of this text, as it is concerned specifically with Southern Scandinavia. Instead of addressing origin, this paper examines the interplay of the main technological elements from which the wheeled cauldron is comprised: the wheels, the cauldron itself and its 'ship-like' curved bars (Fig. 2). The context of the wheeled cauldron in relationship to the body of the deceased will also be addressed with the intent of gaining perspective on other such practices from the same period.

Lastly, dominant and reoccurring iconographical ideas within rock carvings across Scandinavia are considered in the ontological contextualisation of the Skallerup cauldron, as per Johannsen and Kaul's argument that Sweden, Norway, Denmark and northern Germany were part of the same cultural area during the Nordic Bronze Age (Johannsen 2010a, 156; Kaul 2004, 63 and 93). The goal here is to synthesise these

Harzpech

theoretical lines of investigation in order to clarify the prehistoric discourse in which the wheeled cauldron took part and to additionally outline which conceptualisations of mobility and movement it expressed.

Empirical Basis

Wheeled cauldrons appeared across a large swathe of European territory ranging from Southern Scandinavia and Central Europe to Etruria. Treue examines north alpine wagons and wheels both in terms of the technical details of the wheel itself as well as the various meanings and differences between pictorial representations of wheels and wheeled objects (Treue 1965, 173-196). It is possible, therefore, to garner an image whereby wagon technology (and the symbolic wheeled vehicle) arrived from the Caucasus and Near East. Unfortunately, the chronological relationship between those two regions' use of wagons is a more complex matter. Two- and four-wheeled wagons, or pictures and models thereof, have been found in kurgan burials around the Dniepr and Volga rivers. Treue places these burials chronologically at the start of the 1st millennium BC (Treue 1965, 173-174). The shaft graves of Ur, however, also contained four-wheeled vehicles which were dated to 2500 BC (Treue 1965, 176f.).

Several well-preserved specimens of wheeled cauldrons have been recovered in the immediate proximity of Denmark, including the Peckatel cauldron (Fig. 3) from Mecklenburg-Vorpommern (Brøndsted 1939, 118). Likewise, an undercarriage with four wheels found in Hedeskoga, Scania has also been interpreted as the lower part of a wheeled cauldron (Thrane 1962, 152-155). These North European finds have been generally viewed as Bohemian or Austro-Hungarian imports (Treue 1965, 178f.). Such a trade movement would seem to follow the general spread of wagon technology.

Let us, however, return to the Skallerup find. Its manufacturing is usually dated to the 13th century BC (Johannsen 2010a, 161), that is, Nordic Bronze Age Period II. The relative placement of the wheeled cauldron inside the grave and the original placement of cremated bone fragments from the deceased inside the cauldron were determined with relative accuracy during burial salvage efforts at the Trudshøj mound

(Blinkenberg 1895, 361). Other finds within the burial context include: some fragments of woolen cloth, one arm-ring made from a thin, twisted bar of gold, four pieces forming 58 cm of a bronze sword, four sections of a bronze shaving knife, a portion of a knife with a curved back, and some unidentifiable fragments, one of bronze and at least two of horn (Fig. 4). Blinkenberg interpreted the unidentified bronze fragment as the remains of a set of tweezers (Blinkenberg 1895, 365). Furthermore, traces of an oak-coffin (presumably in the form of planks) were recorded as well (Blinkenberg 1895, 364). The whole grave context would fit with what one would expect from the Period II burial of a wealthy, high-ranking male.

The wheeled cauldron find consists specifically of metal fragments which combine to form a bronze cauldron mounted on top of a rudimentary four-wheeled frame (Fig. 2). The Skallerup frame construction was simple and square (reminiscent of the Trundholm sun chariot) rather than the more complex, 'lifted' frame found on other wheeled cauldrons (Thrane 1962, 152-154). Two twisted bronze bars were mounted at right angles to the wheel axles. They were bent upwards and terminate in small stylised figurines (supposedly of birds). The wheels were made of metal and are comprised of spokes placed in a cruciform arrangement.

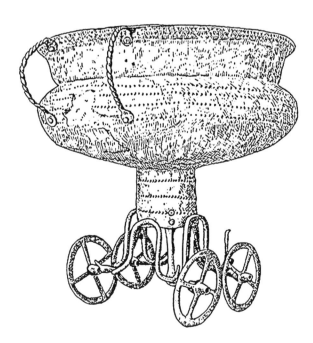

Figure 3. The wheeled-cauldron from Pecktatel near Schwerin, Mecklenburg was found in Konigsberg burial mound in 1843 – after Schubart 1972, 134.

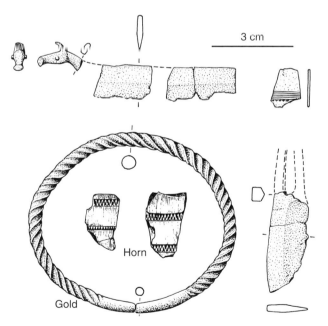

Figure 4. Additional finds within the burial context include fragments of woolen cloth, one arm-ring made from a thin twisted bar of gold, four pieces forming 58 cm of a bronze sword, four sections of a bronze shaving knife, a portion of a knife with a curved back, and other (unidentifiable) fragments: one of bronze and at least two of horn – after Aner and Kersten 1976, 177-178, Tafel 143.

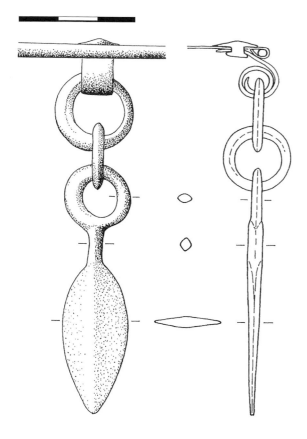

Figure 5. The 'rattle-tin' is comprised of small lancet-shaped pendants, which are attached to the collar by short (two-link long) chains which would supposedly have rattled when the cauldron was in motion – after Aner and Kersten 1976, 178.

The cauldron was mounted on this frame. It was hammered out in three separate pieces before foot, belly and neck were riveted together and the joints filled with resin (Rausing 1997, 994). The foot is riveted to the cauldron by eight brackets, four of which also connect the construction to the frame. Four S-shaped handles made of thin, twisted bronze bars were originally riveted to the sides of the cauldron and the rim of the narrow neck-piece. The flat collar edging the rim of the cauldron is adorned with tiny pieces of so-called 'rattle-tin' (Fig. 5). The 'rattle-tin' is comprised of small lancet-shaped pendants, which are attached to the collar by short (two link long) chains which would supposedly have rattled when the cauldron was in motion. Stylised bird-like figurines connected with lines follow each other in an almost chain-like arrangement on the surface of the cauldron body, blurring the line between symmetrical decoration and realistic depiction.

To summarise, the burial context of the Skallerup cauldron reflected the identity of a socially-pow-

erful person (most likely male). The importance of the deceased was underlined by the inhumation of his cremated remains inside a spectacular wheeled cauldron which showcased a variety of symbols and adornments. Additionally, the use of resin to seal the riveted parts of the cauldron gave it the potential to hold liquid.

Analysis and Discussion

The container seemed to have been cognitively associated with the female body in particular within Neolithic votive and monumental ritual. This interpretation was based on the curvaceous morphology of the vessels, as well as associations with the process of birth (Clausen 2011). However, both the Skallerup and the Peckatel wheeled cauldron contexts contain grave goods which would usually be associated with the masculine warrior ideal; the Peckatel-Mecklenburg composition of grave goods was in fact quite similar to Trudshøj, including a sword, a small knife and a twisted, gold armband (Belz 1910, 193, 203). In the case of Skallerup, a shaving knife seems to secure the gender identity of the deceased to the masculine sphere, at least as far as present interpretations of Bronze Age social identities are concerned:

"With very few exceptions biological sex corresponds wholly to social gender as reflected by burial position and types of grave goods. Gender is thus underlined in the position of the body as well as in the objects applied to the body. The gendered difference is probably the least negotiable in this society" (Vandkilde 2007, 84).

Though the placement of the deceased in the cauldron might still carry the feminine connotation of a uterus to which the deceased returned, the addition of wheels may complicate the story. The addition of the vehicular aspect could recall the vehicle of the journeying sun, as pictured in the Trundholm wagon (Aner and Kersten 1976, 63-64) as well as in rock carvings (Goldhahn 1999). It is possible that a male warrior identity shared certain conceptual connections with the sun. Randsborg's treatment of the Trundholm wagon suggests that its two-sided disc represented both sun and moon (Randsborg 2006). Additionally, a popular female adornment of well-to-do South Scandinavian women in the Nordic Period II was the sun disc-like belt plate, worn low on the abdominal area, i.e. above the uterus. The most well known example of this ornamentation was recovered with the Period II burial of the Egtved woman (Aner and Kersten 1990, 39-41; Randsborg 2006, 68-69).

The iconographic tablets found in the Kivik grave (Nordic Period II) indicate the use of wagons in ceremonies and processions (Wrigglesworth 2005, 564). In her examination of west Norwegian rock carvings, Wrigglesworth makes note of the horse as draught animal which was particularly associated with wheeled vehicles as well as with boats (Wrigglesworth 2005, 564). Likewise, she observes that wagons and boats were often pictured together (Wrigglesworth 2005, 565). She interprets this co-occurrence as evidence for the importance of journeying and mobility as Bronze Age concepts:

> "The journey itself becomes a liminal phenomenon [...] the wagon can thus be attached to the sun on two levels: as a helper of the sun, in the form of draught power, and as a metaphor for the sun itself. The key word is continuous movement" (Wrigglesworth 2005, 565, author's translation).[1]

To summarise, a certain consistency seems traceable in the Trudshøj burial with regards to gender identity and certain cosmological elements. It seems that birth and death were cognitively connected with movement (specifically the movement of the sun). Goldhahn (1999) argued that the movement and the journey of the dead were circular, likened to both the sun and the seasons. He discusses the possibility of a later Bronze Age belief in earthly reincarnation:

> "Heavy and pregnant, the horses on the grave stones drag this sun symbol round and round in its eternal path, urging the deceased to be reborn just as the sun is reborn every day..." (Goldhahn 1999, 204-207, author's translation).[2]

Kaul remains unconvinced of reincarnation *per se*; instead he posits a link between the journey of the (upper-class) deceased and the journey of the sun in a literal, participatory sense reminiscent of ancient Egyptian traditions (Kaul 2005, 268-269). One may remain sceptical as to whether Bronze Age spiritual life can be so closely defined. Nevertheless, as regards the wheeled cauldron, the underlying cognitive impression seems to revolve around several such levels of movement.

Randsborg suggests that the birds depicted on the cauldron body and frame were web-footed, perhaps suggesting that these birds were thought to have been special because of their ability to negotiate all geo-graphical spheres: land, water and sky. He further explains the 'rattling' lancet pendants as a recreation of the sound of rain and thunder (Randsborg 2006, 61). Given the wider context, this explanation seems as good as any.

Johannsen believes the upward-curved framework under the wheeled cauldron to be reminiscent of a ship. According to Johannsen, the wheels had no symbolic function, but were rather included on purely practical grounds (Johannsen 2010a, 161). While the first part of this assessment seems reasonable, especially considering the abundance of stylized ship depictions in contemporary material culture, the wholesale dismissal of the wheels' symbolic meaning might go too far. In downplaying the metaphorical significance of the wheels, Johannsen fails to consider the intimate relationship between functionality and aesthetics. Anthropological as well as archaeological studies increasingly support the presence of such thought processes (see Larsson 2009, 154-159), as human cognition relies very heavily on metaphor. For example, the cross-spoked wheels of the cauldron might have a meaning which reached beyond their technical shape. While they express a technological prototype of the Bronze Age, they also resemble rock carvings of sun symbols. Given Wrigglesworth's observations concerning the frequent combination of wagons and ships in rock art, it is logical to argue for a situation in which the curved, ship-like frame and wheels carried equal symbolic weight. If the figures on the ends of the curved frame and on the cauldron body are indeed birds, than an aerial dimension is added to those already established: land (wheels) and sea (ship frame).

The wheeled cauldron is thus connected to land, sea, sky, and even sun. A vehicle capable of journeying across these spheres must have been a powerful means of transport. Such a capacity for spatial movement must have been fit for the kind of travel a deceased person might have been imagined to undertake.

As noted by Helms, the spatial and the temporal may not always be easily cognitively separated (Helms 1988, 5). In this way, upon death, the life journey of an individual changes from a concrete and temporal zone to one which lies spatially beyond the ken of the living. In her initial argument, Helms first stresses that the 'heartland' of an area was perceived as the known, while remote regions were thought to be increasingly unknown, mysterious and other.

However, she then proceeds to highlight the interplay between a provincial location and the need for communication and knowledge (Helms 1988, 3-19). Helms' ideas fit admirably to the current argument. An ontology which has the concept of the journey thus built into it and which holds a position of such prominence within the mythological discourse is an ontology which, at least partly, conceptualises the world in terms of network and communication, rather than categories of *them* and *us*. It is thereby necessary to propose a balance between network and category, openness and closed-ness. Whatever the exact nature of the journey of the afterlife, *mobility* seems to have been an underlying priority, preferably in or across as many worldly spheres and dimensions as possible.

Many Bronze Age burials include finds which reflect the inhumation and/or cremation of persons of importance. However, only a select few of these burials featured a wheeled cauldron. Such an interment ritual could perhaps have been the send-off of a messenger or representative of the community. Judging from the general standard for European high-profile burials, wheeled cauldrons were a rarity among rarities. A plethora of explanations as to the identity of the deceased interred in this fashion can therefore be suggested here:

It is possible that the deceased was originally a foreigner within the region or village in which he died. As such a person, he would arguably have belonged to the whole world as well as to the locality and his capacity as a travelling man was likely to have defined his identity to a large extent. It is possible, therefore, that the provision of the wheeled cauldron upon his death was provided with the intention that his identity could be distributed equally between the community where he died and the world from which he came. Other alternative interpretations revolve around the idea that the deceased was particularly sacred or important for one reason or another and that this was the origin of his particular burial rite.

In the end, it is impossible to know how many wheeled cauldron burials have yet to be found. Therefore, the identity of the man in the cauldron remains (at least to some extent) shrouded in mystery. The paucity of material artefacts of this type leaves us with the impression that an artefact as powerful as the wheeled cauldron was no randomly issued grave good, even more so if it also served as an important part of other ritual occasions (i.e. a sacred wine vessel).

Summary and Conclusion

The Skallerup wheeled cauldron brings together an impressive combination of metaphors. This text has roamed widely in its attempt to bring together and contextualise the various and sundry meanings associated with this fascinating cult object. The mobility of Bronze Age peoples as well as the importance they placed on mobility coalesced in the form of the Skallerup cauldron. This important object functioned on both the local and the interregional levels in its unique combination of metaphors. The combination of vessel and wheel created an element of duplicity: a vehicle capable of journeying like the sun, while simultaneously being a final home for the deceased. The wheeled cauldron effectively sent the deceased on their journey into the afterlife while at the same time maintaining a local connection. One can easily envisage this phenomenon as a result of a 'hot' cultural climate in which tradition and change were constantly under negotiation. The cyclical nature of tradition and change as well as life and death were not true cycles, continually repeating the same sets of situations, but rather could be thought of in terms of a spiral. The integration of the cauldron with wagon and/or ship elements leads one to imagine that movement and mobility were the norm for Bronze Age peoples. To reference Urry, movement in the Bronze Age was likely the natural state of affairs (Urry 2007). The wheeled cauldron thus reflects a conceptualisation of the world as a mobile, highly communicative and inter-relative network. The burial of a prominent male in such fashion might additionally reflect something of masculine identity, and the place of a warrior within the overall order of things, especially considering that the identity and lifespan of a warrior was likely closely connected with the cyclic journey of the sun.

However, questions remain which the cognitive approach of archaeology and anthropology could not answer. For example, to what degree was the application of metaphor a conscious one? Where exactly did the bereaved imagine that their lost friend or relative would journey? Does the cauldron represent a conscious expression of a spoken mythology, or the reflection of tacit, underlying assumptions and experiences? Alternatively, the situation could also perhaps be approached from a different direction. What caused this emphasis on mobility? Was the adventurous mobility of the European Bronze Age caused by cosmological ideas of the world as a place of movement, or were these cosmological ideas by chance the result of the human experience of such a mobile world? The answers to these questions are not immediately apparent.

As has previously been argued, a causal mapping of the origins of the wheeled cauldron has not been attempted here. However, it is widely agreed that this type of object is most likely foreign and was introduced to South Scandinavia from Central Europe. It is fully possible – or even likely – that the wheeled cauldron carried with it meanings and connotations which were also introduced to the local inhabitants. Nonetheless, it is just as possible that the meaning assigned to the wheeled cauldron concept in Scandinavia diverged from the functions and meanings given to such artefacts by the first wheeled cauldron makers. It is possible that the wheeled cauldron may have had a 'former life' before burial; it may have functioned as a wine vessel for sacred occasions, carrying connotations both similar to, and different from, the meaning it acquired in its capacity as urn and magical vehicle.

This diversity of interpretation is the reason for which the recent directions taken by European Bronze Age researchers and their concentration on networks, movement and agency seem so promising. A holistic and inclusive examination of the evidence rather than one concerned with the categorisation and compartmentalisation of disconnected parts might give archaeologists a better chance of engaging with Bronze Age society on its own terms. The wheeled cauldron was a means of ritualistic travel; perhaps through its study could researchers attain a deeper understanding of Bronze Age thought.

Notes

1. "Reisen I sig selv bliver et liminalt fenomen […] vognen kan dermed knyttes til solen på to plan: som et hjelpemiddel for solen i form av trekkraft, og som en metafor for solen i sig selv. Stikordet er fortsat bevegelse" (Wrigglesworth 2005, 565).
2. "Tunga och dräktiga drar hästarna på gravhällarna dess solsymbol, runt runt i sin eviga ban, manande den avlidne att återfödas – såsom solen återfördes var dag..." (Goldhahn 1999, 204-207).

Bibliography

Aner, E. & K. Kersten 1976: *Die Funde der älteren Bronzezeit des nordischen Kreises in Dänemark, Schleswig-Holstein und Niedersachsen*. II. Holbæk Sorø und Præstø Amter. Neumünster.

Aner, E. & K. Kersten 1990: *Die Funde der älteren Bronzezeit des nordischen Kreises in Dänemark, Schleswig-Holstein und Niedersachsen*. IX. Vejle Amt. Neumünster.

Belz, R. 1910: *Die vorgeschichtlichen Altertümer des Grossherzogtums Mecklenburg-Schwerin. Vollständiges Verzeichnis der im Grossherzoglichen Museum zu Schwerin bewahrten Funde*. Schwerin.

Blinkenberg, C. 1895: Etrurisk Kedelvogn funden ved Skallerup. *Aarbøger for Nordisk Oldkyndighed og Historie* 1985, 360-375.

Brøndsted, J. 1939: *Danmarks Oldtid, II. Bronzealderen*. København.

Clausen, M.S. 2011: Af ler er vi gjort: en undersøgelse af den keramiske beholder som kognitiv metafor i sydskandinavisk Tragtbægerkultur. *LAG* 11, 91-100.

Gamble, C. 2007: *Origins and Revolutions. Human Identity in Earliest Prehistory*. Cambridge.

Goldhahn, J. 1999: *Sagaholm: Hällristningar och gravritual*. Studia Archaeologica Universitatis Umensis 11. Jönköping.

Helms, M.W. 1988: *Ulysses' sail. An ethnographic odyssey of power, knowledge, and geographical distance*. Princeton.

Henare, A., M. Holbraad & S. Wastell 2006: Introduction. Thinking through things. In: Henare, A., M. Holbraad & S. Wastell (eds.): *Thinking Through Things. Theorising Artefacts Ethnographically*. London, 1-31.

Hodder, I. 1990: *The Domestication of Europe*. Oxford.

Ingold, T. 2008: When ANT meets SPIDER. Social theory for arthropods. In: Knappett, C. & L. Malafouris (eds.): *Material Agency. Towards a non-anthropocentric approach*. New York, 209-216.

Jensen, J. 1984: Kedelvognen fra Skallerup. *Nationalmuseets Arbejdsmark* 1984. 138-146

Johannsen, J.W. 2010a: The Wheeled Vehicles of the Bronze Age on Scandinavian Rock-carvings. *Acta Archaeologica* 81, 150-250.

Johannsen, N. 2010b: Technological Conceptualization: Cognition of the Shoulders of History. In: Malafouris, L. & C. Renfrew (eds.): *The Cognitive Life of Things. Recasting the Boundaries of the Mind*. Cambridge, 59-69.

Johannsen, N.N. & S.T. Laursen 2010: Routes and Wheeled Transport in Late 4th-Early 3rd Millennium Funerary Customs of the Jutland Peninsula. Regional Evidence and European Context. *Prähistorische Zeitschrift* 85, 1, 15-58.

Kaul, F. 2004: *Bronzealderens religion. Studier af den nordiske bronzealders ikonografi*. København.

Kaul, F. 2005: Hvad skete med den dødes sjæl? In: J. Goldhahn (ed.): *Mellan Sten och Järn*. Göteborg, 263-278.

Larsson, Å.M. 2009: *Breaking and Making Bodies and Pots. Material and Ritual Practices in Sweden in the Third Millenium BC*. Uppsala.

Randsborg, K. 2006: Opening of the Oak Coffins. *Acta Archaeologica* 77, 1, 1-163.

Rausing, G. 1997: The Wheeled Cauldrons and the Wine. *Antiquity* 71, 274, 994-999.

Thrane, H. 1962: The Earliest Bronze Vessels in Denmark's Bronze Age. *Acta Archaeologica* 33, 109-163.

Treue, W. 1965: *Achse, Rad und Wagen. 5000 Jahre Kulturgeschichte und Technikgeschichte*. München.

Urry, J. 2007: *Mobilities*. Cambridge.

Vandkilde, H. 2007: *Culture and Change in Central European Prehistory 6th to 1st Millennium BC.* Aarhus.

Wrigglesworth, M. 2005: Vognmotivet i en Vestnorsk Bronsealderkontekst. In: J. Goldhahn (ed.): *Mellan Sten och Järn.* Göteborg, 561-570.

The Cosmological Significance of Ships

Birgitte Damkjer

Introduction

Travel and travelling cultures must have been both attractive and important to Bronze Age peoples given the frequency with which they surrounded themselves with travel motifs (like the near ubiquitous "ship"). Rock carvings of ships are found throughout Scandinavia: from Bornholm to Bohuslen and from Oslo to the Baltic, suggesting that the value placed on ships as a means of transportation had an extraordinary and perhaps ritual connotation.

Along the Skagerrak coast of Sweden, more than 10,000 ship carvings have been found on rock surfaces at the sea's edge (Artursson 1987; Kaul 1998; Olsson 1996; Kristiansen 1998). Ship imagery also appears on swords, razors, jewellery and, interestingly, also in grave contexts. The considerable role that ships had in life must have had an influence on the conceptualisation of the ship in connection with death. Since ships were a vital part of cultural mobility, trade and exchange, it is obvious that the inhabitants of Bronze Age Scandinavia may have extended the metaphor of the ship beyond its quotidian, practical form into a mode of travelling into the afterlife.

This article investigates the association between Bronze Age ships and the afterlife by first examining ships and the sense given to them in the world of the living. What was the cosmological understanding of cultural mobility during this period? Why did the ship have a specific meaning in Bronze Age death ritual and iconography? Emphasis is placed on various grave contexts from South Scandinavia which include ship imagery. The basis for this analytical investigation stems from Kaul's archaeological analysis of Bronze Age cosmology and religion.

The Concept of Rock Carving

While rock carving occurred in many places the world over, what remains for archaeological analysis is but a small portion of an ancient practice (Nordbladh 2004,

64). Scholars categorise the Scandinavian Bronze Age as a prehistoric period, meaning that it describes an era before the advent of the written record. However, the absence of writing does not preclude the existence of pictorial evidence, as is shown by the ship carvings. Indeed, the carvings are arguably a better source of information than would be a single written historical account. While both writing and artwork are suggestive, the inclusion of many different viewpoints (such as is presumably the case in an analysis of rock carving rather than historical record) lessens the effects of editorialisation and selective memory (Nordbladh 2004; see also Bradley 2009).

Be that as it may, the picture formed by archaeologists of Bronze Age communities is more solid in some areas than in others. The thought processes of ancient persons, for example, are necessarily unknowable. Researchers are unable to *ask* about the reasons behind the creation of rock carvings, the choice of settlement location and the burial of the dead. In some instances, scholars have used ethnographic studies as a source of analogies with the past. However, there is no way to determine whether people living 3,000 years ago in southwest Sweden were thinking and perceiving of things in the same ways as do modern groups from North America, Siberia or Lapland. The same could be said of comparisons between rock carvings from different locations. The only thing they have in common is their medium, and stone is mute with regards to either chronological development or cosmological meaning.

Archaeologists recreate prehistory on a modern stage coloured by recent memory and modern preconceptions (Hodder 1986, 164f.). The same rules apply to an investigation of ship carvings. Aside from their prehistoric symbolic meaning, ship carvings were also affected by several other filters. By being carved, not only were the ships scaled down from their full size, but they were also altered via the

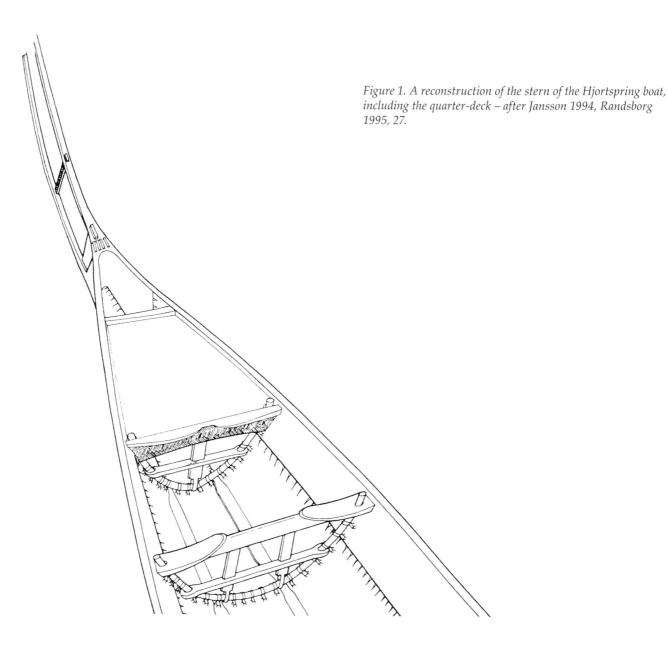

Figure 1. A reconstruction of the stern of the Hjortspring boat, including the quarter-deck – after Jansson 1994, Randsborg 1995, 27.

artistic rendering process. How can the archaeologists access the initial meaning associated with the carvings? Although elevation and sea level calculations show that ship carvings were often found at Bronze Age coastal waterline (Ling 2008), it can be difficult to move from such an observation into the realm of meaning.

Nonetheless, it is likely that the reason behind the production of those carvings was ritualistic. Unfortunately, the religious aspects of Bronze Age research have not been a particularly popular area of research over the last half a century. Malmer, for example, was careful to avoid religious topics in his research (Malmer 1981). He interpreted the rock carvings from the Kivik Grave as imitations of tapestries without any particular wider significance. Rather than engaging with *meaning*, he concentrated on concrete facts (like the establishment of a ship carving chronology). Kaul, by contrast, has engaged directly with

ship depictions and their various associations (Kaul 1998), and has also not shied away from questions of religion on the Bronze Age (Kaul 2004). His cosmological model for the passage of the sun is now a well-used interpretative tool for the investigation of Bronze Age ritual. Thanks to Ling's comprehensive and thorough GPS measurements of more than 5,000 ship depictions and his groundbreaking work relating ship carvings and ancient waterlines, it is now possible to collate a chronological evolution of the ship carving phenomenon (Ling 2008).

Bronze Age Ships

Unfortunately, extant Bronze Age ships are few and far between. Nonetheless, it is known that they functioned in many different aspects of daily life. The vessels were used both for short and long journeys and transported not only people but also knowledge and culture. Journeys by water would have ferried tangible trade items such as bronze and other commodities to and fro and would also have been the means of carrying and disseminating intangible things, such as technological or esoteric knowledge, ideas, innovations and social conceptual changes regarding social status and power (see e.g. Kristiansen 1998; Kristiansen and Larsson 2005).

The shipwreck from Devon is one of the rare archaeological examples known from the Bronze Age. The ship sank off the coast of Britain carrying an expensive cargo of tin and hundreds of copper ingots from continental Europe. Dating from 900 BC, the Devon ship has been described as a sort of ancient cargo vessel (Muckelroy and Baker 1979, 205). Indeed, the 295 artefacts which were recovered from the site of the wreck (including, among other things, 259 copper ingots, 27 tin ingots, a sword blade and three gold arm rings) weigh in at over 84 kg (Muckelroy and Baker 1979, 196-198). Unfortunately, none of the original decking or caulking from the ship survived, thus it is difficult to glean any information about ancient shipbuilding techniques. Nonetheless, this discovery is an important piece of the prehistoric puzzle and points towards the presence of a highly developed trading system between the prehistoric peoples of the United Kingdom and the European mainland (Muckelroy and Baker, 1980).

The Devon shipwreck is not the only source of archaeological information; a single Bronze Age boat was found in Dover (Clark 2004) and the remains of three sewn plank-built boats were excavated in Ferriby (Wright 1990). Additionally, another plank-built vessel was recovered by Rosenberg in 1921-22 from a bog in Hjortspring on the island of Als in southern Jutland (Kaul 1988, 19f.; Kaul 2003). The Hjortspring ship's keel extensions make it very similar in appearance to the vessels depicted in the ship carvings (Fig. 1). Although the Hjortspring boat must have been chronologically later than the ship carvings, its Pre-Roman Iron Age date (350 BC) still earns it a spot as the oldest plank-built vessel found to date in Scandinavia. The boat measured 14 meters in length and would have been able to transport more than 600 kilos, a total equivalent in manpower to the weight of 20 oarsmen and 80 additional warriors (Kaul 2003, 141, 187). Indeed, it is possible that the presence of such warriors could have been represented by the 'pins' present on board the rock-carved ships.

Cosmology

In order to further investigate rock carvings, it is necessary to delve into Bronze Age cosmology. Goldhahn (2005) posits that the conception of the Bronze Age world revolved around the opposing forces of chaos and order. Cosmic order resulted in creation, organisation and life, whereas chaos exemplified the forces of death and decay. These latter forces were dangers which people felt the need to mitigate/control in order to prevent their own downfall and ruin. To the same degree, ancient peoples likely felt the need to ritualistically re-enact their creation myth in order to perpetuate good fortune. These rituals probably involved the binding and/or containment of the powers of chaos. Indeed, when correctly completed, these rituals probably provided the strength to overcome the forces of chaos and the establishment of order (Goldhahn 2005, 25).

Kaul (2004) established an explanatory model of Bronze Age cosmology which is of particular interest here. Depictions from Late Bronze Age artefacts detailed the journey of the sun through the heavens and into the underworld (Fig. 2). This celestial voyage was affected by means of the sun ship and the assistance of mythological fish, snakes and swimming birds. In the earlier part of the period, the horse was perceived as the most significant animal associated with the sun and its journey, whereas in later times, this role was taken over by the (swimming) bird (Kaul 2004, 103). The conceptual link between horse and the ship was exemplified in Northern Europe by the horse-head ship. Therefore, the later introduction of bird-headed seagoing vessels was unlikely to have been problematic, as both animals performed the same cosmological function, albeit in different time periods (Kaul 1998, 215).

Other figures known from rock carvings and bronze artefacts include the wheel cross, cup mark, deer, footprint, hand sign and various variations on the human figure. Additional images include plough scenes, horse-drawn wagons, axes, weaponry, geometrical patterns and house-like structures (Kaul 1998; see also Johannsen 2010; Goldhahn 2006). These motifs have been used with varying intensity throughout the Nordic countries wherever rock carvings were made. Kaul argues that there are two main themes in the interpretation of rock carvings: that of Bronze Age mythology or the performance of rituals. He suggests that the carvings depict a sort of 'ritual reality', as many of the artefacts carved into

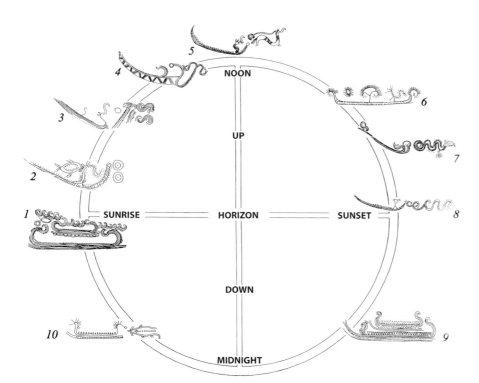

Figure 2. Kaul's explanatory model of Bronze Age cosmology – after Flemming Kaul and Tidsskriftet Skalk.

rock surfaces were items known from archaeological finds (Kaul 1998, 50f.). Nonetheless, it is believed that the creation of rock art in burial ceremonies was an unusual phenomenon and that the pictures created were linked to the eschatology and cosmology of the community by which they were produced (Goldhahn 1999, 2005; Syvertsen 2002; Kaul 2004).

Rock art was created in particular places with particular aims and intentions. Goldhahn (2005) claims that the creation of rock carvings as part of a Bronze Age mortuary ritual was not a passive activity which reflected the beliefs of society. He believes, rather, that it was an active act that created and recreated the mythology and cosmology of the carvers. Likewise, the production of bronze items with social and ideological connotations was also an active means of creating and recreating the eschatology and cosmology of the community with which they should be associated. These actions were cosmologically loaded (Goldhahn 2005).

Ethnographic research lends credence to this theory. The ritualistic thudding of hammer and chisel on stone could have induced the same sort of trance brought about by the beat of the shaman drums from the Sami peoples. In this way, the shaman or the ritual carver could have acted as an assistant for the dead spirit during his or her transition between the world of the living and the world of the dead (Viste

2004, 33f.). Syvertsen (2002) agrees, at least in part, suggesting that the production of rock carving was related to esoteric knowledge and must have been part of the ritual:

"… Egyptian priests' daily performance of the creation ritual was not a narrative of the creation; the performance was creation itself. […]

Perhaps carvings and specific carving motifs were included in the creation ritual not only because they were suitable as symbols or metaphors, but also to communicate a mythological message. Perhaps the myths told about the carvings and the way in which the figures were carved into the rock was itself a part of creation. The role of the carvings within ritual may have been linked to their role in creation and the maintenance of the cosmos […] to carve figures in rock and stone was essential" (Syvertsen 2002, 114, author's translation).

In this way, Bronze Age peoples created and re-created the mythology and cosmology of society. Therefore, rock carvings should not be perceived as depictions of events but rather as part of a ritual process. Scholars must try to understand rock carvings from the context in which they were made and not as a sort of a summary of events. In like fashion, to understand ship carvings, it is necessary for archaeologists to look at questions of context more closely, both in terms of the carvings themselves as well as other contexts in which ships occur. In the preparation of his text on "Ships on Bronzes", Kaul (1998) documented over 400 different bronze artefacts which displayed ships. Indeed, the ship was the most common motif on bronze as well as on rock surfaces. While there are examples of other motifs (such as fish and horses) on bronze items, these figures always occurred in combination with ships. In terms of individual artefact types, the overwhelming majority of bronze ship motifs are found on razors (Kaul 1998, 117).

Is it possible that the ship was metaphorically linked to the male domain? The razor was clearly considered a male item, but should the razor be perceived as a ship symbol in and of itself? Both Glob and Kaul believe that some razors' horse- or bird-shaped handles should place them in the same conceptual realm as that which surrounded ships (Kaul 1998, 124f.; Glob 1969). If one considers razors as being symbolically fungible with ship, then the overall number of ships in grave contexts is considerably augmented.

Ships in Stone and Metal: The Material

Circa 14,000 rock-carving locations are known within the borders of Sweden alone. Of these, some 100 originate from grave contexts (Goldhahn 2005, 21). The following section describes two of these graves from Scania which are useful to this study of ships and cosmology.

The Sagaholm grave mound is situated in the northern part of Småland and was seriously damaged before rescue work in 1971 excavated its central grave. A ring of stone slabs (of which five remain) surrounded the main grave. The grave and the stone ring were covered by a mound made of sod. After the mound was completed (in two sequences), a small circuit of stones was added. Rock carvings were found on the outer side of the middle stone circle (which consisted of an estimated 100 sandstone tiles). All tiles were made of the same material (probably from Visingsö, 30 kilometres to the north) and were shaped to fit together. Clearly, the depictions were not intended to be seen after the completion of the grave, perhaps in an attempt to maintain/contain any magical power (Goldhahn 2005, 36f.).

Geographically, Sagaholm lies in a rock carving 'no man's land'; the closest carving is located some 70 kilometres to the north. Therefore, the discovery of a concentration of rock carvings in the region was completely unexpected (Goldhahn 2005, 23). This is the reason why the Sagaholm mound offers a unique possibility to situate rock carving depictions with the appropriate social and ritual context (Goldhahn 2005, 24). The closed nature of the Sagaholm mound places its depictions within a different context than those found in an open landscape. This does not necessarily imply that the meaning of the Sagaholm carvings differed from those of carvings in an open rock surface, just that the meanings intended for the carvings at Sagaholm were probably more explicitly expressed (Goldhahn 2005, 39). Most of the carvings were of horses, occasionally combined with human figures or a ship (Goldhahn 2005, 22). In total, eleven ships were found within the Sagaholm mound (Goldhahn 1999, 75; Kaul 2004, 165). It is thought that the selection of the remaining slabs would have been representative of the motifs found in the stone circle as a whole (Goldhahn 2005, 42). As to the interpretation of the motifs, Goldhahn writes:

"...there can be no doubt that the horse and the sun held a distinguished position in the creation myth and in the cosmological worldview of Bronze Age people. We find these figures together repeatedly, often in the company of some sort of vessel, sometimes a wagon but most often a ship. In another context, I interpreted this combination as a mythological triad – the sun, the horse and the ship – which may be connected to Bronze Age creation myths" (Goldhahn 2005, 45, author's translation).

Goldhahn further posits that the Sagaholm carvings were intended as a means of reincarnation (Goldhahn 2005, 49). However, Kaul disagrees (Kaul 2004, 172).

The second site to be discussed is the large Bronze Age cairn from Bredarör in Kivik, Scania. The cairn was long used by locals as a source of building stone. In 1748, these deprivations uncovered the central cist. The stone slabs of the cist were decorated with depictions of animals, wagons, weapons, ships and human figures garbed in mantles and/or masks. For the last two and a half centuries, antiquarian and archaeological interpretations have principally described Bredarör as the resting place of an important man. This view is supported by Randsborg's association of the fragmented bronze artefacts recovered with the main grave (Goldhahn 2005, 230ff.; Randsborg 1993, 50f.). Osteological analyses carried out in 2005 concluded that the bones from Bredarör came from several people (at least three teenagers and one adult),

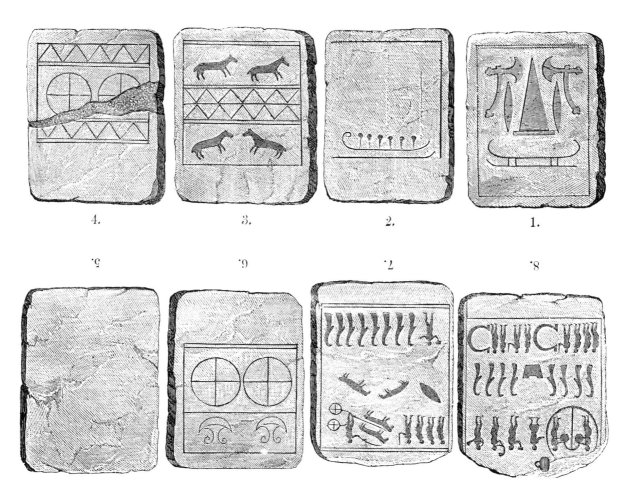

Figure 3. The cist slabs from Bredarör, presumably arranged in order – after Randsborg 1993,21.

and that these were probably interred at different times. This would suggest that the site had been of ritual importance over a significant period of time. This use-phase possibly lasted 600 years (Goldhahn 2005, 249; Goldhahn 2009); the latest dating results place the early phase of the site in Period V (Goldhahn 2005, 244f.). The primary grave was probably constructed in such a way that the head of the deceased pointed northwards, i.e. towards the portion of the cist in which the tiles and abstract symbols were found.

The motifs from Bredarör are nature-themed and include sun symbols, horses and waves. Goldhahn interprets the combination of these symbols as part of the private and individual sphere with essential meanings dealing with personal and esoteric knowledge (Goldhahn 2005, 106f.). There has been some discussion about the individual placement of the stone tiles due to the fact that possibly only one of the side stones is still in its original position. Unfortunately, the remaining tiles were moved in the 1750s by the local inhabitants (Randsborg 1993, 14.). Discussion

about the slabs' original positions is of long duration and began in 1756 with Wessmann's[1] publication of the drawings of the decorated slabs (Randsborg 1993, 25-27.) However, this paper has opted to review Goldhahn's interpretation. Both stones with ship symbols (tiles 1 and 2, Fig. 3) were placed towards the east in the direction of the coast. Therefore, it is likely that they symbolise the underworld's associations with water, death, the past and ritual deposition (Goldhahn 2005, 104). This corresponds optimally with Goldhahn's cosmological model of Sagaholm (Fig. 4). In the Bredarör grave, this tripartite cosmology is apparent in the arrangement of the stone tiles. Although Bredarör was used for several individuals, it can be presumed that the rock carvings were arranged for the first funeral which took place there (Goldhahn 2005, 105, 248).

Despite their differences, both Sagaholm and Bredarör exemplify the usage of ship motifs in a grave context. In both instances, it is clear that the motifs were only visible to the living for a short time and it

The Upper World	The Living World	The Underworld
Future	Present	Past
Rebirth	Life	Death
Sky	Earth/Stone	Water
Sun	Horse	Ship
Grave	House	Depot

Figure 4. Schematic representation of Goldhahn's cosmological model of Sagaholm –based on Goldhahn 2005, 104.

can be presumed that their true purpose was to serve the dead, albeit at a more collective and mythological level at Sagaholm than at (individualised) Bredarör (Kaul 2004, 181f.).

Other examples of ship rock carvings in mortuary contexts were found in Denmark. Three ships were recovered at Dilhøj in northwest Zealand in connection with wheeled crosses on a cover stone (Glob 1969, 17f.). The Breddysse dolmen in western Zealand depicts two ships along with a multitude of carved cup marks (Glob 1969, 17ff.). A ploughed-over mound from Truehøjgårds Mark in Himmerland yielded a single stone decorated with two ships, some cup marks and a single footprint (Glob 1969, 30f.). In Vindblæs near Mariager, a small ship was carved into a stone in the border of a mound (Kaul 2004, 158). Despite these examples, the depictions of ships in stone are comparatively rare in grave contexts.

However, there are many examples of ship depictions recovered from bronze artefacts in funerary contexts. As was suggested earlier, it is possible that Late Bronze Age razors could have been construed as representative of ships, regardless of the specifics of their decoration (Kaul 2004, 56; 1998, 134f.). Following that line of thought, it might be interesting to investigate how far razors could be considered public property due to the fact that they both symbolise and are decorated with ships. If so, the depictions of ships on razors and the razor itself symbolised the community which might lead to a reconstruction of the social position of their owner. Additionally, by viewing the razor as a *pars pro toto* for the ship, one can conclude that ships or what one might consider ships-by-extension were normally present in male graves from this period.

To this end, a brief introduction to the use and the occurrence of razors in grave contexts is necessary. Draiby's (1989) investigation on sex determination in Danish Late Bronze Age graves from Himmer-

land and northwest Zealand should be taken as the basis for this case study. The material included closed grave finds from 679 graves. Of these, 105 graves were defined as definite male graves, 90 of which contained razors. A total of 120 graves were not allocated a specific sex. (None of these contained a razor, as those items were employed as a sexing criterion) (Draiby 1989, 159ff.). If one presumes that half of the individuals of unknown sex were males, this adds an additional 60 male graves to the dataset, resulting in a total of 75 male graves without razors. Compared to the 90 male graves with razors, the data indicates that there was a strong tradition for placing razors in male graves.

Another potential means of investigating the symbolic application of ships in the Bronze Age death cult would be through an examination of ship settings. A mere 35 ship settings are known from the Bronze Age. In these graceful and unusual prehistoric sites, stones were placed so that they increased in size from the port and starboard sides of the boat to the bow and stern. Most settings are found on Gotland, although others have been found in Halland and Schleswig and range in date from early Period III to Period V (Capelle 1995, 71-75). The stone settings could be understood as a symbolic means of enabling the dead to sail to the underworld. It is possible that individuals interred in this fashion had a special connection to the sun and the sun ship, or were local leaders.

However, the use of ships and ship imagery was not limited to grave rituals. Tens of thousands of ship carvings have been found on the coastal parts of Sweden and Norway and a few sacrificial boat finds have also been recovered (i.e. Kaul 1998; Ling 2008; Widholm 2007). Taken together, these indicate a clear and definite use of boats in ritual contexts. The discovery of 100 small gold foil boats found in Thy (Denmark) in 1885 supports this conclusion (Jørgensen and Petersen, 1998, 90). The gunwales and frames of the miniatures were made of bronze and were subsequently covered in gold foil. The foil was decorated with circular ornaments. While the dating of these items is uncertain, the decorations and the material from which they were made are indicative of Bronze Age production. This unique find may provide some hints about the way in which full-scale Bronze Age boats were constructed. Regardless, the rarity of the materials and the care taken with the assembly of the miniatures acts as a clear sign of the significance of ships to Bronze Age persons.

The Significance of Bronze Age Ships

To further unpick the cosmological significance of Bronze Age ships, it is necessary to take an iconographical approach[2]. Panofsky (1955) presents three important art-historical levels of examining icons: (1) the pre-iconographic level, in which individuals perceive pure form, devoid of any added cultural knowledge; (2) the iconographic level, in which the understanding of the icon is crafted in relation to cultural and iconographic knowledge and (3) the iconological level, in which the comprehension of an image is created via personal, technical and cultural history. In this last, deepest understanding, the icon is placed within a historical environment. The combination of these different comprehensions creates a synthesis between knowledge and emotion (Panofsky 1955, 28f.).

If one continues with the idea that rock carvings (especially those present in grave contexts) were religious or cosmological in nature, then Panofsky's three-part analysis could be used as a theoretical entry point to creating an understanding of rock art. An analytical correlation of these levels would firstly involve the thorough description of artwork (including the choice of materials employed as well as the geographical situation of the piece and the surface of the stone carving as well as such details as colour and the presence of cracks). Following this, any motifs employed must have been analytically identified. The third and final section of this discussion must, therefore, seek to interpret the motif by means of theological analogy.

Ritualistic activities are a sort of social communication. They carry echoes of many current social and environmental phenomena, including ideologies, social status, kinship ties, social tension and economical conditions. Religious activities also function as an adaptive mechanism which contributes to the maintenance of society. In this sense, ritual can buttress the position of those climbing the social ladder or could alternatively cause a narrowing of the gap between social elites and those of lower rank. Ritual can even act as a means of organising mutual obligations between groups of social equals. When carefully and correctly employed, ritual can manipulate social relations (Levy 1981, 103f.). In this sense, ritual and religion can form a buffer zone during the negotiations necessary for the creation of a new social order.

Van Gennep's model for the analysis of the ritual process can be employed to untangle the forces which powered its presence in past societies (van Gennep 1960, 146, 166.). Society goes through a series of three phases when faced with death: separation, marginality and then a third, liminal period. This concept is best illustrated by means of example; when someone dies, he or she must be removed from living society. This procedure brings about a phase of separation. This absence leads to a marginal phase in which the deceased conceptually moves from the land of the living to that of the dead. This is a dangerous period, usually rife with rituals and taboos (Kaul 2004, 170). The final, liminal phase involves the incorporation of the deceased (or their spirit) into a new context.

Death rituals in the Bronze Age may belong to this practice of aiding and abetting the movement of the deceased from the world of the living to the realm of death. The building sequence of the Sagaholm grave would fit admirably into this ritualistic sequence. The deceased was presumably separated from society. Next, they were confronted with the carvings on the stone tiles, the production of which was likely completed by ritual specialists possessed of esoteric knowledge. Finally, the grave was closed, effectively sealing off the deceased from the world of the living.

The presence of ships as part of these processes mark them as conceptual symbols possessed of many meanings. On the primary level, they were indicative of transportation and the secondary conditions of the sharing of goods and knowledge as well as the creation and maintenance of cultural contacts. Metaphorically, the ship could also be understood to be a means of transporting the sun and the dead. Vertical differentiation associated with ships suggests that they might also have been employed as markers of gender.

Some Concluding Thoughts

Ships had a major cultural and conceptual impact on Bronze Age Europe. Ancient peoples carved tens of thousands of ships on rocks in Scandinavia. Ship motifs-covered bronzes, and ships were modelled in miniature out of precious materials. Many ships sailed the waters surrounding Scandinavia and the European mainland…but how did the ship gain such importance in the first place?

Thedéen sees the origin of the ship's popularity in its symbolism. The ship represented different forms of journeys, mental as well as physical, which traversed both time and space (Thedéen 2002, 130). Kaul supports this symbolic emphasis on travel; the presence of ships and horses in the grave must be understood as symbols of the sun and its journey. In this sense, rock carvings in funerary contexts could have represented the cosmological wishes that the living maintained for the deceased in their travel to the underworld (Kaul 2004, 172).

The ship was part of a mythological triad (sun, horse and ship) which can be connected to Bronze Age creation myths (Goldhahn 2005, 45). The reproduction of ships in rock carvings and the esoteric knowledge associated with said work also formed part of the religious *status quo* (Syvertsen 2002, 114). Bronze Age ship settings should be seen as symbolic expressions of ships created for and by seafaring humans. For example, stone settings are evocative of the original shape and size of Bronze Age ships (Capelle 1995, 74f.).

Researchers agree that these ships were symbolic, although the meanings associated with the ship-as-symbol vary. It is probable that ships were the means rather than the end for Bronze Age people as a ship epitomised freedom of movement.

The aim of this paper was to demonstrate that ships had a significant cosmological and practical meaning for Bronze Age society. It is likely that ships functioned in terms of the rituals associated with both death and the quotidian. Moreover, it is probable that their important role in daily life influenced their perception in relation to death; namely that life's journey presumably continued into the underworld.

Ship motifs in grave contexts support this argument. However, how does this relate to other ship decorations and models within the Bronze Age world? Should they also be conceptually associated with death? The meaning associated with a symbol may easily have varied in terms of the context in which it was found. Many Bronze Age symbols have multitudinous meanings, and the ship is not the least of these. It is possible that, like the sun's journey through the skies of morning and evening, the ship was intended both for the living when at sea and for the dead when in the grave.

Acknowledgements

Many thanks to the editors of this book whose suggestions and knowledge helped me to transform my article into its current form. I especially want to thank them for the many helpful comments they provided during the peer-review process which enabled me to see my chosen theme from new, previously unconsidered angles.

Notes

1. Various drawings were made by N. Wessmann around 1756 which can be found in Stockholm's "Kungliga Biblioteket."
2. Iconography is the study of pictorial religious motifs in terms of their religious content and function (Panofsky 1955, 28f.).

Bibliography

Artursson, M. 1987: *Mast-, rig- och segelliknande konstruktioner på Götalands Hällristningsskepp.* Lund.

Bradley, R. 2009: *Image and audience. Rethinking prehistoric art.* Oxford.

Capelle, T. 1995: Bronze-Age Stone Ships. In: Crumlin-Pedersen, O. & B.M. Thye (eds.): *The Ship as Symbol in Prehistoric and Medieval Scandinavia. Papers from an international research seminar at the Danish National Museum, Copenhagen, 5th-7th May 1994.* Publications from the National Museum. Studies in Archaeology and History 1. København, 71-75.

Clark, P. 2004: *The Dover Bronze Age Boat in Context. Society and Water Transport in Prehistoric Europe.* Oxford. Draiby, B. 1989: Kvinde- og mandsgrave i yngre bronzealder. Regionale variationer. In: Poulsen, J. (ed.): *Regionale forhold i Nordisk Bronzealder. 5. Nordiske Symposium for Bronzealderforskning på Sandbjerg Slot.* Aarhus, 159-167.

Glob, P.V. 1969: *Helleristninger i Danmark.* Jysk Arkæologisk Selskabs Skrifter VII. Højbjerg.

Goldhahn, J. 1999: *Sagaholm: Hällristningar och gravritual.* Studia Archaeologica Universitatis Umensis 11. Jönköping.

Goldhahn, J. 2005: *Från Sagaholm till Bredarör. Hällbildsstudier 2000-2004.* Gotarc serie C. Arkeologiska Skrifter No 62. Västra Frölunda.

Goldhahn, J. 2006: *Hällbildsstudier i norra Europa. Trender och tradition under det nya millenniet.* Gotarc Serie C. Arkeologiska Skrifter No 64. Göteborg.

Goldhahn, J. 2009: Bredarör on Kivik: A monumental cairn and the history of its interpretation. *Antiquity* 83, 359-371.

Hodder, I. 1986: *Reading the past. Current approaches to interpretation in archaeology.* Cambridge.

Jansson, S. 1994: Nordsvensk Hjortspringbåd? *Marinarkæologisk Nyhedsbrev fra Roskilde* 2, 16-17.

Jørgensen, L. & P.V. Petersen 1998: *Guld, magt og tro. Danske skattefund fra oldtid og middelalder.* København.

Kaul, F. 1988: *Da våbnene tav. Hjortspringfundet og dets baggrund.* København.

Kaul, F. 1998: *Ships on bronzes. A study in Bronze Age religion and iconography.* PNM Studies in Archaeology and History 3, 1. København.

Kaul, F. 2003: The Hjortspring boat and ship iconography

of the Bronze Age and Early Pre-Roman Iron Age. In: Crumlin-Pedersen, O. & A. Trakadas (eds.): *Hjortspring. A Pre-Roman Iron-Age Warship in Context*. Roskilde, 187-207.

Kaul, F. 2004: *Bronzealderens religion. Studier af den nordiske bronzealders ikonografi*. København.

Kristiansen, K. 1998: *Europe before History*. Cambridge.

Kristiansen, K. & T.B. Larsson 2005: *The Rise of Bronze Age Society. Travels, Transmissions and Transformations*. Cambridge.

Levy, J.E. 1981: *Social and Religious Organization in Bronze Age Denmark. An Analysis of Ritual Hoard Finds*. BAR International Series 124. Oxford.

Ling, J. 2008: *Elevated Rock Art. Towards a maritime Understanding of Bronze Age Rock Art in northern Bohuslän, Sweden*. Gotarc Serie B. Gothenburg. Archaeological Thesis 49. Göteborg.

Malmer, M.P. 1981: *A Chorological Study of North European Rock Art*. Antikvariska Serien 32. Stockholm.

Muckelroy, K. & P. Baker 1979: The Bronze Age site off Moor Sand, near Salcombe, Devon. An interim report on the 1978 season. *International Journal of Nautical Archaeology* 8, 189-210.

Muckelroy, K. & P. Baker 1980: The Bronze Age site off Moor Sand, Salcombe, Devon. An interim report on the 1979 season. *International Journal of Nautical Archaeology* 9, 155-158.

Nordbladh, J. 2004: Hällristningar som allmän bild – och som speciell. In: Milstreu, G. & H. Prøhl (eds.): *Prehisto-ric pictures as archaeological source -Förhistoriska bilder som arkeologisk källa*. Gotarc Serie C. Arkeologiska Skrifter 50. Göteborg, 63-67.

Olsson, L. 1996: *Skeppets väg till Hälleberget. En komparativ bildanalys av hällristningsskepp i Sverige och skeppsbilder från medelhavsområdet*. Stockholm.

Panofsky, E. 1955: *Meaning in the Visual Arts. Papers in and on Art History*. Michigan

Randsborg, K. 1993: Kivik. Archaeology and Iconography. *Acta Archaeologica* 64, 1, 1-147.

Randsborg, K. 1995: *Hjortspring. Warfare and Sacrifice in early Europe*. Aarhus.

Syvertsen, K.I.J. 2002: Ristninger i graver – graver med ristninger. In: Goldhahn, J. (ed.): *Bilder av Bronsålder*. Stockholm, 151-183.

Thedèen, S. 2002: På resa genom livet och landskapet. Tankar kring bronsålderns skeppssymbolik. In: Goldhahn, J. (ed.): *Bilder av Bronsålder*. Stockholm, 129-150.

van Gennep, A. 1960: *The Rites of Passage*. Translated by Vizedom, M.B. & G.L. Caffee. Chicago.

Viste, S. 2004: Rock-art and Shamanism. In: Milstreu, G. & H. Prøhl (eds.): *Prehistoric pictures as archaeological source -Förhistoriska bilder som arkeologisk källa*. Gotarc Serie C. Arkeologiska Skrifter 50. Göteborg, 33-47.

Widholm, D. 2007: *Stone Ships. The Sea and the Heavenly Journey*. Kalmar.

Wright, E.V. 1990: *The Ferriby Boats. Seacraft of the Bronze Age*. London.

The Meaning of Hands

A Semiotic Approach to the Interpretation of Hand Stones

Thomas Rune Knudsen

Introduction

The creation and meaning behind hand stones is a conundrum within current research. Not only are archaeologists uncertain of the reasons behind the creation of hand stones, but further study has yet to offer a satisfactory explanation for the basis of the unrealistic way in which they were depicted. What did they mean? Can this meaning be reconstructed? This paper addresses these questions by examining the stone slabs and motifs from Sandagergård and Jenriksbakke on the Danish island of Zealand.

The purpose of this article is to reconstruct the initial meaning of hand stones by means of the study of motifs. Due to said concentration on original meanings (as opposed to the meanings associated with later use, adoption or abandonment), discussions of landscape, adjacent settlement and the interconnectivity of different motifs have been sidelined in this study. However, although this specific approach to the material does not leave much room for agency or past negotiations of meaning, this should not be perceived as an argument for a single, static state of affairs in prehistory. Hand stones should not be viewed as simple and passive carriers of meaning. In the same sense, this paper should be considered an exploration of a particular aspect of hand stones rather than an all-encompassing interpretation of the hand stone phenomenon. In order to attain its goal of reconstructing the original meaning of hand stones, this paper isolates various significant elements of their depiction.

These motifs are analysed via semiotics and cognitive linguistics. The reasoning behind the use of this line of inquiry includes analytical value and methodical experimentation. The aim here is not merely to attempt to reconstruct the initial meaning of the stone slabs, but also to investigate the analytical value of a specific semiotic approach. To this end, this paper is divided into two sections. The first portion presents the analytical mode of academic inquiry in terms of the central premise of the paper: namely, that the visual expression of prehistoric art was predominantly intentional and conscientiously created. It follows, therefore, that early artworks can and should be considered as meaning-laden human expressions. Following discussion of this concept, an analytical framework is put forward by which the meaningful aspects of the depictions can be assessed. A subsequent section contains a brief introduction to the material and goes on to analyse two chosen examples in accordance with the analytical framework. Previous hand stone interpretations (Brøndsted 1939, 140; Larsen 1955; Marstrander 1963; Glob 1969; Johansen 1970; Malmer 1989; Kaul 2006) are compared and contrasted with those derived from the current analysis. The final part of the paper includes a summary and an evaluation of the methodical approach as well as any attendant theoretical concerns associated therewith.

The Interpretation Issue

Because of the degree to which both semiotics and cognitive studies rely on the concept of cognition, it is vital cognition be clearly defined here. 'Cognition' as a term does not merely refer to rationality and common sense; it also includes emotions and subconscious elements like perception and categorisation. It is an organic and continuous process which has inspired some scholars to write of "visual intelligence" (Hoffman 1998, xi). Very broadly defined, cognition includes everything which is done by the brain.

Unfortunately, it is beyond the scope of this paper to define either art or aesthetics. (For discussion see Croce and Romanell 1965, 3-27; Dissanayake 1988, i-ix) Nonetheless, this text must utilise these concepts, as it is based on the premise that prehistoric art was intentional rather than either passive reproduction or purely aesthetic. In other words, prehistoric art contained within it an initial meaning, and it is this very meaning (in terms of the hand stones) which this paper attempts to access. Naturally, one can argue that the original sense or message of any piece of prehistoric art was ambiguous, that it was perhaps intended only for the eyes of the artist or even as an offering to the divine. Alternatively, one might suggest that it was the *production* of the art and not the resulting end product which was the goal of art creation. Although any (or all) of these scenarios might be true, they give no indications of the reasons for which a motif like the hand stones would be produced in a particular way.

A potential means of grappling with the original intentions involved in producing a particular piece of prehistoric artwork is to investigate artistic choice, location and means of expression by which said artwork was created. This concept can be illustrated quite conveniently in terms of hand stones. Hand stones are unique in that they are distorted rather than realistic. Instead of rendering the features of hands objectively, the artists of the hand stones actively chose to depict them in a specific way. The analytical investigations of this phenomenon, however, must be carefully constructed.

Bundgård's paper on the creation of meaning in art divides any particular artwork into three levels: medium (the physical object or subject of the artwork), motif (representation) and the particular presentation thereof (Bundgård 2002).[1] It is essential to differentiate between these categories. Motif is essentially the representation of medium. Presentation, however, refers to the particular *style* employed in that depiction. British colonists in India critiqued local images and statues of erotic nudes with enlarged breasts, wide hips and waspish waists for being unrealistic. Realism may have been an artistic movement in and of itself in the mid 19th century, however, proponents of that style ignore art's great potential for changing reality by enhancing and/or distorting it (Ramachan-dran and Hirstein 1999, 16). Distortion is a vital and easily recognizable aspect of art, and so, therefore, it is our means of engaging with artistic choice and production of meaning.

This focus on distortion and enhancement must necessarily spill over into a discussion of style and the reasons behind the selection of a specific motif. In other wards, why was a *hand* depicted rather than a leg, sword or other object? One must also account for what one might call 'portioning' or 'partiality'. Was it *only* hands that were depicted, or were forearms and elbows included in the images? All interpretations should take the totality of the evidence into account.

Indeed, not only inclusions but also exclusions and embellishments must be addressed in such a study. What was the role of distortion, or even of realism? Although they cannot be summarily dismissed, it is problematic to explain away depictions purely by classing them as 'normative' or as the 'evidence of a passive style'. Certainly, the original hand stone(s) were consciously planned productions without previous examples to passively copy. In this context, conscious planning can be sharply contrasted with passive reproduction, suggesting that the artist made active decisions in deciding how a particular motif should look. Therefore, it is necessary to address representation: the style and medium of the motif.

Any motif must be made out of, in or on some sort of medium. Just as the medium of the *Mona Lisa* is a wood panel and oil paint, so is stone the medium of rock carvings. Engagement with rock as a medium must necessarily extend into a discussion of context, as one must also address the wider context and position in which rock carvings were situated.

Thus far we have addressed questions of medium and motif and the ways in which these aspects could have been employed or manipulated by a prehistoric artist in his or her quest for meaning creation. However, this is not a complete representation of the creation of art. Either separately or in tandem, these three categories could have modified the execution of any specific piece of artwork, and therefore affected its intended meaning. One of the primary concerns in such an analysis would be the artist's technical competence. The creation of a realistic image of a hand would have been dependent upon the possession of the technical skills required for that process. To what degree the technical competence of the artist would have affected a carving's overall appearance is unclear. If the artist had strived for a realistic depiction, then the artist could simply have used his or her own hand as a template. While the absence of proof is not proof of absence, no clear evidence for realistic hand 'sketches' has been found, intimating that the continuity of more abstract hand stones was the result of intentional artistic decision-making.

However, the technical abilities of the artist are not the only area of concern. The shaping of stone is not without limitations. Rock surfaces make the expression of small details and delicate elements difficult. Therefore, it would be logical to suggest that the stylistic expression of hand stones could have been influenced by the limitations of the medium in which they were expressed. Due to practical concerns, simple, clean shapes would have been preferable. Even so, this does not mean that it was impossible to create realistic motifs. The foot sole motif from Godensgård in Himmerland, Denmark proves that fairly realistic rock carving was within the grasp of prehistoric persons (Fig. 1). Other aspects cannot be explained by the limitations of the medium. Stone alone cannot have been responsible for such things as strange proportions, extra features and/or orientation.

The Hand Stones

At present, 27 hand stones have been discovered in Scandinavia. The presence of some specimens in grave contexts allowed for relative chronological dating; the majority of the hand stones were created between 1100-900 BC (Montelius' Period IV), although both earlier and later examples are known (Goldhahn 2009, 96; Goldhahn 2007, 47; Glob 1969, 85). The majority of hand stones are stray finds. However, when linked with other prehistoric materials, they most often appear in association with mortuary contexts, specifically in mounds or as the cover stones in cremation burials (Goldhahn 2009, 95f.; Malmer 1981, 56; Norling-Christensen 1941, 49; Glob 1969, 85 and 209) The hand stones from Sandagergård are the exception to the rule as they were found in association with a ritual building (Kaul 2006).

Hand stones differ from other Scandinavian rock carvings in several significant ways. They are only found on portable stones rather than on rock surfaces (Goldhahn 2009, 95). The distribution of hand stones is predominately Danish with the highest concentration on northern Zealand (Johansen 1970, 171; Goldhahn 2007, 46f.). Other rock carvings – such as depictions of ships – are more prominent in the

Figure 1. A foot sole motif from Godensgård, Himmerland, Denmark – after Glob 1969, 92.

rest of Scandinavia (Malmer 1981; see Damkjer, this volume). Finally, hand carvings are decidedly homogeneous in both style and the depiction of the subject matter (Goldhahn 2009, 95). The horizontal lines above the arm usually occur in sets of four, although examples with five or six lines are not unknown (Malmer 1981, 57). Interestingly, the 'thumb' appears most often on the right (Goldhahn 2007, 47). Whether this indicates the presentation of the back of the left hand or the palm of the right is unclear. It is interesting to note that the hand is often carved slightly deeper than wrist, arm or fingers, and could perhaps be construed as indicating a right palm, insomuch as it would echo the concavity of this feature (Goldhahn 2009, 95; Johansen 1970, 177). Although this question must remain unresolved, for the sake of consistency, such depictions will henceforth be regarded as being those of a right hand.

As was mentioned above, depictions of hand stones are very uniform, having only very slight variations (Goldhahn 2009, 95). Therefore, it is likely that the two examples chosen for this analysis contain elements which are representative of a larger body of data. The first case from Sandagergård (Kaul 2006) includes a hand and part of the forearm, while the one from Jenriksbakke (Glob 1969, 87 and 209) includes these elements with the addition of the elbow. Both examples were found in northern Zealand.

Figure 2. Hand stone from Sandagergård, Zealand, Denmark – after Kaul 2004, 109.

The motif from Sandagergård (Fig. 2) was made on a flat, tear-shaped rock of c. 50 cm in length and was recovered approximately three meters from the southern side of a Bronze Age building (Kaul 2006, 100). It was found in the company of three other hand stones. It represents a hand with spread fingers and forearm with four horizontal lines scored above the hand. While the depiction is recognisable as hand and arm, upon closer inspection it is clear that this representation deviates noticeably from a reality. The forearm, which is the major feature of the motif, is thin and uniform. Anatomically correct forearms would be significantly thicker and would taper from the elbow to the wrist. The palm is unusually small and is triangular in shape.

The fingers of this hand stone are particularly remarkable. These digits are disproportionately long in comparison to the palm, but remain (more or less) proportionate to the rest of the forearm. Additionally, the fingers have no size gradation; the little finger is too long in relation to the index, middle and ring fingers. Even the thumb deviates from the anatomic norm with regard to thickness and length, although not to a significant degree. The sharp lateral bend of the thumb at the last joint must have been as an inten-

tional presentation choice, which Kaul has previous described in terms of an exaggeration (Kaul 1986, 6).

Another aspect of particular note is the position in which the hand is depicted. A position in which the hand has widespread fingers is not a natural pose; the same can be said about the sharply bent thumb. It seems to be a suspicious coincidence that the motif should be depicted in this way solely by chance, suggesting instead that it was the intentional choice of the artist.

This unusual depiction fits in with the concepts of suspicious coincidence (Ramachandran and Hirstein 1999, 27-30) or non-genericity (Darrault-Harris 2009). These ideas can perhaps best be illustrated by means of the representation of a jumping horse. When airbourne, the horse is not in a sustainable situation, gravity would soon return it to the ground. That the horse is depicted at this particular moment in time is a suspicious coincidence, and as this is the marked result of intentional artistic choice, it must also, therefore, have an impact on meaning. The same situation applies to the unusual pose in which hand stones were depicted.

The motif from Jenriksbakke (Fig. 3) is most likely from a burial mound. The stone slab is three sided, the most even side of which was carved with the motif. The stone is slightly over half a meter long and is a quarter of a meter thick (Glob 1969, 209).

The carving includes a clear representation of a hand with forearm and elbow joint. Four horizontal lines were placed above the hand. As with the previous example, the hand stone from Jenriksbakke is unrealistic. While the forearm is the widest portion of the carving, it is far narrower than would be anatomically correct and is missing the natural tapering from elbow to wrist. The latter joint is indicated by a simple bend in the groove representing the arm. While the palm is too small, its shape is more accurate than that from Sandagergård (Fig. 3). As was the case with the previous example, the fingers of the Jenriksbakke hand stone are remarkably uniform, showing no differentiation, even between fingers and thumb. All digits emerge from the palm at even intervals, showing to special differentiation from the thumb's natural position lower on the hand.

As was previously the case, position merits further discussion. The Jenriksbakke arm bends naturally at the elbow, while the fingers remain rigid and extended, as with those at Sandagergård. As has been argued, this unusual positioning of the hands must

Figure 3. Hand stone from Jenriksbakke, Zealand, Denmark – after Glob 1969, 87.

have been intentional and could therefore provide an indication of an artist's initial meaning in creating the piece of art.

Previous Interpretations

Although the discipline generally holds that South Scandinavian rock carvings should be understood within a ritual frame (Thedéen 2002, 137), scholars have suggested various ritualistic uses for the process. For the purposes of this text, these interpretations have been grouped together according to the following themes: mythology, luck, separation and transition.

Proponents of a mythological interpretation suggest that hand stones represent the hands of a thunder god (Brøndsted 1939, 140) or sun deity (Larsen 1955, 51f.). In an analogy which would fit with the abnormally long and slender nature of the hands, scholars suggest that the fingers should be understood as representations of lightening bolts or sun rays. A variation of the sun god theory posits that the horizontal lines above the hands represent the

sea at sunrise (Larsen 1955, 52). Unfortunately, neither theory is easily reconciled with hand stones' aforementioned association with mortuary contexts (Goldhahn 2009, 95f.). These mythology-based interpretations are weak analogies and assume a rich mythological tradition for which there is little empirical evidence.

The following explanatory device is more solidly grounded in the facts and conditions in which the material culture was recovered. Given that hand motifs were principally found in grave contexts, they have also been interpreted as a form of protective totem (Malmer 1989, 96). Regrettably, this analogy does not address the presentation of the hand motif, the horizontal lines accompanying it, the presence of forearms or a particular predilection for the depiction of the right hand. One could understand an association between protection and hands, given that those body parts are one of mankind's primary means of physical defence. A similar interpretation proposed by Marstrander suggests that hand motifs might have been intended to bring luck (Marstrander 1963, 223).

The third slant taken on hand motifs is similar to the former in that it is also well based on the material evidence. It suggests that the depiction of the appendages was intended to separate the living from the dead and to ensure that the peace of the grave was maintained (Kaul 2006, 109; Johansen 1970, 185). Hands could either have been intended as a deterrent for the living (Marstrander 1963, 223) or as a means of ensuring that the deceased remained in their resting places (Kaul 2006, 109; Johansen 1970, 185). It is also possible, of course, that the hand stones served both purposes at the same time. This interpretation is particularly interesting insofar as it is equally engaged with representation as well as context. If we imagine that the hand represented a person standing with his or her palm and spread fingers raised toward the spectator, it could be easily associated with the modern gesture of warning (Johansen 1970, 182). The horizontal markings could be indicative of motion, in which case the outward hand could represent aggressive force (Johansen 1970, 184). Another scholar has suggested that those same markings intimate the presence of some unknown weapon (Brøndsted 1939, 140), threatening would-be disturbers of the deceased. Unfortunately, the reason for which the images include the forearm or the preference of ancient artisans for depicting a right hand remains elusive within this analogy.

An alternative 'transitive' interpretation branches off from the previous 'separatist' one. Kaul suggests that the hand motif symbolises a transition to the land of the dead (Kaul 2006, 109f.). Hands could have been connected to certain rites of passage, marking distinct phases in the human life course. If modern interpretations of these transitional rituals as a form of death and rebirth (i.e. Van Gennep 2004) are true, then the horizontal lines could represent time (Kaul 2006, 109) either in terms of the cycle of the seasons or the phases of night and day. A variant on this theory posits that the hand motifs symbolise rebirth. The addition of the five fingers and four horizontal lines accompanying them add up to a total of nine, which equates with the length of a human pregnancy (Glob 1969, 90). This latter interpretation is dependent upon a numerical system in which fingers and lines could each symbolize numbers as well as a measurement of time similar to our own. While a transition-focused view of hand stones dovetails with the contextual evidence as well as the horizontal markings on the stones, it falls short of explaining the presentation of the hands in particular, the tendency for right hands and the marked inclusion of the forearm.

In summary, while each of the previous interpretations has its strengths, each has weaknesses as well. Those interpretations of hand stones which concentrate on the themes of separation, transition (Kaul 2006, 109) and protection (Malmer 1989, 96) have the greatest potential, as they consider both grave context and the particularities of hand stone representations in their analyses. Unfortunately, they do not include discussions of the presentation of hand stones (i.e. the way they appear). Therefore, at present, there is no all-encompassing interpretation of hand stones which touches upon their representation, presentation and context.

The Meaning of Hands

This section presents an alternative interpretation to combining the representation, presentation and context of hand stones and is an extension of the transition theory described above. In order to adequately explain the approach, we must begin by examining the concepts of metonymy and conceptual metaphor.

Metonymy is specific figure of speech in which the subject is replaced by another item with which it is closely associated. For example, when the captain of a ship orders 'All hands on deck', the 'hands' to which he refers are sailors rather than dismembered body parts. In other words, a part can reference the whole of a thing (or person, as the case may be). Although originally relegated to the realm of linguistics, metonymy is now considered as a cognitive phenomenon. Metonymy is not merely the oral expression of a 'handy' figure of speech; it represents the way in which our minds work (Ungerer and Schmid 2006, 117f. and 127f.).

How does this concept relate to hand stones? The inclusion of forearms (and perhaps the occasional elbow) allows the hand to be more easily recognisable as a hand (rather than a five-pointed sunburst, for example). As with metonymy, it is possible that hand stones were not intended as depictions of fingers, wrist, palm and arm, but rather as partitive representations of whole persons. In this way, the hand could have represented the body. It seems plausible that hands could have been an obvious representative symbol for the whole person, even in the distant conceptualisation and thought processes belonging to prehistoric persons. Superficially, hands are similar between people in a way that faces are not. Because of the fact that they are extremely complex and possessed of such a range of diverse movements and actions, the hands are mankind's most important means of interacting with the world (Tilley 1999, 144). In light of this, it is logical to view hand motifs as a means of getting or maintaining contact. The function of hands is to manipulate. To make an abstract thing – like death – more tangible or handle-able in this way seems a universal human inclination (Johannsen 2010). Given that the find contexts of hand motifs are dominated by graves (Goldhahn 2007, 47), it is perhaps not so great a leap to suggest that hand motifs were intended to make a connection with death.

Several important concepts are implicated by any mediation between life and death. Liminality (Turner 1967, 93) counts among their number, and is an important concept which refers to the idea that the world in which we live is separated from the next by only a very thin border. Insofar as death can be understood as a transition between two different worlds, the hand motif could then have been employed as a symbol or a tool for (or within) this transition. Such a focus on the junction between what *is* and what is yet to come is a common religious theme (Eliade 1958, 375; 1961, 41-47), and could be a modern echo of an ancient concept.

Even if we accept hand motifs as symbols of or tools within a liminal life-death division, we have yet to address the way in which this symbolism was expressed. The transition from life to death has been conceptualised as a journey in many cultures. Often, the deceased's voyage is thought to be guided by some specific form of transport or support (Johannsen and Laursen 2010, 50). In this way, the potential for the presence of a travel analogy for death within Bronze Age Europe rests entirely within the realm of possibility. Other academics have presented travel metaphors, particularly by drawing parallels between the boat motif and mythological journeys (Thedéen 2002, 140; Artelius 1996; Kaul 1998, 14f.).

The meaning of hand motifs in Bronze Age Europe could have been similar. If the function of hands is to manipulate the external world and there were firm contextual links between hand stones and the mortuary domain, as evidenced by the archaeological material (Goldhahn 2009, 95f.), it follows that hands could have easily functioned either as symbols or ritualistic elements in the transition to a different world. The hand is an obvious means of symbolising contact, particularly when emphasised (as they are in the hand stone depictions by the presence of spread fingers). Furthermore, it is a symbol to which most people can easily relate. Hands are executers of hominid interaction or connectivity and so are likely symbols of, or media for, a transition to the world of the dead or contact with the afterlife

Conclusion

This paper has attempted to approach the initial meaning of hand stones and has also addressed the question of their unrealistic depiction. The summation of the various modes of analysis presented here suggests that these motifs were most likely connected with the conceptualisation of death and acted as symbols or tools for engaging with death and/or the afterlife. This theory addresses both representation (i.e. the choice of hands as subject matter) and presentation (i.e. why the hand stones looked the way they did, and why they were linked to the contexts in which they have been found).

Unfortunately, certain aspects of hand stones remain unknown. Thus far, no comprehensive explanation for the horizontal markings associated with hand stones has been proposed, while it is certain

their almost exclusive occurrence in sets of four should be investigated further. Moreover, this paper has not engaged with the medium of rock as regards portable stone slabs, nor has it addressed the reasoning behind this choice of medium. It is possible that rock had a metaphorical linkage with death in the Bronze Age worldview. Alternatively, it is possible that rock had a degree of permanence absent from the Late Bronze Age cremation burials with which hand stones were often associated. In this sense, the perceived permanence of hand stones could have acted as a 'soft' transition from long-lasting burial mounds to the ephemeral anonymity of cremation graves. Finally, this paper has not attempted to explain the tendency for right hands (although this preponderance does not negate the conclusions reached by this study.)

Despite its problems, the semiotic approach has been useful to this investigation. Employing the concepts of conceptual metaphor, metonymy, and suspicious coincidence segued into an investigation of meaning-making and its employment with the hand stones. This resulted in a more grounded explanation of the reasons for which hands were depicted in the first place as well as the distinct way in which they were carved into the stones.

This line of inquiry offers a clear alternative to reconstructing Bronze Age mythology from rock carvings, which can be highly problematic (Malmer 1989, 92). However, the approach is not without its limitations. Firstly, it focused on universal human meaning-making, and so is not geared towards meaning-making within a specific culture. Universal meaning-making, like metaphor and metonymy, can most likely be found in any time and place. While the specifics of the application of meaning-making can enlighten our understanding of the Bronze Age as a period, drawing parallels between modern times and European prehistory can be problematic. Moreover, the analytical framework on which this paper is based was not assembled with such a purpose in mind. This framework focuses on the ways in which meaning-making occurs in modern art rather than prehistoric meaning-making. Nonetheless, the guiding principles which enable study of the divisions between art and anatomic reality have assisted in creating a better understanding of hand stones, if only insofar as they revealed as many new questions as answers.

Notes

1. The author acknowledges that this is a simplification of the original analytical framework which does not account for aesthetic experience. However, as aesthetics is not the object of this paper, that aspect has been disregarded here.

Bibliography

Artelius, T. 1996: *Långfard och återkomst. Skeppet i bronsålderns gravar.* Kungsbacka.

Brøndsted, J. 1939: *Danmarks Oldtid. II. Bronzealderen.* København.

Bundgård, P.F. 2002: Presentation and Representation in Art. Ontic and Gestaltic Constraints on Aesthetic Experience. *Visio* 7, 1-2, 187-203.

Croce, B. & P. Romanell 1965: *Guide to Aestheics.* Indianapolis.

Darrault-Harris, I. 2009: Non-Genericity as an Invariant of the Readability of Pictures. *Cognitive Semiotics* 5, 93-102.

Dissanayake, E. 1988: *What is Art for?* New York.

Eliade, M. 1958: *Patterns in Comparative Religion.* London.

Eliade, M. 1961: *Images and symbols. Studies in Religious Symbolism.* Kansas City.

Glob, P.V. 1969: *Helleristninger i Danmark.* Jysk Arkæologisk Selskabs Skrifter VII. Højbjerg.

Goldhahn, J. 2007: Dödens hand. En essä om brons- och hällsmed. In: Goldhahn, J. & T. Østigård (eds.): *Rituelle spesialister i bronse- og jernalderen* 1. Göteborg, 1-379.

Goldhahn, J. 2009: Rock art for the dead and un-dead. Reflections on the significance of hand stones in Late Bronze Age Scandinavia. *Adoranten* 2009, 95-103.

Hoffman, D.D. 1998: *Visual Intelligence. How We Create What We See.* New York.

Johannsen, N. 2010: Technological Conceptualization: Cognition of the Shoulders of History. In: Malafouris, L. & C. Renfrew (eds.): *The Cognitive Life of Things. Recasting the Boundaries of the Mind.* Cambridge, 59-69.

Johannsen, N.N. & S.T. Laursen 2010: Routes and Wheeled Transport in Late 4th-Early 3rd Millennium Funerary Customs of the Jutland Peninsula. Regional Evidence and European Context. *Prähistorische Zeitschrift* 85, 1, 15-58.

Johansen, E. 1970: Med hevet hånd. *Kuml* 1970, 171-188.

Kaul, F. 1986: Hændernes hus. *Skalk* 4, 3-8.

Kaul, F. 1998: *Ships on bronzes. A study in Bronze Age religion and iconography.* PNM Studies in Archaeology and History 3, 1, København.

Kaul, F. 2004: *Bronzealderens religion. Studier af den nordiske bronzealders ikonografi.* København.

Kaul, F. 2006: Kulthuset ved Sandagergård og andre kulthuse. Betydning og tolkning. In: Anglert, M., M. Artursson & F. Svanberg (eds.): *Kulthus and Dödshus.* Stockholm, 99-112.

Larsen, K.A. 1955: Solvogn og solkult. *Kuml* 1955, 46-63.

Malmer, M.P. 1981: *A Chorological Study of North European Rock Art.* Antikvariska Serien 32. Stockholm.

Malmer, M.P. 1989: Principles of a non-mythological explanation of North-European Bronze Age rock art. In: Nordström, H.-Å. & A. Knape (eds.): *Bronze Age Studies.* Stockholm, 91-100.

Marstrander, S. 1963: *Østfolds Jordbruksristninger.* Oslo.

Norling-Christensen, H. 1941: Et Bronzealders Helligtegn. *Nationalmuseets arbejdsmark* 1941, 5-59.

Ramachandran, V.S. & W. Hirstein 1999: The Science of Art. A Neurological Theory of Aesthetic Experience. *Journal of Consciousness Studies* 6, 6-7, 15-51.

Thedéen, S. 2002: På resa genom livet och landskapet. Tankar kring bronsålderns skeppssymbolik. In: Goldhahn, J. (ed.): *Bilder av bronsålder. Ett seminarium om förhistorisk kommunikation.* Stockholm, 129-150.

Tilley, C. 1999: *Metaphor and Material Culture.* Oxford.

Turner, V. 1967: *The forest of symbols. Aspects of Ndembu ritual.* Ithaca.

Ungerer, F. & H. Schmid 2006: *An Introduction to Cognitive Linguistics.* Harlow.

Van Gennep A. 2004: *The Rites of Passage.* London.

List of Contributors

Helle Vandkilde

Most recently, Vandkilde has served as the coordinator of the Marie Curie ITN Forging Identities Project. In addition to her multiple publications on a variety of different Bronze Age topics (especially warfare), Vandkilde is also the director of Aarhus University's "Materials, Culture and Heritage" research programme.

Constanze Rassmann

Starting her archaeological meanderings at the University of Cologne and laying over at the University in Kiel, Constanze Rassmann completed her PhD on Middle Bronze Age connections ("Crossing Blades and Crossing Borders – A Re-examination of Octagonal-hilted Swords and their Paradigms") at Aarhus University in 2013. Since November 2013, Rassmann has been employed by the Museum of Middle Jylland as their Head of the Archaeological Department.

Samantha Reiter

Reiter is a PhD Fellow at Aarhus University, Denmark and a member of the Forging Identities Project (Marie Curie Actions ITN). Her thesis ("Being, Doing and Seeming: Identity, Mobility and Culture Change at the Early Bronze Age Cemetery of Jelsovce, Slovakia") is currently under evaluation by committee for promotion to doctoral status. Since April 2013, Reiter has been employed as an archaeologist and researcher in Frankfurt am Main by the German Archaeological Institute (DAI) working on the Early Bronze Age settlement and cemetery of Fidvar-by-Vráble.

Majken Tessa Tollaksen

Tollaksen recieved her Master's degree in 2013 from Aarhus University ("Who Owns Cultural Heritage? An Archaeological Study of Jelling and its Influence on Students with Different Ethnic Backgrounds"). Thereafter, Tollaksen continued working with heritage and culture, most recently as a communications officer for VitaPark Odder and as a field archaeologist for Museum Østjylland.

Heide Wrobel Nørgaard

A current doctoral candidate, Nørgaard finished her Magister Artium at the Freie Univerität in Berlin in 2008 (entitled «Die Halskragen der Bronzezeit in Nordeuropa und Südskandinavien). She published this thesis in 2011 within the Universitätsforschungen zur Prähistorischen Archäologie series (Band 200). In 2009, Nørgaard recieved a Marie-Curie ITN Fellowship and continued her PhD studies at Aarhus University. Her doctoral project is entitled «Craftsmanship, Production and Distribution of Metalwork in the Early and Middle Northern Bronze Age". The paper presented in this book was awarded the EAA Student Award 2011 at the 17th annual conference in Olso.

Karin Johannesen

Johannesen's Master's degree was completed in 2012 with a thesis entitled "Exploring Ritual: Ritual Wetland Deposits in the Late Bronze Age and Pre-Roman Iron Age in the Danish Region". She is currently employed at Aarhus University and Museum Østjylland as a PhD student. Her doctoral project also concerns wetland depositional rituals in the Early Iron Age of Southern Scandinavia.

Disa Lundsgård Simonsen

Simonsen completed her Master's Degree in 2013 ("Spirals and Wavy Bands: An Investigationof Transmission and Transformation in the Early Bronze Age"). The publication of said thesis is expected in late 2014 in the Danish archaeological journal Kuml. She is currently employed as a field archaeologist by Museum Lolland Falster.

Zsófia Kölcze

Kölcze's interest in design, ideology and Bronze Age weapons is of long standing. After finishing her Master's degree in 2010 ("Design and Ideology: Early European Bronze Age Swords as Material Agents") at Aarhus University, she continued on at the same institution as a PhD student. She is preparing her doctoral thesis (on mobile weapons and transculturality in European Bronze Age c. 1600 BC) for submission in 2014. Currently, she is working as a freelance lecturer on various archaeological topics.

Rannveig Marie Jørgensdotter Spliid

Spliid obtained a Master's degree in Early Celtic Studies at Cardiff University in 2008 her thesis concentrated on the ethos of specific female figures in Celtic myth ("The Woman in the Middle: A structural examination of the mytheme of Deirdre, Grainne and Iseult"). Thereafter, she continued her archaeological studies both by means of several archaeological courses at Aarhus University as well as at Moesgaard Museum. Her interests center around cognitive studies and the cross-disciplinary interface between archaeology and ethnology.

Birgitte Damkjer

Damkjer finished her Master's degree at Aarhus University in 2012. The topic of her thesis ("The Symbolic Value of Bronze Age Clothing in Ritual and Social Contexts: Reconsidering the Oak-coffin Graves") is one in which she continues to be engaged. She is currently working as an independent textile artist for Moesgaard Museum by reconstructing Bronze Age costumes for the new museum exhibition opening in the autumn of 2014.

Thomas Rune Knudsen

Following his course of study at Aarhus University, Knudsen was awarded a Master's degree in 2013 for his thesis "Between Gifts and Markets? Monetary Economy and Exchange at Gudme-Lundeborg, Dankirke and Ribe c. 200-800 AD", thereby maintaining a long-standing research interest in Viking and Iron Age economics, exchange, metrology and social change.